DRAWN
from the
HEART

Illustration from Julie Hunt's, *The Coat*

DRAWN
from the
HEART

a memoir

ron brooks

ALLEN&UNWIN

For my family,
and for Yvonne Burger

First published in 2010

Allen & Unwin
83 Alexander St
Crows Nest NSW 2065
Australia
Phone: (61 2) 8425 0100
Fax: (61 2) 9906 2218
Email: info@allenandunwin.com
Web: www.allenandunwin.com

Cataloguing-in-Publication details are available from the National Library of Australia
www.librariesaustralia.nla.gov.au

ISBN 978 1 74237 155 9

Cover design Ron Brooks
Text design by Sandra Nobes
Set in 11 pt Stempel Garamond by Sandra Nobes
Printed in China by Imago

10 9 8 7 6 5 4 3 2

Australian Government   Australia **Council** for the Arts

This project has been assisted by the Australian Government through the Australia Council, its arts funding and advisory body.

Contents

The Ant, the Grasshopper and the
Remarkable Rocket

WHEN A TEACHER read Aesop's 'The Ant and the Grasshopper' to my Prep/Grade 1 class, in the old shelter shed out the back of Mallacoota Primary School, I knew I was meant to decide whether I wanted to be an ant, or was going to be a rather silly grasshopper.

Of course, the ant was the sensible one, but I had sympathies for the grasshopper. He enjoyed life, in the moment, and wanted to express that joy, share it around. I felt he should not be quite so self-righteously condemned for that.

But, yes – to be an ant, industriously gathering supplies and stocking up against hard times, was the prudent decision.

The years meanwhile have only confirmed this. Over and over.

It was many years later that I read Oscar Wilde's 'The Remarkable Rocket' – a story about a firework rocket who is convinced he is going to stun the whole palace with his brilliance. The King, the Queen, all the courtiers attending the wedding of the Prince and the Princess, and all the other much less impressive fireworks – are all there to do honour to him; to see and hear just how marvellous he is. This is his destiny. He and the rest of the palace are just waiting for the right occasion, for the very best moment…

But when the time does come, he not only fails to take off but fails even to fizz, and is thrown over the palace wall into a ditch. Nevertheless, still convinced of his own grandness, he believes he has been sent away to 'some fashionable watering-place' for a rest.

When moment after likely best moment passes him by, it is most certainly not that he is being overlooked – surely not; it can only mean he is destined for even greater things, not just within the palace but in the wider world.

Finally, on a bright summer's day, a couple of small boys use him as a piece of kindling, for their fire. But because he has become so damp – from being in the ditch for so long, and from all that fond weeping about himself also – it takes some time for him to dry out sufficiently for the fire to catch.

All of which, he believes, allows the world more time to be properly ready (in the middle of the day) to witness his full magnificence.

The palace has meanwhile forgotten all about him, the farmers and villagers are entirely unaware of his existence; the frog and the duck have swum away, the dragonfly flown. And stretched out on the warm grass, waiting for their water to boil, the boys are dreaming their own dreams, asleep in the sun.

At last the fire catches. 'Now I am going off!' he cries. 'Now I am going to explode. I shall set the whole world on fire, and make such a noise that nobody will talk about anything else for a whole year.' But no one sees him, no one hears him. All that is left of him is the stick, which falls on the back of a passing goose.

'Good heavens!' cries the Goose. 'It is going to rain sticks'; and she rushes into the water.

'I knew I should cause a great sensation,' gasps the Rocket, and goes out.

———

A collection – a collage, a montage – of memories, musings, reflections and explorations … by a bit of an ant, a bit of that grasshopper, and by whatever remains of a most unremarkable rocket. (Not to mention a bit of a goose.)

PART ONE

Spring has returned.
The Earth is like a child that knows poems.
Rainer Maria Rilke

Mallacoota to Melbourne

I THINK IT was the English earthwork artist Richard Long who said (roughly paraphrased) that one possible definition of the artist is that he, or she, continues to do as an adult that which they most liked to muck about with as a child.

So, did I have a whole lot of books? Read a lot? Draw?

None whatsoever. And, no – not at all.

In many ways, my childhood was a little impoverished. Not enough money. Food, clothes and accommodation were all pretty basic. Not a happy family. This was nothing special at the time, of course – there were plenty of others in a similar boat in Genoa and Mallacoota, in the beautiful far eastern corner of Victoria. After World War II such families were fairly run-of-the-mill in small country towns all over Australia. Still are, I know.

I was the first of two children from my mother's second marriage.

She had come from an extremely wealthy family on the south coast of New South Wales, and grown up as some kind of protected princess, the youngest of three, in an Edwardian mansion, with private governesses – the lot.

Her father, John Ronaldson Logan (simply 'JR' to everyone who knew him), had moved from western Victoria after his father died, and established a large grazing property near Bombala in the Eden–Monaro

A shorter version of this piece first appeared in *Island* magazine, no. 91, 2002–03, under the title 'Drawn from the Heart'.

region of New South Wales. And then – because the hills, the sea mists and the coast there reminded him of Scotland – he bought a substantial tract of what once had been Ben Boyd's land on the southern side of Twofold Bay. Boyd was an entrepreneurial squatter of sweeping ambition and dubious method, who in the 1840s had embarked on a number of huge projects in the south-east of New South Wales, but had left it all behind before the decade was out.

In 1910, just around the bay from Boyd's whaling station, JR began building the new family home: a grand Edwardian pile that he named Edrom, after the ancestral property just out of Edinburgh.

The setting – on a headland directly across the bay from Eden, near the mouth of the Towamba River and with sandy beaches to each side – was picture-postcard perfect. And with its vast, multi-gabled and orange-tiled roof forested with tall white chimneys (JR had a particular passion for big fireplaces, they were in almost every room) and huge bluestone verandah, Edrom was a handsome and imposing building, and commanded stunning views right across the magnificent bay.

The large front entrance door (displaying the Logan coat of arms in stained glass) led into an entrance hall the size of a small house but twice as high, wood-panelled all around, with a soaring pyramidal vault to a skylight above. There was a large open fireplace in a typically Scottish inglenook to one side, curtained with long, pure wool drapes in the Logan tartan, and beautiful bookcases on the other. JR's father having imported the first red deer into Australia, there were antlers mounted above doorways opening into the drawing room, to JR's study and the even larger central courtyard conservatory, which had a fountain playing into a fishpond in the centre, and stairs going up to a minstrel gallery. The large dining room – again, wood-panelled all round – with its long table and chairs, sideboards and dressers, was a cornucopia of fine craftsmanship and beautiful timbers: cedar, oak and blackwood, myrtle and maple. Beyond the dining room was a no less impressive kitchen with a huge wood-fired combustion stove, ovens, its own small bakery and a fully stocked pantry big enough to park a small car in.

The fireplaces in all the main rooms were veritable celebrations of bluestone, granite, basalt and water-worn sandstone.

There was an abundance of bedrooms for the family of course, but also for the 'help' – governess, gardeners, cook, housekeeper – and plenty more for visitors and guests. Large, arched bluestone entrances under the massive verandah led into a series of rooms, one of which was a classroom for the three girls, with windows looking out over the bay. Wide stone steps led down to the beautiful gardens, with Norfolk Island pines, palms, magnificent rose arbours and large flowerbeds, and gently undulating lawns (kept cropped by wallabies and kangaroos) sweeping all the way to the shore, to the private jetty and beaches.

At one time there had been a beautiful little cottage there, that my grandfather (alas) knocked down to clear the view and make way for the lawn – very sad, especially as the original occupant was Oswald Walters Brierly, manager of Ben Boyd's many businesses for some years and a talented painter and diarist, who showed considerably more respect for the local indigenous people and their culture than did most of his European contemporaries. The painting of Brierly's for which I have a particular affection is *East Boyd*, done in the 1840s. This almost luminescent little watercolour shows little sign of the romanticised European view of the landscape so typical among painters in Australia at the time. Brierly's washes and touches of body-colour capture perfectly the dryness, the rough textures, the gentleness and the transparency of the bush; his gum trees are real gum trees, the bush and foreshore scraggly.

My grandfather had left school at thirteen, but was something of an autodidact, always searching out knowledge, ordering and buying books in from Sydney, Melbourne and London. Over the years he built up a substantial library. A successful grazier and prominent businessman in the Eden–Monaro region, in his semi-retirement, and with all the confidence (dare I say arrogance?) of a largely self-educated and self-made man, JR became a bit of a mover and shaker at Twofold Bay, passionate about all sorts of plans and involved in all sorts of projects.

He built and set up Eden's first power station, and founded and built the Eden Killer Whale Museum (primarily to house the skeleton of Old Tom, the leader of the group of Orca whales – the so-called 'Killers of Eden' – that used to help the local whalers by rounding up and herding the baleen whales into the bay). He was a very early advocate of the Snowy River Hydro Electric Power Scheme, bringing surveyors and engineers out from England and Scotland to work on his ideas and help him finalise proposals with which he would then lobby politicians.

With his schooner, *White Heather*, always ready to ferry influential visitors back and forth across the bay to Eden, and RAAF sea-planes to and from Canberra or Sydney, JR frequently hosted large gatherings at Edrom – long weekends and meetings, at which all sorts of ventures and plans would be discussed. Many of these, like the schemes of Ben Boyd before him, came to not much at all, at least not in his own lifetime.

My mother, much the youngest of the three sisters, was born and brought up in this house, among all this activity. She enjoyed all sorts of privileges, had her own horses and pair of English setters, and certainly had her share of fun and adventures with her father on *White Heather* – occasionally helping to tow a whale or one of Davidson's green whaleboats in to shore, or, in an encounter with Old Tom when he threw his bulk across the stern of the boat, holding on 'for dear life' to the rear mast. But her life there was generally somewhat sheltered. For the most part she didn't spend much time with other children her own age; only later, when JR built the log cabin in Eden for the Girl Guides did she begin to mix with other girls, and that was for a limited time. I suspect she had even less to do with boys or young men.

Somehow, with both her older sisters long married, and gone from the family home, she took herself off to London to study nursing in 1937 – only to have to return later in the same year when she learned of her father's illness. It was during the Great Depression and she later recalled JR on his deathbed, saying to her, 'I was very silly, darling, I trusted people I shouldn't have…' He had lost everything, and my grandmother eventually had to sell Edrom. With the darkening clouds of World War II already gathering and the Girl Guides losing their leaders, the troop disbanding, my grandmother bought back the log cabin, and moved in there to live.

By her own account, my mother's marriage soon after to a pianist and singer was a disaster. The marriage ended unhappily, with him accidentally blowing himself up some months after they had separated, attempting to weld a leaky petrol tank under his car. Suffering from the most horrible burns, he took some time to die. I'm not sure that my mother – a deeply unhappy single mother then, and pregnant with their third child, no longer living in the palace, but in a small fibro-cement and timber cottage in Eden – ever visited him as he lay there in the hospital.

My father, meanwhile – from south of the border and very much indeed the wrong side of the tracks – had a very different story. Born in 1918, he had only ever lived in shacks, huts or tents. He moved with his family from place to place around East Gippsland, wherever his father could find work – on farms, felling trees, cutting timber.

Dad attended school for just four years, from when he was nine to thirteen, in a small bush school just outside Cann River. He then had to go to work to help support the family – working as a farm labourer, cutting timber with his father, carting the mail by horseback through the forty or fifty miles of bush from Cann River to the lighthouse keeper's place at what was then known as Cape Everard, and cutting firewood for them there. Pop himself was a relieving keeper for some years at Everard.

In 1933, when Russell Grimwade bought Captain Cook's family cottage in Yorkshire, England, and transported it to Melbourne to have it rebuilt in the Fitzroy Gardens, he decided to have granite quarried from Cape Everard (Point Hicks), and transported back to Yorkshire, to there build a replica of the monument to Captain James Cook and Lieutenant Zachary Hick(e)s already standing by the Everard lighthouse. My father, at the age of just sixteen, was foreman of the crew which did that work – in charge of drilling and setting the dynamite charges into the rock, blowing off great chunks and cutting them down to smaller blocks, which were then dragged by horse and sled along a track (still just visible) around the shoreline to a wharf on the lee side of the point, where it was loaded aboard a cargo boat bound for Port Phillip, thence onto a ship to England.

But at the time he first met my mother, when he was eighteen or nineteen and she four or five years older, he was working as the handyman, caretaker and river guide at the Gipsy Point Hotel and Guest House, on the beautiful Wallagaraugh River, inland from Mallacoota Inlet.

Mum's whole family and extensive 'parties' of relatives, guests and friends regularly drove down in their Buicks, Chevrolets and Plymouths for a week or two at Gipsy Point – staying in the guesthouse, boating and fishing on the river and downstream lakes, and shooting in the surrounding bush. Collectively, these splendid Logan entourages – the men with their canes, hats and suits, their fishing or hunting gear, the women in fashionable great floppy hats, fur coats and collars and heels – must surely have been quite a sight.

My father could well have thought them altogether beyond his class, might well have been a little intimidated; but he was nothing if not a little cheeky at the time. Possessing great good health, extremely fit and strong from all his years of solid physical work, and with a broad range of skills, he probably felt capable of doing just about anything. And was quite handsome, a bit dashing actually.

'For all his brute strength, your father was a beautiful dancer, you know,' Mum used to say. 'He could glide across the floor, barely seeming to touch it, all night long. He was so light on his feet. People used to just stand back and watch the two of us, and we won some prizes, I can tell you, with our dancing.'

In those couple of years just before the war – after my mother's father had died – at the end of a day's work, Dad would scrub up, change his clothes and drive the sixty or so miles to pick her up and go to a dance in Eden. Or drive another however many miles to somewhere else; to Bega, Tathra, Pambula, Merimbula, Bemboka, Bombala. Or all the way back down to Genoa, perhaps – wherever a dance was happening – so they would dance the hours away together, before he took her home at god knows what time of the night, and then drove back by himself to Gipsy Point in time for work again in the morning.

He was in love.

Substituting 'Gipsy Point' for 'Mexico', they used to sing, 'South of the bo-order, down Gipsy Point way…' That was *their* song.

However, at some point just before World War II – when my father was about twenty, and had declared he wanted to marry her – she told him 'Oh, George, you silly, silly young boy. Go and join the army, and grow up.'

So he did that – he joined the army. But I suspect he was no more grown up after the war, simply unhappier, and most certainly none the richer for any of the experiences thus provided him. Though he was never able to speak about it, over the years I've managed to deduce the nature and events of those years for him, the reasons for his guilt and shame. Fresh out of the army and now driving transport trucks between Bairnsdale and Sydney, he had of course heard of my mother's marriage, of her having two small boys, and of her husband's death. He'd drop in boxes of vegetables, and loads of firewood that he would then chop and split for her.

My mother's third child, a daughter, was born… Dad would later tell me, many times, how 'this lovely little thing, barely able to walk, would waddle up the front path to me whenever I visited, and grip me by the trouser leg for support, and say, "Daaa"'.

And my father fell in love with her too.

He finally persuaded my mother she needed him, and they married.

I'm not really sure it was a great idea, but there you go.

They moved into a small fibro house – still there, now derelict, overgrown and full of rubbish – at the edge of Genoa. My arrival on the scene a year or so later did not make my mother any happier. She certainly told me often enough: 'Five minutes pleasure, if you can call it that, for nine months pain, and then you were the ugliest little blighter I ever saw. Couldn't possibly be mine. I told them to take you away.'

I think it went downhill from there.

The dairy farm Dad took up just across the road on the flatlands of the Genoa River didn't work – a flood one year took most of the paddocks away. Nor did the move to Mallacoota, to another small fibro, 'first red-roofed house on the right, as you drive in'. Neither was within the walls of the now long-lost palace gardens. The populace had no need of a princess, and the feeling was probably reciprocated.

At home, however, Mum ruled comprehensively, aided by the ever-threatened horsewhip. It was always laid at Mum's place at the table, alongside her cutlery – fork, plate, spoon, knife, whip – and regularly used.

Home was not a very happy place.

Quite possibly my older (half-)siblings, John, Ted and Tess, will have very different memories of this time, but for the most part, I cannot remember them ever playing with me.

One incident with my two older brothers does however stand out. They had been mucking about in the bush across the road from our house, and come across a large anthill. I think I'd probably just been following them around, hanging about too much. My brothers stirred the nest open with sticks and whacked away at the ants, making them as furious as they possibly could. They then pulled off my shorts and underpants, sat me right down on the scene of destruction and held me there among the raging inhabitants, all of whom took their understandable anger out on me. I later crawled the couple of hundred yards home with the more vengeful ants still attached and biting. My mother stripped off the rest of my clothes, plonked me into the galvanised iron hip-bath, and poured kerosene all over me.

The one entertainment I remember my sister enjoying with me – time and time again – was to lay me on my back on the floor, sit astride me and pin my arms down with her knees, and tickle, tickle, tickle me, or repeatedly drum my chest, hard, with the tips of her fingers. Until I eventually, inevitably, always wet my pants.

My younger brother, Gilbert, was five years away.

Very sadly, I have few memories of much involvement at all with my father during those years. He was then working for the Country Roads Board on the roads around Genoa, from the Wingan River to the New South Wales border on the Princes Highway, and down to Mallacoota, on the coast.

One of the happiest moments I do remember was when I visited the bark hut he lived in on the banks of the Genoa River, while the rest of the family were in Mallacoota. He joined us at weekends. I think.

I still love the smell of diesel, dirt, graders and gravel, but I especially loved that little hut beside the river – just big enough for a bed, a small table, a chair, a couple of shelves, with a fireplace and a big corrugated-iron chimney at one end. Le Corbusier – in his retirement after all those gorgeous buildings (and the somewhat larger, more misguided visions) – built himself and his wife a couple of not dissimilar small hideaways somewhere in the south of France, overlooking the Mediterranean. 'All you need,' he said.

There were rides on Caterpillar bulldozers and graders with Dad, a couple of fishing trips, picnics maybe, and I remember one very special evening when I had bad 'growing pains' in my legs, when he massaged eucalyptus oil into them, so gently, and told me the pains meant I was growing good, healthy big muscles. But there weren't many such moments; there wasn't much else. Poor old Dad.

And, yes, there was a lot of waiting outside the Mallacoota and Gipsy Point pubs, and far too many extremely scary drives home.

I recall being woken in the middle of the night by my mother, shouting awful things at Dad. 'Your son knows far more about you than you realise, George Brooks!' – the last two words absolutely spat out, in complete contempt.

Earlier on I had no idea what my mother meant by some of these things, and would lie awake for hours trying to figure it all out.

He drank too much, of course. Almost all the adults in Mallacoota drank too much at that time. The town's children, their children, regularly witnessed the most appalling behaviour – drunken fights between friends, parents, brothers, uncles (all, by the way, of Anglo-Saxon stock).

We were poor; the whole town was poor. We lived in a small weatherboard and fibro-cement house. Tess had a room to herself, which had a built-in wardrobe with hanging space and drawers for all the kids' clothes, and it was the throughway into the boys' room, which was barely big enough to fit the two home-made double bunks we all four slept in. I had one of the top ones, close to the (gaping apart at the seams) water-stained masonite ceiling. Rambling briar roses – planted at the back corner of the house by the two tank-stands – had grown up and along the wall of the house, under the eaves and in through the roof, and small yellow-green leaves and pale pink blooms poked through the gaps between the masonite just above my head.

My pet kookaburra, Jacko – just a baby when Dad rescued him from the side of a road (after the tree its nest had been in had been struck by lightning) – sometimes slept up there with me. Normally he would perch on the head of my bunk, head tucked around between his wings, but I awoke one Christmas morning to find a halo of his droppings neatly distributed on the pillow around my head. Dad always insisted there were exactly twelve of them.

Belonging more to John, Ted and Tess, there were two free-spirited magpies, Billy and Jacky, both real characters, who were allowed to range a little more widely than Jacko. They were nevertheless emphatically part of the family, and would fight off the 'wild' magpies who had sufficient courage to attack them in the garden, the many kookaburras that would regularly attack Jacko, and any of the neighbourhood kids they didn't like, chasing them around the house (pecking away at their bare running feet and heels) and out the gate or over the fence.

They were more effective as guard dogs, our parents reckoned, than Soxy. A mixture of labrador-retriever, he had long, wavy black hair, and four white socks. He would accompany us kids everywhere we went – into the bush, to Davis's Creek, the lake, along the foreshore, to the beaches. He loved the beach especially, loved to chase the seagulls, and would swim with us all day long. His favourite thing, our favourite thing, was to tell him, 'Sit, Soxy, sit!', and he would wait while one or other of us dived in and swam right out somewhere, turned around and then called him, waving. He would then positively burst into the most joyful of runs, an ecstasy of galumphing, leap into the water and swim out to us, smiling hugely all the way. And when he reached us we'd say, 'Good boy, Soxy, good boy!', and turn him around, take hold of his tail, and let him tow us all the way back to shore.

Mum always believed that if Soxy was with us, we'd be okay. And indeed, we were one day down on the beach, just inside the entrance (the quite dangerous *exit*, actually, if an ebb tide was in full flow) and right where one of the local fishermen swore he'd seen a white pointer shark as long as his trawler; it had followed him as he came in over the bar. Tess had swum too far out into the channel and got caught in the current. I don't know whether she called him, or whether someone told Soxy to go, but go he did, and towed her safely back to shore.

Though I look back with great fondness on those years in that small house with no electricity (it hadn't come to Mallacoota yet) – and no wireless, no telephone, but with kerosene lamps and candles, a wood-fired stove and a bark-hut bathroom/laundry just outside the back door, the old copper in one corner, and our dunny down by the back fence – there was not a lot of laughter, most times, in that house. Not a lot of fun.

This was before television (I never even saw a television set until I was about fifteen), and having no electricity, no radio, we heard no music in the house either. There was a lovely old piano that my mother would occasionally play – and she did try to give me lessons, but all I ever got from that were sharp cracks over the knuckles with the edge of a wooden ruler whenever I made a mistake.

Apart from a bookcase containing books from my mother's childhood (I used to sit for hours on the arm of the couch, staring through the always-locked glass doors at the beautiful lettering on the embossed and gold-stamped spines), there were no books at all. I had none of my own, and no one ever read to me.

There were seldom any encouraging words; those few were only ever spoken by my father, and quickly squashed, jumped on, by my mother. I came dux of the school one year, was duly presented with the much-coveted and highly varnished wooden map of Australia that sat above the blackboards all year round, and my father gave me the ten-shilling note he'd promised me if I did. He told me how pleased and proud he was.

'Nonsense!' Mum scoffed. 'There's nothing so unusual about working hard – so he should, we all have to. You're a blasted fool giving your money away like that. He's already got his shiny little piece of wood...he certainly doesn't need any other prizes!'

There was little or nothing in the way of beautiful language. Just the odd glimpse, later. Which made me wonderfully hungry for it.

Oddly enough – or perhaps not – the most abiding memory I have from that house is of a picture that hung on a wall in the lounge room. This wasn't a room I generally spent much time in – having only one small window looking east out under the roofed verandah at the front of the house, it was dark in there most of the day – and I felt I wasn't really allowed to, because it had so many of my mother's special things in it: the piano, the bookcase, nice vases, the good crockery, glassware and porcelain, shells in a sideboard, pictures on the walls, and a big old dark-varnished clock that donged resonantly every quarter-hour, all day and (especially deeply, especially reassuringly) all night. But sometimes – perhaps because I felt I wasn't likely to be seen – I would sneak in to sit on the arm of the couch, to peer again at the books in the bookcase, but more often to look at that picture.

There were other pictures, of course: old photographs from the Edrom time; large black-and-white lithographs (*The Thin Red Line*, another large one of galloping horses, two just of horses' heads); a couple of small landscapes – all pinks, greens and pale blues; and pictures of Scotch terriers advertising whiskey. But the picture that most fascinated me was a large steel engraving, late nineteenth-century I think, which hung above the fireplace.

The image is of an interior even darker than our lounge room, close in, with an old dog (a long-haired English setter, I think), lying on the floor. The front legs of the dog are stretched out; its head, with its big soulful eyes, is resting on both paws, and those on a pair of gloves... Heavy embroidered drapery hangs down in big folds from above, mostly covering (only the near corner of it is visible) a coffin. But never did I see any of this – despite staring at that picture, again and again, fascinated by what I thought I saw – never, when I was younger, did I see what was really there. Never did I see that it was a picture of the inside of a room; never did I see the coffin, the dog, the drapes or the gloves.

Instead, every time I looked at this picture, I saw a landscape, a mysterious image of a place I knew well: the back of the sand dunes between the mouth of the Betka River and the ocean, as seen from the bridge. Instead of the long, curly hair on the body and head of a dog, I saw hills and clumps of acacia, banksia, callistemon, hakeas and grasses. Between them, instead of the outstretched front legs, I saw long ridges of sand dune; instead of the fingers of a glove under those paws at the ends of the legs, I saw lying across the end of one of those dunes a figure, a man. I wondered what he was doing there. I thought perhaps he was dead.

For a very long time, for years, whenever I looked at the picture, I saw only this. And wondering about it, disturbed by it, I dreamed about it also.

I don't recall ever asking anybody about it; I felt there was a private mystery between me and the picture, between the picture and me, and was happy to keep it that way – wanted to keep it that way, because I looked forward to each quiet time when I would again find myself alone in that dark room, sitting there, looking and wondering.

While it remained hanging on that wall all those years, I only ever saw the man lying among the sand dunes. We left Mallacoota when I was eleven, at the end of my fifth grade.

Years later, when we lived in North Balwyn, in Melbourne, the dog with his paws resting on his (dead) master's gloves had appeared, and the man in the sand dunes had gone. By then, I was sixteen or seventeen.

Apart from my fascination with that picture, my love of the kero lamps and candles, the roses above my bed, Jacko, and the bark-hut bathroom, there was not a lot of fun to be had in our house at Mallacoota. So I spent most of my time outside. I just went outside.

––––––––––

Ours was a small house, closer to what most people would refer to as a shack, but from the front verandah I could look over our fence, through the trees, down the hill, out over the town and across the expanse of the bottom lake with all its islands, all the way to the mountains and hills on the eastern side, to where the original town settlement had been. I could see 'Fair Haven', the dairy farm from where the Hansen boys ferried the milk across in big aluminium barrels every morning to the town wharf, where we'd fill our billy (before we had our own cow), and then swing it in full circles all the way home, around and around, but careful, also, not to spill any… You could look a bit further north to where the Spotted Dog gold mine had been; or south across the face of those hills to the lower marshland flats and ancient banksia forests, to Lake Barracouta, the sand dunes, the ocean beaches, to Gabo Island and the lighthouse, to Bass Strait and beyond. We looked out over all of this, all the way to the horizon, from our house.

No matter what the season, the weather or time of day or night, the view out there was always beautiful. The colours of the sky, the hills, the water – of everything, depending on the light, the air, the wind – were constantly changing. One day the lake would be vivid ultramarine, or deep Prussian blue, on another it would be polished platinum, a mirror; on the next, as wind moved sheets of rain and the seemingly impossible luminescence of a rainbow across it, it could look like lead, heavy, dark and dull, with the islands almost black, or steel grey, under banks of heavy cloud. And in summer – blessed days, the lake shimmered a transparent turquoise – the islands lay like promises in the sun.

With the sunrise out here every morning, lighting all this up, and all sorts of waterbirds – gulls, terns, cormorants, sandpipers nesting among the melaleucas, tussock grasses and sands of the islands – with the cacophony of all these birds beginning their days, I had pretty much the ultimate *son et lumière* show to begin mine.

Most beautiful of all these birds, to me anyway, were the pelicans. There were always so many of them. I would watch them in flight above the lake – their big black-and-white wings in that lovely, slow flapping motion – or gliding down out of the blue of the sky and across the hills, turning, dropping altitude, coming down and in to land on the water. They come in fast, their great vast wings blades now, cutting through the air…the whole magnificent creature levelling and stretching out as it comes closer to the surface, still at substantial speed, and then somehow it just seems to condense its overall length a bit, shortening the neck, turning the wings slowly back to vertical (acting as flaps now), and then actually cupping, spooning them – the first big brakes. The feet and legs (the undercarriage) – which all this time have remained almost unnoticed, laid back against that soft white underbelly – are detached, uncoupled, swung down; the big orange webbed feet spread, twist, adjust and drag, and then the legs move forward, almost ahead of the whole body, the head pulls back, and that massive, extraordinary beak is up, but tucked and still pointing, the whole body almost vertical now. The legs stiffen as the maximum forward position is reached…and suddenly, the feet, that before were dragging, have come forward and up, now at an angle of forty-five to sixty degrees to the legs, and pretty much perpendicular to the water surface…and we have the final brakes.

(Am I embellishing – making and mixing the whole performance up with some of those remarkable Disney animations that we saw for the first time in Billy Bruce's picture theatre, an old World War II mess-hall he brought in from the aerodrome, and set up with a generator in the main street?)

The massive bird is still moving pretty damned fast at this point, but immediately those brakes begin to make first contact with the water – depending how smooth, how rough the surface – there will be a bit of skimming, (just) feeling, touching, testing; then, as the heels of those brakes begin to dig in, sending up two fanned and beautifully symmetrical bow waves, the bird is coming in like a big old sea-plane now – a massive great Catalina, the tummy, the fuselage, creating its own wake. The huge wing-flap brakes fold in to the body, which condenses just that little further, and then drops down, slowing, deeper into the water.

She, he, is there.

The whole thing, the whole performance, is astonishing.

There's a shake of the head, of the wings (probably also some adjustment of the undercarriage, the legs and feet, but we can't see that)…and the beak, that beautiful great pearly-pink, apricot bill, is dipped, once, perhaps twice into the water and shaken; its almost transparent underside swings and slaps; the head will move up and down, turn this way and that, once or twice, and there'll be one last, small quiver of both wings… All instruments checked and re-set, the great kings and queens of the lake are now into slow, majestic surface-cruising mode.

I loved it.

Immediately behind our house, and starting right at our back fence, was the bush. It went for miles – mostly stringybark forest, but a mix of other eucalypts also, with an endlessly interesting under-storey of all sorts of native plants which would flower at different times of the year: the creams, yellows, pinks and reds of different acacias, banksias, boronias, grevilleas and hakeas, and in among all this the hanging purple blooms of the rambling hardenbergias, the smaller yellow-and-black flowers of the 'egg-and-bacon' plant, and beautiful spider orchids and brown- and green-hoods; and as we ventured deeper into the bush, there were various ground ferns, others which grew up the trees, and increasingly dense melaleuca forest the closer we came to Davis's Creek.

There were snakes of course, lots of them – red-bellied blacks mostly, but tiger snakes also, and copperheads; and an endless variety of spiders – funnel-webs, trapdoors, red-backs and all sorts of extraordinarily beautiful small coloured ones suspended in their webs strung between bushes, grasses and ferns. Birds galore – magpies, kookaburras, currawongs, choughs, parrots, mudlarks, thrushes, warblers, wrens, and more that I couldn't name, and kangaroos (big reds and greys), wallabies, wombats and the less often sighted and therefore all the more fascinating echidnas, and blue-tongues and goannas; lots of goannas. They would regularly come through the back fence to raid the Bruces' chookhouse next door, decimating the flock and leaving behind a mess of feathers and eggshells. We would see them halfway up the trunks of the big gum trees just outside the fence, or resting, stretched out on the lower branches, not having bothered to go any higher – or barely able to, so full, round and heavy were their bellies.

I spent most of my childhood building cubbyhouses – in the bush, out on the beaches, up in the branches of a tree hanging out over the lagoon, from where we could see ships and the Sydney–Hobart yachts going by on the horizon. Or we'd be mucking around in billycarts, messing around in boats, homemade canoes, rafts – paddling and rowing about the inlet, going ashore and exploring the islands. On summer nights, we'd go out cicada-ing – more often than not without torches, trying not to think about spiders – feeling about the trees in the dark with our bare hands for the unhatched larvae, taking them home to put in cages so we could watch them hatch. We played all around the long foreshore to the lake, endlessly climbing trees, wandering about the bush, and spent days on end out along the ocean beaches and cliffs, exploring caves filled with bats or heading out to the old aerodrome where there'd be the big red kangaroos come in from the surrounding bush to graze on the grasses around the airstrip.

We'd go to the old World War II air-raid shelters hidden away in the bush around the aerodrome – massive concrete structures, half underground, all now covered in fallen branches, bush litter and grown over with lichen. Stale air rose to meet you as you descended the stairs into their dark, smelly interiors – always damp, always dank – with old newspapers, empty beer bottles, broken glass lying about, and the walls blackened here and there by fires a good deal more recent than 1945. Fertile ground for the imagination, great places for war games. You be the Germans (or Japanese) this time, we'll be the Australians.

Cowboys and Indians would more often than not happen in and around Mortimer's Paddock and Devlin's Gully, or out the other side of town around Black-Fella's Point (apparently an old Aboriginal burial ground), near E.J. Brady's old home, where he and others (including Henry Lawson) once dreamed of some sort of utopian community of kindred spirits. We'd go further, to Roly Davidson's place – a big old house set in acres of beautiful gardens with terraced lawns, beds of roses, dahlias, lilies – great cascading banks of colour – with orchards, greenhouses, vegetable gardens and a long, dark arbour, tunnel-like, with a small, white figure, a girl-woman, standing in a pool of light at one end. So bewitching did I find the darkness of this long tunnel with the small figure that I dreamed about it for years after the one time I saw it. The whole place was beautiful – and mysterious, all hidden away as it was behind dense cypress hedges. It was like another world. It was another world. We would try to find a gap in the hedge to look through, thinking to raid the fruit trees, but we never did – instead we just ran around the hills for days on end playing Cowboys and Indians with our home-made (everything was) guns and bows and arrows, running among the tussocks or from one clump of blackberries to another, jumping up from behind a fallen log to shoot at somebody hiding behind a fencepost, or sneaking through a grove of silver wattles, a stand of stringybarks, to surprise our foe.

We played those games for days on end during our long, hot summers, immersed in the perfumes of eucalypt, hot dry grass and seaside air, and accompanied always by the constant din of thousands of cicadas, the clicking of grasshoppers, the relaxed chortling of magpies and the sudden laughter of kookaburras, the cries of gulls – and from time to time, the distant, steady rhythm of a single-cylinder diesel engine from a water pump somewhere, or maybe from a boat moving slowly across the lake sparkling below us.

It was an unhappy family, but I did have all this: the lakes and the islands, the beaches, lagoons, rocks and cliffs, the bush and creeks, the foreshore, wharf, sheds and slip-yard, the fishermen's nets (the smell of them), the paddocks, the hillsides, the skies and – especially – the trees. God, I loved the trees! Mallacoota was an extraordinarily beautiful place. Still is.

I honest-to-god believe I spent just about my entire childhood outside in the landscape, simply loving what my eyes were seeing. I drank it all in. In great greedy gulps.

I believe it was the riches of the natural world all around me that got me through the disunity in the family, the sadness, the poverty, the wordlessness – the chaos. My heart and my soul were nourished by beauty (as James Hillman would say), 'in perception', in the moment of recognition, in the very act of breathing it in.

I felt so glad, so lucky to be in that place. Enriched by it, I might almost say now, by the sheer beauty – what Hillman refers to as the 'divine face of things' – of each and every thing, calling for my attention, which I happily, gratefully, gave.

But that's all. I didn't do anything at all with any of it…

———

It was the 1950s, just a few years after the end of the war. We were familiar with men on crutches, with one leg and a stump (the other trouser rolled up, or cut off and stitched up), or just one arm, with the empty sleeve tucked into the jacket pocket. Not that I had any idea – despite having an unhappy father who was trying to bury or forget too many things in drink – of the horror they were evidence of.

Nor did I understand or properly appreciate a mother who – bitter for all she had lost – would wade in the lagoons at night with lantern and net to catch prawns, and pump pipis among the islands during the days, and sold it all as fishing bait to tourists. With the proceeds she bought a good milking cow which provided more than enough milk for the family, enabling her to sell the extra along with copious jars of cream; a mother who must once have imagined such a different life.

At times when I felt a particular unwantedness, when I was perhaps eight or nine years old, I would be outside somewhere among the trees, under the sky – loving it all, but perhaps feeling a little intimidated by all the beauty, by the sheer scale of the world, feeling small, useless – and the question would come to me (and god knows, it isn't an original question), What are we here for, what am I here for?

Feeling unwanted in there, much more engaged out here, but faced with all this beauty… What can I do? What should I be trying to do? Every time I asked that question, and I did ask it many times, the answer was the same: Well, you've just got to try and add to what is. You've got to look at all this, and figure out some way of making something that is not there already. You've got to add something, *of your own making*, to the world.

Well… How to do that?

Another, equally unoriginal, also not unreasonable question.

———

Mallacoota Primary was a one-and-a-half-teacher school, at that time with only three buildings. The old main building (moved from its original location around the lake), was just one room, where the 'main' teacher taught all subjects to all kids from Grades 3 to 6, all together. In the built-in verandah was a shelf with maybe thirty or forty books on it: the *Famous Five* and *Secret Seven* series by Enid Blyton; *Biggles*, and *Noddy and Big Ears*, and a selection of Golden Books. This was the school library.

Out the back, behind the old building, was a small shelter-shed, open to the weather on one side. The kindergarten and younger grades used to be in there for a while, and that's where I learnt to read the alphabet, sitting at my little wooden table with maybe a dozen or so other children. Then a new portable classroom was put up and that was where Mrs Cav McLeod, a local, taught Kindergarten and Grades 1 and 2 from then on. Physically tiny (and I thought she was about a hundred years old at the time), Cav was there for years, but we tended to get a regular turnover of the 'main' teachers – all men, most of them married and not anywhere near as wonderful as Cav.

One of them must have seen the whole town as requiring serious missionary work; we sang hymns at the beginning of each day, and he would hold bible and religious instruction classes after hours, in his residence.

Another I remember as being totally uninterested in us, pissed off at being posted to such a godforsaken place, I think. He did, however, have a very pretty daughter, whom my cousin Brenny and I 'shared' – making a tunnel through the dense melaleuca just outside the school grounds beside the residence to a secret cubby we built especially for the purpose, where we'd all three just sit together. Brenny and I took it in turns to hold hands with the teacher's daughter, feeling very pleased with ourselves.

There was another one, unmarried, who was always angry, shouting and making liberal use of the big leather strap he had in his desk, thrashing boys for no good reason at all. One day he actually hauled one of my older brothers from his desk, and threw him onto the rough concrete block on which the briquette heater stood, cutting and grazing his leg badly. The Education Department, bowing to pressure from the townspeople, removed him at the end of that year, but only to an even smaller school some miles up the road, which closed down only a year or two later when he was similarly removed from there.

And then kids from that school had to travel down to Mallacoota with Cliff Hatfield, the one-armed driver, in his old brown bus. I liked Cliff. He was funny, but scary too. He used to yell, 'Watch out, watch out! I'm gonna getcha,' and shake his stump at us whenever we saw him, usually going into or coming out of the pub.

Of all the kids who travelled on that bus, the Johnson kids were the most extraordinary. There were something like thirteen kids in the family, and they all lived in a tumbledown old farmhouse a few miles down the river from the town. They would have to be up at god knows what hour in the morning – rain, hail or shine – to do odd jobs about the place before breakfast, then run down the hill to the river, and row across in an old dinghy. They'd then catch a couple of horses in a paddock and ride bareback (two or three to a horse) through I don't know how many miles of bush to the turnoff to Gipsy Point, where they left their horses and waited for Cliff to come along and take them the ten winding miles to Mallacoota. And they'd go back home again the same way, every day, in summer, autumn, winter, spring…catch Cliff's bus, get off at the Gipsy Point turnoff, see if they could find and catch the horses, ride through the bush to the river, to the boat, and then home to do more chores before teatime.

Sometimes younger kangaroos or wallabies would wander into the school grounds, causing great excitement and much running around. The two older Johnson boys would say they could catch one for us if we liked. 'Betcha can't!' And off they'd go, belting across the oval after the poor wallabies, leaping the fence and disappearing in hot pursuit into the bush beyond, leaving the rest of us well and truly behind. After half an hour or so, maybe an hour, back they'd come, with an exhausted, panting wallaby draped over one shoulder. 'Easy enough, mate. Just a matter of runnin' 'em down. Wearin' 'em out.'

When I was in Grade 4, we had a truly extraordinary teacher, a young man in his first year out from teachers college in Melbourne – Don Wordsworth. He used to write stories for us on the two blackboards at the front of the room on either side of the small briquette heater. Every Monday morning, after standing in line and singing the National Anthem under the flagpole, we'd march into the room, look up and find the board on the left completely filled, top to bottom, with a story he had written up there during the weekend, all in the most elegant copperplate script, perfectly angled, in white chalk, with proper paragraphs, beautifully decorated margins and all the initial capitals coloured in. The other board to the right would be similarly filled with a beautiful coloured chalk drawing of whatever the story was about. Written especially for us, the story might be about one of the local shipwrecks – the *Monumental City*, say, just off Tullaberga Island, or the *Riverina*, near Cape Everard – or about the building of the lighthouse on Gabo Island.

Or it might be about all the bird life on the lake. On the right-hand board there'd be a whole series of smaller drawings of the five or six islands in the bottom lake, all of them so different from one another, with the hills all around – and close-up pictures, all exquisitely drawn, of the different waterbirds, the different sorts of nests they built, and the different sorts of eggs they laid.

Spectacular!

And he did this every week.

He had amazing enthusiasm and energy, together with a real knack of combining work and play. Work *became* play.

The school had a fenced garden around it, and a small shed tucked away in a corner for tools. Suddenly we all had spades, forks, rakes and hoes, carefully labelled with our own names; we would work out there for several hours every week, and we loved it. We planted flowers, creating banks of colour around the lawns, and put in twenty vegetable beds – each about six feet by four, two students to each small bed – which we framed in timber, filled with soil and compost, and planted and maintained ourselves, while Mr Wordsworth went around helping, advising, and down on his hands and knees, pulling out weeds with us, joking and laughing. And we were able to take home bags of beans and beetroot, cabbage, carrots and corn, lettuce, parsley, potatoes and pumpkin...

He had a great work ethic himself, and expected us to work also. But he had a singular talent for helping us get there. On days that promised to be hot and sunny, for example, he would say to us, 'We've all got a lot of work to do today, but how about we work twice as hard, and get the whole day's work done this morning, all of it, before lunch? We could then all take our lunches, and head out into the bush for the rest of the day, and have a bit of fun in the cool of the trees.'

And sometimes, after we'd lunched under the trees somewhere (Vegemite or jam sandwiches, in brown paper bags, an apple and maybe something to drink), he'd say, 'What say we all get stuck into building a jolly good cubbyhouse?' And we'd be into it, for the rest of the day, until home time.

Or we'd do nature walks. Most of the local kids, viewing the whole area for miles and miles around as our own back yard, probably thought we already knew all there was to know out there – but through his stories and drawings, and on these walks through the bush, Mr Wordsworth pointed out all sorts of things we hadn't known before, hadn't even guessed at. He gave us the proper names for birds, pointed out their nests – some high in the foliage of trees, some inside hollow branches or trunks, some on twiggy little bushes, some on the ground, hidden in the grasses. He knew all the spiders, and taught us which ones we needed to be careful about, and which ones merely looked scary. He knew bugs and beetles, and could do great birdcalls. He was amazing.

He would also take us all to the beach, to our favourite swimming place, the stink-hole (which was anything but, I have no idea why we called it that) – teaching those who didn't already know how to swim. Sometimes my mother came also, to help him with the younger kids.

There were times when I didn't really want to go home at the end of a day, when probably a whole lot of kids didn't want to.

I loved him. He was like a great big, beautiful gift. I think the whole town loved him.

DRAWN *from the* HEART

Every so often we'd drive to Eden to visit Ganny, my mother's mother, along sixty miles of winding dirt road, stopping frequently so I could throw up at the side of the road. On one such rest stop, between these dreaded heavings, I spotted half-buried among the bracken a small pewter vase, which I fell in love with – fifty years later it is still on my desk, used to stand brushes in.

Ganny lived in the log cabin my grandfather had built a quarter of a century before. It had small windows, and was always a little dark inside with candles specially mounted (on what we used to call 'Blackfella's bread' fungi) around the walls. There was still the handmade bush furniture (made originally for the Girl Guides), the antlers and the heavy Logan tartan drapes from Edrom, and Ganny's beautiful big brass bed looking like something out of a book, and a collection of swords stuffed into a big pot just inside the door, a couple of lovely old wooden chests and a magnificent great fireplace, built with big, rounded, water-worn smooth stones.

Visiting Ganny, in that cabin, was like visiting heaven. She dressed beautifully, in boldly patterned fabrics, and was always gracious, generous and kind. She was also cheeky; she joked, smiled and laughed a lot, and told stories in a language unlike any I'd ever heard before. And she always smelt delicious, as did the whole cabin.

I dropped in again, with my own young family, some years ago when the cabin was serving as the local library. And as soon as I opened the door, there it was: (almost) the same smell! The smell of the logs, the oil that had been used on them, of the handmade log furniture, the fabrics, the curtains, the rugs. But not quite the same… This time, there was no Ganny welcoming me with hot scones fresh from the oven and jam and cream on the table, no great strawberry-blonde head of hair with combs stuck all over the place, no round, soft cheeks and laughing eyes, no more bold orange pattern swirling on white skirt… There was no more Ganny, smelling of good things to eat.

––––––––

Towards the end of my primary school years, the family moved to Paynesville on the Gippsland Lakes, where Nanna and Pop (my father's parents) lived in their old house just out of town. We moved into a run-down rental house immediately across the street from the school where I would do Grade 6. At the end of that year, much to my amazement, I was awarded a scholarship that would cover all my school costs for the next two years. The family moved again, to Bairnsdale, and I began Form 1 (Year 7) at the Technical School there, just above the river.

It was a pretty rough school in a lot of ways at the time. The (boys-only) Tech. was seen as 'the trades school', less academic than the co-educational high school across the other side of town. It certainly had its share of bullyboys and thugs among the students – there was rough behaviour, the odd spasmodic fight and downright ugly brawl in the schoolyards, just as there were some extremely unpleasant members of the teaching staff – starting with the Principal himself (quite different from the friendly old Headmaster). I believe his idea of a really good way to start a day was to have as many boys as possible lined up in the corridor outside his office, waiting for the belt.

There were the gentler souls on staff, too – the new Science teacher, for example, who really was a very clever young man and so clearly wanted to be a good teacher, but who, faced with us, was so nervous. His right hand was almost always fiddling in the pocket of his brand-new dustcoat, jiggling car keys or marbles or something; the more nervous he became, the more his wide, gentle mouth would open and close, and the more his thin, pale hand would dart into that pocket, to grab and fiddle about with whatever was in there.

Before the beginning of class one day, a couple of particularly unpleasant boys had slipped two or three small bird eggs, gone off already, into the right-hand pocket of his coat while it was still hanging on its hook just inside the door. When class was in, they began to disrupt proceedings, slowly at first, just every now and again – enjoying the build-up, savouring the moments – harassing the poor bloke to the point where finally he snapped, and in went the hand…

The whole class had been primed of course, and we were all watching closely as the hand went in, and began fiddling…

Suddenly, the hand stopped. The poor wretch's face turned paler than pale, and twitched, almost uncontrollably, and then became quite still, before he suddenly left the room almost at a run – almost, if not actually (I know this now), crying.

Appalling. Absolutely appalling.

But it wasn't *all* bad, Bairnsdale Tech. I enjoyed most of my time there, and, in a school that used a system of 'streaming' with the 'better' students in Groups A and B, the 'strugglers' in F – as it happened, my own results at the end of each year always put me among the top three or four of the very good group of students I went with – I mostly remember only a good-hearted competition.

The one I think most about now is Robert Jones. Not that we were particular friends at the time – we weren't. I spent much more time mucking about with other kids. We were in the same group, A, all the way through. He was different from the rest of us in lots of ways – not so physical, or sporting, much more civilised and sensitive, actually gentle; a quiet boy who actually enjoyed reading and listening to classical music. Highly focused academically, he came top of the top class every year. The rest of us were not so serious about school and tended to belt about the town, haring up and down the riverbank on our bikes and getting into fights and generally causing our fair share of trouble throwing the odd stone on the odd roof, pinching the odd bottle of milk from somebody's front doorstep, throwing cakes around inside one of the showground pavilions when we'd actually been sent there to help clean and tidy up. We'd swim across the Mitchell River to steal cobs of corn from the Italians' farms on the other side, stuffing them down our bathers ('Waddyah reckin about that? Bewdy, eh?'), laughing, swimming back to cook them over a fire on our side of the river. We'd climb out on overhanging branches, swinging out on ropes as far as we could, dropping into our favourite swimming hole, doing our damnedest to land as close as possible to a mate's head, just as he was coming up. We came damned near, on any number of occasions, to killing one another, or at least breaking a neck.

Robert never joined us on any of these escapades – though for a couple of those years he and I lived just round the corner from one another.

The rest of us all had families to go home to – not all of them were picture postcards of perfect happiness, but we all had mothers and fathers, and most had both brothers and sisters. Among all the boys we knew in that school, in that whole town, Robert was the only single child we knew, and the only one with a single parent.

I suppose we would have been able to imagine the possibility of there being only a single parent in a family, if that single parent were a mother – fathers have accidents, after all; they fall off roofs, under tractors, out of boats and drive off the road – but Robert was especially unusual because his single parent was a father!

We couldn't imagine what might have happened to his mother. It was so extraordinary that I, for one, wasn't ever even game to ask. But perhaps most puzzling of all was the closeness of his relationship with his father. A couple of times I invited Robert to come around after school, 'We could read comics, or go for ride maybe, down the river…'

He would say, 'Thanks, but my Dad'll be there, and we're going to work in the garden.'

His dad'll be there? They're going to work in the *garden*?

I'd ride by a bit later and, sure enough, there they'd be, happily working away together in their garden, one of them pruning, the other nearby, digging or weeding. Another time I saw them sitting on the front verandah of their modest little cottage – white weatherboards I think, with a green, corrugated iron roof, lace curtains in the windows – sitting together in the late afternoon sun, both of them reading, and music coming softly through an open window from somewhere inside the house.

Robert and his father were friends. You could tell. But I never actually met Robert's father; we never spoke.

One of our teachers, Chester Eagle, years later, told me Robert's dad was a real gentleman. 'As was Robert,' he said. 'Two of nature's gentlemen.'

————

One of the things that stands out most vividly, still, from all my time at Bairnsdale Tech. is that once inside the distinctive Art Deco building, you'd find framed reproductions of paintings by Rembrandt, Van

DRAWN *from the* HEART

Gogh, Cézanne, Pissarro, Manet, Sisley, Vlaminck, Degas, Picasso hanging on classroom and corridor walls, everywhere. A simple enough thing, but, god how I loved those pictures! I began to dig out art books from the school library – books on Leonardo da Vinci, Raphael, Holbein, Rodin, Michelangelo – and could not believe, was stunned, in absolute awe of what those blokes had done, with what their eyes had seen. I would sit or stand in front of those pictures and be amazed at their beauty – at the compositions, the colours, the brushwork, the drawing; amazed at the sheer skills involved.

I found heroes.

And Don Wordsworth again! He was there at the Tech. teaching Mathematics (which rapidly became my best subject), but he would still, if we'd got all our work done in the first period and it was a sunny day, take us down along the riverbank immediately behind the school – not to build cubbyhouses any more, not to go on nature walks, but to draw.

'Get your sketchbooks,' he'd say, handing out black-lead pencils. 'I want you all to choose a tree you like, look at it carefully, and draw it. Now off you go.' Once we'd all settled to the task, he would wander around, looking at what we were doing, giving advice and commenting. Then, when he figured we'd all got far enough with that exercise, he'd take back the pencils and hand out sticks of charcoal, perhaps, or bottles of black India ink and pens, or brushes, and say, 'I want you all to look at your tree again, think about it, and draw it again' (with the charcoal this time, or the pen, or brush and ink, or whatever).

So simple. But amazingly instructive.

In those wonderful, 'stolen' hours, down on the riverbank, I learnt something about how many very different ways of drawing there are; how many different ways of looking, seeing, thinking and doing. And though Maths remained by far my best subject – the subject I was most successful in, closely followed by Science – I slowly began to feel that it was somehow a little too easy. You either understood the method of the particular problem or not, got it right or not. And mostly I understood the methods, and got the right answers. I began to see Mathematics as being simply uninteresting; whereas with drawing, you could look at a tree, see a tree a hundred different ways, and still have more to explore. You didn't always come up with a good drawing, of course – I very rarely managed to do a drawing quite as I'd 'seen' it in my head – but that just made it all the more interesting. I would simply have another go, and maybe use a different tool or medium for trying to 'get it' this time. Slowly I began to think, 'Now, this is something I'd really like to try to do.'

In addition to Mr Wordsworth, we had a couple of other pretty good teachers – Mr Ferguson in the Art department, but especially, in the English department – Kevin Murray and Chester Eagle. Together they covered the entire curriculum in spelling, grammar and punctuation, clear thinking and 'coloured writing', and the structure and art of the essay. We read and wrote essays constantly in my last couple of years at Bairnsdale Tech. Most notably, Chester read to us all sorts of things: not your Greeks, and not exactly the canon of Great English Literature; rather, he chose writing (and subject matter) that I suppose he felt we could more easily identify with and that meant primarily Australian novels, a lot of short stories, and especially tall stories set in the country. He was a wonderful, passionate reader, extraordinarily expressive; he brought these texts and all the characters in them vividly alive for us.

Chester would be standing, usually, at the front of the room while he was reading. Well, actually not just standing, and not just reading – he'd be pacing, gesticulating, enacting, living; he'd be breathing life into the characters, while we'd all be sitting with the text of the day open on our desktops, following. We had to follow, because every now and again he would ask one of us to take over. Woe betide any boy who was spotted gazing out the window daydreaming, or, much worse, with his head bent over a comic instead of the required text. A chalk missile or a (bigger, heavier) chalkboard duster would be hurled at the offending head, with a (literally) stunning accuracy, always. If the offence was judged to be more serious, Chester, still reading, would calmly walk up the aisle beyond the offender to the back of the room, turn, and without skipping a beat quietly close the book (but continue reciting as he approached – he knew the texts well enough to be able to do this), come down behind the boy, and belt him hard on the back of his head with the now closed book; then he'd demand that the lad continue reading from where he had just left off.

The stunned boy, in all likelihood having his book open at the wrong page, would start reading the wrong passage, from three pages back or – taking another stab – perhaps three pages forward. Chester would allow the poor bugger to stew in his own juice for a while there – no fun for the victim, but certainly edifying for the rest of us – then ask him whether he had been enjoying the story after all, whether he would like to explain some particular detail or nuance in the text to the rest of the class.

'Ah, no, that's okay…'

'It's bloody well NOT okay, Mister! You miserable little wretch. God knows why you bother to come to this class! God knows how you got into the class at all! And God alone knows, for that matter, why on earth you would think you are even remotely welcome to come into my room! MY room. Because you most certainly are not! So you can just–get–out! Get OUT! I say.'

And then (as the boy headed to the door) he'd call out, 'No, no, wait! On second thoughts, we'll go this way.' And he would drag the offender over to one of the old multi-paned sash windows, which he'd throw open with an almighty bang. Chester's room was on the upper floor, and the drop to the asphalt below was around twenty feet. He would shove the poor kid headfirst at the open window, and threaten to throw him out. 'Perhaps that would knock some sense into your un-bloody-believably thick head! I seriously doubt it myself, but it's got to be worth a try. GOD KNOWS, everybody in this place has tried everything else with you for quite long enough now, and all you've done is proven yourself a complete WASTE OF TIME AND ENERGY!'

In Year 9, Chester somehow blended all the curriculum requirements with his passion for Ned Kelly. All our work in English that year – whether it was spelling, grammar, clear thinking, essays or whatever – had Ned Kelly as its subject. He read all sorts of Kelly texts, stories and histories to us, and had been working on his own play about Ned, which he read aloud also. We became almost as obsessed as Chester was with the mythology that surrounded Ned. We did a whole lot more than just English in English that year; we made sets, costumes and props, painted scenery and even built the stage itself – at the base of the slope between the back of the school buildings and the riverbank – and all the seating for the audience, in fact a whole amphitheatre running right across and up the slope.

Just about the entire population of the school seemed to be involved in one way or another – if not as performers, then as carpenters, painters, costumers. There were three or four acts, and the entire cast changed with each act, different classes taking different acts. (The less interested boys in each class were trees; they simply stood about holding eucalypt branches in front of them.) In the weeks leading up to the actual performance we rehearsed over and over and over – for both of them – for Chester, and for Ned. Ned was Chester's Magnificent Obsession. He became ours, too.

Chester Eagle's 1963 production of *Ned Kelly*, by the banks of the Mitchell River, just behind Bairnsdale Tech. – it was fantastic.

Maybe the trees among us were not so persuaded, but a whole lot of us, I know, thought Chester himself was *totally* magnificent, for all his madness.

Hell and damnation, he could get angry – he'd threaten to drop blithering idiots, missing links and philistines from the second-storey window to the asphalt below; or mime the grabbing of some unfortunate by the throat – absolutely wring it with gusto, tying it in a thumping great knot, then throw open that window again, and hurl it out. He'd crash the window closed, spin around and stride back to the front of the class, vigorously wiping his hands on the sides of his jacket as if to remove all traces of contact with the boy. 'God damn! Black dogs.' He'd turn this way and that, snorting through his nose, pulling at it, flustered and furious, grabbing a piece of chalk from the shelf at the base of the board as if about to write something up there, but instead, spinning round again and throwing it at the rear wall of the classroom. And all the while he'd be running his hand wildly, again and again, through his unruly black hair – whipping and pulling not only at the nose, but at the cheeks, the chin, the forehead, the whole head, and snorting, snorting…

It does sound a bit crazy, I know – sad to say, he quite possibly wouldn't be considered employable nowadays – but he wasn't. He was *wonderful*.

While he is thrashing around at the front of the class, throwing open (then banging closed) cupboard doors, grabbing papers from the top of his desk then throwing them down again, we are all just sitting there, watching. We are not surprised by any of this, really, because of course we've seen it all before, many times. But we are stunned yet again by the sheer fury, the power of it; by the whole performance, the theatre. Enthralled, actually. Enthralled, and humbled. Because, critically, we also did know that he was passionate about language, about story, about beauty, about art. The love and passion he had for his subject was plenty enough reason to respect him.

We all looked forward to his classes, loved his flamboyant and firebrand style of teaching; his more extraordinary fireworks we simply regarded as fabulous symptoms of his anything but ordinary enthusiasm. We understood that he really did want to share beauty with us, wanted to help us see, hear, and enrich our lives with beauty.

We more than respected him. We loved him for that. Well, I sure as hell did.

And, of course, he never actually threw anybody out that window – it was just theatre, and entirely effective. In fact, for all his pyrotechnics, I don't remember Chester ever really hurting anybody. Oh, okay, the odd head banged onto the odd desktop, but all pretty harmless and ordinary stuff compared to the Machine-Shop Nazi and Sheet-Metal Slapper. I don't even remember Chester ever giving anybody the strap.

I am unsure, though, about what happened that time when our young Science teacher ran from the room. Some moments later, the door crashed open against the wall and an absolutely volcanic Chester exploded in, white-hot with fury, snorting and raging that we all ought to be bloody well ashamed of ourselves, that most of us were clearly still soaked in the primeval slime from which we had, quite obviously, only very recently dragged ourselves. A couple in particular.

He didn't ask anybody to name them, but made it clear he'd be waiting for them in his room – they'd better be there within the next few minutes, or we'd all be in trouble. Then he stormed out of the room, damn near wrenching the door from its hinges behind him.

Of course he knew who they were. But he wanted us all to sweat a bit further, which we did. There was a long silence after he had left the room. Then the two boys who had put the eggs in the teacher's pocket got up from their desks, and left the room, looking very unhappy indeed; looking sicker, even, than the rest of us were feeling.

I would not have liked to be in their shoes going up the stairs and along the corridor to Room 18 that day.

Chester also started a kind of music club, in a small spare room near the back of the main building. Some of us would go along and try to understand what he wanted us to hear in a piece of Bach, Beethoven or Mozart, and for a while, a few of us, including Robert, would sometimes visit his house towards the western edge of the town. We'd go in through his wildly overgrown garden (the first 'native garden' I'd ever seen); he'd welcome us with great fanfare, and we'd sit or lie around in his lounge room, which was crowded with books, records and pictures, simply listening to music. We'd be on the couch, in armchairs or on the floor in front of the fireplace – talking about Mahler, Stravinsky, Mendelssohn, Wagner. Though I was stunned by the power and sheer mystery of the music, I'm not sure I did any better in that particular exercise than I had in my rather middling role in *Ned Kelly* – as a foreman on the railway line to Glenrowan.

I had been in costume of course – appropriately grubby overalls – and was delivering my few lines to (it seemed) half the town, when I was distracted by the sight of Chester in the front row gesticulating at me, repeatedly running and rubbing both his hands through his hair. Nervous anyway, but confused also, I initially interpreted this (somewhat hopefully, desperately), as an expression of enthusiasm on his part, and ploughed on, smiling straight ahead. But as his thrashings became increasingly wild – he was positively tearing at his hair – and having no idea at all what he was trying to indicate, I chose to try to ignore him altogether and focus on finishing my delivery.

DRAWN *from the* HEART

When next I looked at him, Chester had collapsed sideways on his seat, whether with total exasperation, or relief (that my brief moment in the spotlight was over), I couldn't tell.

Come the interval, he left me in no doubt at all. It was both. He strode up to me, grabbed at my oh-so-carefully combed hair, and messed it right up. 'You're meant to be a worker for Christ's sake! A filthy–bloody–railway–worker! And instead, you're looking like a prissy little mummy's boy, standing up there with your beautifully brushed blond quiff, for god's sake! Bloody unbelievable!' And he almost threw himself off the stage.

I felt horrible that I'd let him down so badly, horrified to think that I'd ruined the entire scene, and absolutely sure that I'd very obviously made a total git of myself. (Needless to say, I've never gone anywhere near a stage since.)

I'll never forget Chester Eagle, or Don Wordsworth.

————

The other big thing that happened in Year 9 was the Vocational Aptitude Test. It was the latest thing: an amazingly clever test, supposedly – especially formulated by the very best minds in Australian education to not only help teachers work out what students would be best suited to doing for the rest of their time at school, but also to help us work out what kind of job we might look for after we left. This was clearly very important because it might, after all, turn out to be what we ended up doing for the rest of our lives.

The test was announced months in advance and we were reminded about it again, just weeks out, to make sure we would all be at school. I was a reasonably diligent student, so I approached the whole thing seriously. I read all the pages, all the questions. They seemed to deal with every conceivable thing: whether we were more interested in Mathematics (numbers) than English (words); whether we liked reading more than writing, animals more than people, working manually (with our hands) more than with our brains (thinking), indoors more than outdoors, night more than day, dark more than light, etc., etc., etc. Ridiculous. But (perhaps even more ridiculously)

I took it all seriously. I thought about all the questions – and took all the time I needed to consider the answers – carefully. I bent over the desk there, laboured away at it…for five days. It took an entire week!

Having already changed my mind a few times about what I wanted to do, I was interested. And if this test (obviously put together by people who knew what they were about) was going to help me sort any of that out – well, great.

As a five-year-old, I had wanted to be a doctor (I think that was when my dad had become an ambulance driver). But, fairly quickly, I remembered that I didn't like blood very much, and moreover, realised that doctors had to be really intelligent.

Being reasonably good at sums, and always loving being outside, I then thought, again encouraged by my father, that perhaps I'd be a surveyor working out where roads should go through the bush, and measuring everything.

Years later at the Tech., when I had Don Wordsworth for Maths, and it became my 'best' subject, I decided I would become an engineer. Dad was there again. Roads, bridges, buildings.

Next, not altogether losing my interest in mathematics, but wanting to be a bit more creative, enjoying drawing up ideas for houses, at thirteen or fourteen – I was thinking of becoming an architect. This was around the time I discovered art, and drawing. Dad was again supportive, although a little less certain.

Anyway, I did the test, and I was interested, open and ready, to receive the results, the judgment…

Some weeks or months later, we each received back a single page, with our name, year and class at the top and, in the middle of the page, a single dotted line over which was written the occupation they suggested for us.

So here it was at last, the occupation the experts thought would best suit me, the job that they were suggesting I should work toward trying to get, and that quite probably I'd have for the rest of my life…

Petrol Pump Attendant.

And, underneath that, the reasons: 'Likes being outdoors, likes dealing with people, good with numbers.'

I was stunned.

Not that I had then (nor do I have now) anything at all against petrol pump attendants. Why should I? The world needs all kinds of people. But being a petrol pump attendant wasn't anywhere on my radar screen. Even one of those good old-fashioned ones who would not only fill your petrol tank for you but wash the windscreen too, maybe even check your tyre pressure. The sort of bloke who would ask how the missus is, the kids, whether you've still got that dog, and whether your dad is still doing as much fishing as he used to…

It took me about two seconds to get over the shock, and dismiss the whole thing as a joke; a little longer for me to draw conclusions about so-called experts, figures of authority and institutions, and longer still for me to begin to find my own way.

––––––––

My eldest brother, John, was still living at home with us, and doing his plumbing apprenticeship in Bairnsdale. He had his own car already, a Ford Anglia, a pale yellow, funny-looking little thing, with a much too narrow wheelbase. He loved it.

Ted was boarding in a Legacy boys' hostel in Melbourne, studying illustration at the Royal Melbourne Institute of Technology in the city, coming home during term breaks and summer holidays. I don't recall him ever talking much about his studies there; we weren't that close. The only involvement I had was to take a photograph of him, back when we were living in Paynesville, to include in his application papers for the course.

Tess was living in a hostel attached to a hospital in Melbourne, studying to be a nurse. Sometimes John would drive to Melbourne to pick up Tess, and bring her home for a weekend. He loved the drive. It didn't matter to him that it was so far, one hundred and eighty miles or so each way. He'd drive up after work on a Friday, collect Tess in the evening, and drive back – stopping somewhere along the way for something to eat – arriving home later that night. He'd have the radio going, full bore, to keep him awake. It was fun.

Towards the end of my third year at Bairnsdale Tech., in the small hours of a Saturday morning, John and Tess went off the side of the road on their way back from Melbourne. The car rolled over the bank, and ended upside down in a creek. They were both still lying there when a passing motorist heard the music from the car radio.

John wasn't seriously hurt – he had a torn ear, a head like a football, and a few scratches here and there – but Tess's legs were very badly smashed up, so severely in fact, that the doctors at the local hospital thought both legs might have to be amputated.

A specialist from Melbourne who was passing through Traralgon early the next morning had dropped in to say hello to a colleague and fortunately happened to see her, just in the nick of time. He decided he would give the operation a go – give it a try, at least – and see how it all went.

The initial operation was a success, happily, but later, when my parents realised that Tess would need still further operations and a lot of follow-up specialist attention, maybe for quite some time, they decided the whole family should move to Melbourne.

I was fifteen, and had by now decided that I wanted to go to art school – that I really wanted to learn how to draw. I didn't know what I wanted to be, I didn't know what sort of a job I wanted to do, I only knew I wanted to learn how to really draw. Properly.

I told my parents I wanted to go to a school I'd heard about – Swinburne Tech., in Hawthorn – that offered students the possibility of specialising in Art in Years 10 and 11, after which I could go on to Swinburne Institute of Technology and do a Diploma of Art. I had made my decision; I was excited. Really excited.

My father thought I'd be much better off doing something with my mathematics – engineering, or surveying. He didn't even want to talk about 'the whole art thing – it's just plain bloody ridiculous! Van Gogh cut off his own damned ear, before he killed himself! Rembrandt! You love him. Even he died poor, they all died poor, for god's sake! You're not going to do it, and that's it!'

He was angry – said I'd damn well go to whatever school they sent me to, and bloody well continue with sensible subjects. 'None of this nonsense about spending half your bloody week doing art, for

Christ's sake! You'll bloody well do something sensible with your life – something that you'll actually be paid for!'

Being more concerned about Tess, my mother wasn't actually very interested, one way or the other. But she was sympathetic, if not to him (for a change), towards his argument at least.

We had huge arguments, all three of us. None of us would budge.

I was determined. I said I wasn't moving with them if they wouldn't let me go to Swinburne.

'And just where do you think you are going to live down here, if we're in Melbourne?'

'I'll figure something out,' I said.

And they went.

I shared some of this information – about the accident, my family's move to Melbourne and my parents' refusal to allow me to study art there – with my Art teachers, with Mr Ferguson in particular. He told me Bairnsdale Tech. didn't even offer Art as a subject at Year 10 level, let alone the possibility of specialising in it, but that if I was really serious about it, and if I could find enough other people in Year 9 going into Year 10 who were interested also ('Try rounding up a few, half a dozen would do'), then they'd let us do it.

'But you'll have to design and run your own course, pretty much. We won't have much time to help you, with all the rest of our teaching. A bit of advice here and there, maybe – we'll be able to look at what you're doing from time to time – but mostly you'll have to just get on and do it by yourself.'

Amazing, when I think back on it now.

I rounded up some mates, who probably thought it was going to be a damn good bludge, and they all signed up. At the ripe old age of just sixteen, I would be running my own art course.

My family – Mum, Dad, John, Ted, Tess and Gilbert, now about ten years old – moved to Melbourne, and I went back to live with Nanna and Pop, whom I adored, in their old house just out of Paynesville.

But my so-called art course became, predictably enough, a bit silly, a bit of a farce. Mostly I just dragged my mates around wherever I wanted to go, drawing trees along the riverbank, or the ramshackle tannery buildings by the bridge, or any other building I liked – the courthouse, or a shopfront in town. I loved it, but my mates became a bit bored after not very long at all. They all started to fade away. I also realised I wasn't really learning very much; I needed proper teachers.

Mr Ferguson would occasionally see me setting off somewhere with my sketchbook, wave hello, ask how it was going. He probably saw that more and more I was just wandering around by myself. He suggested I attend the evening art classes the school ran once a week. They were for adults but he would make an exception for me because he knew I was serious and wouldn't waste time or muck about, knew I'd work at it. That Mrs Brownbill, a very nice woman who lived just over the road from my grandparents, came to the classes, he'd talk to her – he was sure she'd be happy to bring me up and back each Thursday night.

'I know Mrs Brownbill,' I said. I'd seen her working in the garden.

'They're Life classes,' he said.

Life classes, I thought. The human figure. *The Nude*, I thought. Naked!

'I'd love to,' I said.

I liked the idea of driving up and back with Mrs Brownbill too.

I had recently discovered Degas – his charcoal and pastel figure drawings, his beautiful dancers. I loved Toulouse-Lautrec also, for his brush line work, and for the washes and touches of body colour; Ingres, for his forms, compositions and all that velvet-smooth pale skin; Maillol's sculptures of women with small breasts and torso, heavier pelvis and thighs – strong, refined, graceful. I loved them all.

And then there was Joy, a lovely girl who lived up the road past Nanna and Pop's place. Olive skin, thick, wavy black hair and big brown eyes. Delicious.

But the night classes at the Tech. were a disappointment.

Life classes in drawing, okay...but these were 'still-lifes' of things like bowls of fruit, teapots, jugs, bottles, chairs, flowers in vases. I was not exactly transfixed, and really it was a class of hobbyists simply trying to make pretty pictures. I wanted, and knew I needed, something much more.

Nanna and Pop's house was a small, late nineteenth-century weatherboard with a verandah right across the front and down one side. The floors had gentle slopes, undulations, as you walked from room to room over the patches of carpet and rugs. Pictures cut from magazines were glued all over the whitewashed, wallpapered, hessian-lined walls – wall to wall, floor to ceiling, throughout the entire house – hundreds and hundreds of pictures, stuck on the walls to cover up mouse holes.

The central hall was dominated by the Royal Family towards one end, with a few cats and dogs, including the corgis; in Nanna and Pop's bedroom the pictures were of flowers and birds mostly; mine might have had only birds in it, I think, the lounge had flowers and shells, the dining room was for landscapes, and the kitchen with its old wood-fired stove – run like a ship by Pop, who was an old sailor, seaman, lighthouse keeper from way back – was nautical in theme. Beautiful.

Only one room – originally a bedroom, but now a place for Pop to store his tools – and the lean-to bathroom and laundry were without these embellishments.

And then there was Pop's shed out by the back of the house, where there were more tools and dozens and dozens of jars and old tobacco tins full of nails, screws, nuts and bolts; the dunny down the back (past the vegetable garden and fruit trees); the woodheap under the big old oak tree, the chookyard over past the clothesline, and more fruit trees; paddocks all round the back and both sides. Cows, sheep, and a pig farm about a mile or two up the road.

I loved that place, absolutely everything about it, but what I loved most of all was simply being there, living there, with Nanna and Pop.

They were both around seventy at the time, married for just about half a century, and completely different from one another: Nanna was always chatting, full of gossip (often not very nice) about everybody, a bit impatient and always fussing about with something or other – cooking, cleaning, gardening; she was almost completely unable to sit still. Pop was so quiet, just going about his business – mending a chair, building a fence, servicing his car, cleaning his shotgun, sharpening his axe or his saws, working in the vegetable garden, pruning the fruit trees, mowing the lawns; taking his time, but getting it all done. He was a good cook, too; he cooked the most wonderful roasts – lamb, beef, chicken, pork, rabbit – with perfectly cooked vegetables always, the roast potatoes golden and crusty, and sauces and gravies the magic of which I can only guess at, and certainly have never mastered.

An excellent axeman, and still incredibly strong for his age, at about seventy he could still cut and split a ton or two of wood without breaking a sweat, simply working steadily away at it. I would help here and there where I could – in the garden certainly, digging and weeding, and with the firewood, mostly just with the carting and stacking. We rarely spoke while working together like that – neither of us really needed to. I was happy just to be there, and Pop was more for doing things, rather than talking. And he was so capable in the way he went about everything, I learnt a lot by simply watching him. If he did have something to say, it was always worth hearing. He possessed wisdom, he was modest, had a cheeky sense of humour, a lovely irony, and never had an ill word to say about anybody.

Their lives were simple, every day pretty much the same. Pop would get up at about 5.30 every morning, light the fire in the old cast-iron combustion stove in the kitchen, put the kettle on to make a pot of tea, make toast through the open door of the firebox, and then take Nanna her breakfast in bed. Usually she wanted just tea and toast, maybe with egg and bacon, and sometimes it would be porridge. She'd be sitting up by then, with a bedjacket round her shoulders, reading some trashy novel or magazine.

'There you go, Mum,' he'd say, and kiss her on the forehead. Every morning, for god knows how many years.

'Bless you, Dad,' she'd say. 'It looks wonderful!'

'He's an angel, your grandfather,' she would tell me. 'And, do you know, I can't imagine ever not wanting to sleep together with him in the same bed. After all these years, I love feeling him next to me, still. No matter how old you are, no matter how sick one of you might be, if a husband and wife don't sleep together in the same bed [as though she already knew that my parents, her son and his wife, would end up not sleeping together for the last twenty or so years of their marriage], it can't be much of a marriage.'

For six months I shared in the simple rhythms and daily rituals of my grandparents' life – all pretty much unaltered for years – chopping and stacking the firewood, working the garden, feeding the chooks, and doing the washing; cooking while listening to the ABC on the old bakelite wireless in the kitchen, and spending the evenings in front of the fire in the lounge room, reading or playing Scrabble, each with our glass of sherry. So quiet, and peaceful, without television. It was all a total pleasure, and a complete and utter privilege for me. I loved every minute of it, every minute of them.

Towards the end of my time with them, however, I did occasionally disappear after dinner, to meet with Joy. Frustrated at feeling unable to sit next to one another on the school bus to and from Bairnsdale every day – for fear of what might be said, wanting simply to avoid stupid innuendoes – Joy and I had taken to sometimes meeting in the comparative safety of the dusk, in the paddock beside her house.

I think Nanna probably telephoned my parents to say she was concerned; my father suddenly phoned, after not speaking with me the whole time I had been at Nanna and Pop's.

'It's time you came to Melbourne,' he said.

'Only if I can go to Swinburne.' (They were living in a flat in Cotham Road, just a tram ride away, down Glenferrie Road.)

'We'll talk about that when you get here.'

'I'm only coming if you agree to let me go to Swinburne.'

Eventually he relented, and a few weeks later, at mid-year, I was in Melbourne, living in a flat above Mrs Hazlehurst (Noni's mum), and enrolled in Year 10, with twenty-two periods a week of Art, at Swinburne Junior Technical School for boys.

I was sad to leave Nanna and Pop. Their house, furniture, garden, and the rhythms and patterns of their life together – all that went, fifteen years later, into *John Brown, Rose and the Midnight Cat*, and 20 years later again, into *Old Pig*.

————

Although I felt like a bit of a country bumpkin for a while, I settled in reasonably quickly at Swinburne, found new friends and thoroughly enjoyed my eighteen months there. Drawing, painting, sculpture, art history (using the bible, Gombrich's *History of Art*), and more drawing – with the wonderfully generous Frank Hall and Ros Press, fresh out of art school herself, and with whom we were all somewhat smitten.

Apart from having the opportunity to spend so much of every school week studying and practising art for those eighteen months, I discovered a whole new world of art, culture and ideas, a whole new way of thinking, in the galleries and museums in and around the city. In a wonderfully dark little café in Glenferrie Road – the atmosphere thick with the aromas of real coffee, cigarette smoke and rich, hearty soups – where I first heard Bob Dylan, the owners happily hung some of my drawings on their walls (my first exhibition!). There was also a small second-hand bookshop, spectacularly crowded, not with people but with books – books spewing from the floor-to-ceiling shelves onto the floor, tunnels and towers of books, all tucked into a hole in a wall alongside the Glenferrie railway station. There I discovered Tolstoy, Dostoevski, Orwell, Shaw, Wilde. And further up Glenferrie Road was Martin and Rosie Smith's art materials supply shop, full of originals by Boyd, Nolan, Blackman, Dickerson and Olsen, all just lying about, or stacked against and hanging on the walls. Rummaging around in the shop one day, I went to the stairs to listen more closely to some music I could hear coming from upstairs, and was invited up by their two daughters…into a world so exotic and, yes, bohemian, that I was stunned. The music I thought must have been African turned out to be the Rolling Stones – it was the first time I'd ever even heard of them, and there were records and books lying about and art everywhere, with not a bare surface in the whole place. The girls seemed almost to be from another planet, wafting around in their fabrics and jewellery, stunning in their worldliness and their familiarity with art and literature; articulate, open, friendly and generous, unlike anybody I'd ever met, inhabiting a world unlike anything I'd even been able to imagine. We lounged about on couches, cushions and rugs on the floor, listening to more Stones, Dylan, The Kinks, and to still more

Dylan. It was 1965. I was seventeen. Those two totally lovely girls poured me my first wine, my first real coffee… It was all so fabulously new and exotic to me, I might have been in a Bedouin tent somewhere, or living in a Toulouse-Lautrec.

The building on the corner of Glenferrie Road and Liddiard Street in Hawthorn – with two big arched windows and the jam-packed art and supplies shop at street level, and their other-world residence upstairs – was close to my idea of some kind of earthly paradise. It is now a real estate agency.

I was painting all the time, or if I wasn't actually painting I was at least thinking about it; studying the history, reading the books, looking at the works and reading the letters of the great artists. Ray Bowler and I (Ray was also studying at Swinburne) used to go drawing and painting down by the Yarra at Studley Park, and we were constantly visiting the National Gallery, which at that time was behind the State Library and the old Museum in Swanston Street. God, how I loved being able to get up that close to a real Rembrandt, a real Cézanne, able to look that closely at the real colour, the real brushstrokes.

At night I would do almost nothing but draw and paint, and at weekends I would walk for miles with my sketchbooks, sheets of masonite and paints, from North Balwyn out through the apple orchards and hills of Doncaster, and do my best possible imitations of Pissarro, Sisley, Monet, Van Gogh. Later, it would be trains to Williamstown, pursuing Cézanne, Derain, Braque, even a little Perceval. Later still – nostalgic for the country and in awe of the early works and sketches of Streeton, in love with Conder and Roberts, with just one particular Withers, and fond of (only some) McCubbin – I went backwards, in more ways than one – I'd catch trains to Castlemaine, or hitch to Daylesford, Blackwood and Trentham.

After Year 11 at Swinburne Tech., gaining a studentship and working as a gardener to pay my way, I began my Diploma of Art at Swinburne Institute of Technology.

Thrilled to be in a 'real art school' at last, I stayed, however, only for one year. I found the overall direction of the course to be too commercial for my taste; the course there was aimed at graphic design and advertising – and my main interest was still simply in learning to draw in what I have to admit was a fairly traditional manner – sound, solid draughtsmanship of the sort I so loved in Rembrandt, Degas, da Vinci, Holbein. For all its many other very good qualities, there was not much of an interest or emphasis on (any sort of) drawing at Swinburne. We had life- and figure-drawing classes, but I didn't find the teaching good enough. I knew from my brother that in the illustration course at RMIT, there were still a couple of 'old-fashioned' drawing teachers there; it sounded as though that was just about all they did – draw, draw, draw. I decided to leave Swinburne, and apply to RMIT for the beginning of my second year.

I went to the interview, showed my folio, did the test, and got in. I was in heaven just walking through the front door into the art school every day, through the smell of oil paint, linseed oil and turpentine, and up the stairs to the big drawing studios with their large windows looking across Latrobe Street to the State Library, the Museum and National Gallery.

It was not all plain sailing. A year earlier, those of us who had come from eleventh year at 'technical' schools into first year at Swinburne had to pick up Year 12 English in addition to doing the first-year art subjects. Not that I saw this as a problem – I loved English, and still had the example and inspiration of Chester Eagle in my heart and head; moreover, though his name now escapes me, we had a great teacher at Swinburne (who happened to be on the board of examiners for the state examinations). He would frequently read bits of my essays out loud to the class and say, 'You can actually write, my boy! You won't have any trouble at all.' At the end of the year I came out of the four-hour examination on top of the world; I felt I had never written so well in my life.

Come January or February the next year, when the results were published, and just as I was about to begin at RMIT, I found I had failed. I damn near died of shame.

Looking back now, I wish I'd had the spunk to question the result, but (still a country boy) I didn't. I just re-enrolled in English at RMIT, to do it all again during my second year.

I felt so deeply shamed by my failure, crippled by it, that I was barely able even to read the texts, unable to write a thing, and certainly lost all confidence about joining in on any class discussion. In fact, I almost lost all power of speech – I shrivelled up inside myself, felt like an idiot, barely spoke at all, to anyone, anywhere, for the whole year.

It was 1967, the year Fred Williams had a show of absolutely astonishing paintings at the Georges Gallery in Collins Street. I was stunned by them. I visited that exhibition of around twenty or so paintings again and again and again, almost unable to believe them. But believing them utterly.

I had been looking at and loving the Australian landscape and admiring Australian landscape painters for years – from Martens through Buvelot and Glover to Streeton, Roberts, Conder – but had never seen anything like this.

The earlier artists had produced pictures as though looking through frames or windows, all beautifully composed, with natural perspective. Everything was there in Williams' pictures – the trees and hillsides (of Upwey), the horizon line, the skies, the space, the light – but he had flattened the whole picture field dramatically, simplified all the detail, abstracted it, distilled it all back to two dimensions, and enriched it hugely. All the marks – the brushstrokes themselves, the transparent washes of colour and the more opaque areas, and the daubs, dribbles and splotches of thick paint straight from the tube – all the actual building up of the painting was itself at least as important as, and somehow at one with, the image. Everything was right there, on the surface, on the one picture plane, on the canvas. This, I felt, was what painting is about.

His paintings were not mere pictures of things, of scenes – they were incredibly strong, emphatic creations in and of themselves, unbelievably compelling, powerful representations of the landscape, but not needing the scenery itself for any sort of justification. His paintings existed for their own reasons.

It may sound silly now, I know, raving about Williams like this, but I was a very old-fashioned boy – somebody who had grown up in the country, inside the landscape, and I'd only ever been able to read landscape paintings as images of three-dimensional objects in three-dimensional space. Fred Williams knocked all that for six. It was a revelation. He had obviously always loved landscape too, just as he had also looked at all those earlier paintings – especially Roberts' *Bailed Up* – but he had looked at our landscape, seen and recreated it all anew. He created a whole new way of seeing, a whole new language.

I was never able to look at landscape the same old way again.

––––––––––

At the end of that second year, having hardly read the set texts at all this time, not having written all year, I didn't believe I had a hope of passing the English examination, I almost didn't see the sense in sitting for it. But I did. I sat the exam and struggled all the way through it. And at the end of it, I knew – with every bone in my body – that I had failed miserably.

My tail now firmly between my legs, I disappeared. In the summer holidays – shouldering a huge old World War II army sleeping roll and massive backpack stuffed full with paints, brushes, sketchpads, masonite sheets, and with a collapsible easel strapped on top, I hitchhiked to Bairnsdale to visit Pop, who was then in hospital, to Mallacoota where I camped in the dense tea-trees by Mortimer's Paddock (making the mistake of stretching my swag between trees either side of a kangaroo and wallaby track), on to Boydtown, to Eden, and Wolumla. Then, for two or three weeks, I simply walked inland, kept company by chortling magpies all the way, stopping to paint whenever I came across a hillside or gully that demanded my attention, and camping – rolling out my swag, lighting a fire, putting the billy on, and cooking up some tucker – whenever and wherever I felt like it, and sleeping under the stars. Heaven. And eventually ended up in a cosy little hollow under a couple of willows on the riverbank, in the heart of lovely Candelo, nestled among the hills.

I was well enough intentioned, but looking back, all the landscapes I did were a pale imitation of Williams, and I became an embarrassment to myself (didn't have a clue what I was doing) when it came to painting the village of Candelo.

By the time I got back to Melbourne, I had decided I wanted to make another switch – this time out of the design and illustration department on the third floor of RMIT into the painting department on the fourth. Having that summer of painting behind me, and discovering that I had in fact passed English with a Distinction, I somehow found the confidence to speak to my lecturers about it. The painting lecturers were happy for me to come across, but none of the design and illustration lecturers wanted me to leave.

Unable to make the decision for myself, I rang my old art teacher from Bairnsdale, Mr Ferguson, who I knew was now an art inspector for the Victorian Education Department.

'Ron, we have far too many painting students coming in to teach art at our schools, none of whom can draw. You can. You may not know this, but you were the highest-scoring art student in the state among all the studentship applicants at the end of Year 11. It would be a pity to throw all that away. I think you should stick with illustration, stick with Harry and Murray. They are great teachers.'

I didn't have the courage or self-confidence to go against his advice, so I stayed with design, and with Harold Friedman and Murray Griffin, who were indeed great drawing teachers.

Harry was nearing the end of his time at RMIT by then, but he was still ferociously effective as a life-drawing teacher. He had no tolerance at all for sloppiness in attitude, no patience (no forgiveness, almost) for weak, poor drawing. He could be quite unpleasant, in fact. I remember our first life class with him.

'All right,' he said. 'We're all here. And there's your lovely model, Joan, just waiting for you. Now, show us both what you can do!' Then he promptly left the room, for quite a long time. When he finally reappeared, he walked slowly around, pausing behind some students, bypassing others, constantly snorting, harrumphing and clearing his throat as he did so. Going out to the middle of the room then, and standing next to the model, he said, 'Well…I was told some of you people in this class could draw, but doubting that myself, I was nevertheless hoping to be pleasantly surprised, and I was thinking Joan here might like to have a look at how you all see her, too. But looking at what you've been doing today – what have you been doing for the last forty-five minutes, for the last ten or fifteen years for that matter? Hmmmph? I can see now that some of you probably think you can draw, in fact one or two of you probably think you've been pretty jolly good at drawing for quite some time. Well, I am terribly sorry to have to disappoint you, but I am now telling you that absolutely none of you has any idea at all of what real drawing *is even about*! Dreadful! This is all absolutely dreadful! I've never seen such rubbish. And there is no way [he was now pacing around between the students and the model, gesticulating wildly] I'm going to invite Joan here to walk around and see what you've done to her – she'd be a mess! We wouldn't be able to get her to continue, would we? And we can't have that – good heavens no. We couldn't have that.

'Sooo…I'm terribly sorry to have to do this to your poor, fragile, self-important little egos, but I am going to take you right back to the beginning, right back to square one, and teach you all over again how to draw properly. And we are going to take our time about it; there'll be no rushing it. The first thing you're all going to do is throw out any pencils, anything with a point on it – there'll be no silly little line drawings in my class; I'm not remotely interested in seeing every single one of Joan's lovely eyelashes, all the wrinkles round her eyes, or her finger- and toe-nails. I certainly don't want to see some pretty little outline around her leg, if the leg itself doesn't look as though it could stand up – let alone support the weight of her body, for god's sake!'

He'd make us all go down to the shop and buy the very thickest sticks of charcoal they had (10 to 12 millimetres), break them into short lengths, and then using only the flat sides, show us how to draw the figure as a series of simple gestures, rhythms, weights, with no details at all.

He would determine the pose, set up the model – bossing her about while we organised our charcoal sticks and clipped our paper onto our easels – tell us what he expected, then leave the room. Reappearing ten or fifteen minutes later, he'd stalk round behind us all while we worked, pausing here and there, snorting with irritation. Then he'd launch into some poor student's drawing.

'Were you actually listening when I told you what I wanted you to do? Hmmm? Were you? No, no, I don't think you were – you couldn't have been, because this is absolutely awful [here there was much spluttering and spraying] what you've done to this poor woman here! I mean – where's the body? The *body*. Where's the weight? Where's the strength? Where's the bone, the muscle? How does she manage to stand up? For goodness sake! Nobody could stand on a leg that looks like that! Looks as though it's going to float away, or just collapse. And then what'll we do for the rest of the day with a model who can't even stand up? Eh? Eh? Hmph?'

He'd scribble all over the poor student's work, hacking it about and then, finally losing all patience, he'd call us all around to watch as he did a small demonstration drawing in the corner of the student's sheet. And he did them so easily, so solidly, those little demo drawings of his, it was almost shocking. All the weight, the tension, the movement, the form – whatever it was he was asking us to find and explore, it was always all right there, in just a few marks and strokes. Astonishing.

It was months before he let us use any line at all, and then – just when we had got used to not being allowed to use any lines, he'd make us use nothing but line; looking only at the model, sometimes even without looking at the drawing as we did it, without lifting the charcoal stick or pencil from the paper at all, we were to draw one long, never-ending line. Taking Paul Klee's line for a walk. Or then, Rodin-style, we'd use broad brushes and watercolour. He forced us to move from one way of looking, one way of seeing, to another, from one way of drawing to another. Only after a year or eighteen months of all that did he offer us any freedom, invite us to search for our own way of looking, seeing and drawing.

As abrupt and unpleasant as he could be, I hugely appreciated the rigour of his teaching. But when he was retiring to take up his appointment as the inaugural State Artist, and he invited me to leave RMIT at the end of third year to become his apprentice – without any hesitation at all, I said no. And later, when I saw what he had been doing in his new job (which he had tried to persuade me would be on a par, if not surpassing, any position Michelangelo himself attained), I had no regrets, none at all.

We then had Murray Griffin – back from semi-retirement to teach figure- and life-drawing for our last year – he was as unlike Harry as it was possible to be. An absolute gentleman, patient and generous with students, his particular passion was planes, volume and form.

'Forget the available light,' he would say, 'ignore the incidental light and shade, those dark shadows thrown by the light from the windows that just happen to be there; we don't want any black holes in the middle of the form. Imagine instead that the light comes from your point of view – as if you have a miner's light on your forehead – and so the planes of the body facing you are lightest, the planes going over the top of any of the forms the next lightest, the ones around to the sides having just that bit more tone; and the planes going under the forms – whether forms as small as the brow, the nose, the lips, the jaw, or the larger ones – the arm, the torso, the buttocks, the leg – make them the darkest, the strongest.

'Look at Holbein's heads,' he would say. 'It is the strength of the tone on the plane *under* the jawline – whether it is done with a single line, continuous tone or with hatching – however it is done – it is the strength of that tone, the strength of that *plane*, that holds the *whole* head.'

Several other teachers also made an impression: the incredibly modest and gentle Mr McDonald, who took us for nature drawing – trees in the Exhibition Gardens, stuffed birds and animals from the Museum across the road, plants and shells; a 'Methods of Production' teacher, Frank Campbell, but whose classes are memorable only for how many cigarette butts he might have had lined up, standing on his desk at the end of a long, droning hour or two; and John Mason, who ran the illustration department after Harry left, whose own specialty was making pictures using thousands of nails, and who encouraged us to work in whatever medium and in whatever way we liked. He was a breath of fresh air in what had become, finally, a slightly stuffy old place. It was John (he was English) who brought in picture books and introduced to us some of the illustrators from the 'new wave' of English picture book makers in the 1960s – Brian Wildsmith, Victor Ambrus, Charles Keeping, Raymond Briggs. Collectively, they became heroes among all the illustration students. I asked my lecturers whether they knew of anything going on here. As far as they knew, there was nothing. All the picture books were brought in from England, America or wherever. Nobody was originating them in Australia.

I explored all sorts of media in my fourth and last year, in 1969; in fact I was all over the place with paintings, collages, drawings, printmaking, assemblages, sculpture, but in among all that I had also done a lot of pen-and-ink line drawings. At the end of the year, we held our graduation exhibition, to which all sorts of people from industry were invited – art directors, designers, television producers, magazine and newspaper editors, and publishers. The studios were crowded with people drinking wine and eating cheese and biscuits, with the students huddled somewhat self-consciously in a corner. Mr McDonald – beside himself, almost – came over to me. 'Oh, Ron,' he said, 'Mr Eyre, *Frank Eyre*, is here. He wants to meet you.'

We had heard about Frank Eyre – he was the Managing Director of Oxford University Press in Australia. In his previous position with OUP in London, before he was sent out to the colonies, he had been very largely responsible for that new wave in English picture books. He was now (almost) some kind of god, apparently – and I was to be ushered into the Very Presence.

He had a full head of wavy grey hair, wore horn-rimmed glasses, a brown tweed jacket, a knitted tie, and (I think) green trousers. He struck an imposing figure, a bit larger than life, with an even larger and very English voice. Booming, in fact.

Yes, just like God, I imagined. And yes – everybody around him was just about scraping…

'Wellll, Mr Brooks…' [this should all be set in loud, bold type, all in capital letters – but still it wouldn't be loud enough] 'it seems you have almost learnt how to draw, hmmm?'

(Imagine now, a very squeaky, thin little voice, barely audible.) 'Gee…thank you, Mr Eyre.'

'I have been having a bit of a look at your pen-and-ink drawings on the walls here; they're not bad, not bad at all – actually quite good, young man.'

'Ummm, gee, thank you.'

'I am wondering whether you might like to do a book with us.'

'Well, gee, gosh, of course I'd love to… Really?'

'Of course, my boy! Now, why don't you come down to my office some time next week, and we'll have a bit of a chat about things.'

And I did.

It was nothing much, of course – a dozen or fifteen pen-and-ink drawings to be scattered throughout the text of a little (read *tiny*) book about Wilsons Promontory, written by Ross Garnett, in OUP's educational 'Life in Australia' series. But I did have fun doing it. I spent a couple of weeks camping at Tidal River, bushwalking, swimming, sketching – all in all a very pleasant holiday at the end of fourth year, it wasn't really like working at all – and then took the sketches back to Mr Eyre, who liked them, paid me $225, and asked if I'd like to do another, and then another.

I did three or four of those little books for Oxford, and a whole lot of scraperboard portraits for the covers of their equally small-format 'Famous Australians' series…and never thought anybody would ever see any of them, anywhere at all. But in fact they went everywhere, certainly into every school library in the country.

Australian publishing was a small industry back then, and before I knew it other publishers were calling me up, wondering whether I would like to have a look at a manuscript by David Martin, Mavis Thorpe Clarke, Joan Phipson…

And then Pat Thomas from Macmillan sent me a story by Jenny Wagner.

It was *The Bunyip of Berkeley's Creek*.

PART TWO

When you are a Bear of Very Little Brain,
and you Think of Things,
you find sometimes that a Thing which seemed
very Thingish inside you is quite different
when it gets out into the open and has other people looking at it.

A.A. Milne, from *The House at Pooh Corner*

The Bunyip of Berkeley's Creek

*Late one night, for no particular reason,
something stirred in the black mud at the bottom of Berkeley's Creek.*

*The fish swam away in fright, and the night birds hid their heads
under their wings.*

*When they looked again, something very large and very muddy
was sitting on the bank.*

'What am I?' it murmured. 'What am I, what am I, what am I?'

I HAD MOVED out of home after art school, into an old flat in
Prahran. I was working as a freelance illustrator and graphic designer,
doing a lot of large, messy paintings in the lounge room, arranging
little pieces of theatre – written and visual assemblages in the front

window overlooking the corner of Punt Road and High Street (just small invitations to wonder, really), for the passers-by – and met Jay, who had a baby, Michelle, and eventually they both moved in.

In among the paintings, the 'window-dressing', the illustration, design, and the nappies, and not long after I had illustrated my first 'Life in Australia' books for OUP, I had begun to get calls from editors in other publishing houses asking me to provide illustrations for novels and book covers. I did quite a few, but was not very deeply engaged by them – had little or no input into the overall design of the book.

And meanwhile, though my relationship with Jay was rocky (and continued thus, more or less, for five years), I adored Miche and books had slowly become a big part of our life together. I was buying picture books and reading with her all the time. We loved it. We loved discovering the books; we loved the reading, the sharing.

I began to think how wonderful it would be to design and illustrate these kinds of books myself, and have more control over how the whole thing looked, felt and worked. I began to think how good it would be to produce really good picture books here, in Australia, but whenever I asked editors whether there was any possibility, they all said no – there was not enough of a market for them, certainly not enough to justify all the trouble and expense of trying to originate our own. So I continued on for a couple of years with my work as a freelance illustrator with advertising agencies, design studios and publishers, and with my own clients as a designer.

It was a slightly messy time. Jay and I fell apart; I moved with friends into a share house above a photographer in Coventry Street, South Melbourne. I had a big studio out the back where I was putting together the bi-monthly film and television magazine *Lumière* (I was art director, paste-up artist, general dogsbody and gopher), as well as doing all the promotional material for St Martin's Theatre in South Yarra, and all the advertising, posters, labels, signage and some of the shop concept work for Saba and Staggers.

Somewhere in there Jay and Miche moved back in, and I had also begun studies at the Victorian Technical Teachers College in Hawthorn at the beginning of the year (as required by the studentship

I had received throughout college), and was teaching two or three days a week at the sorely neglected Altona Boys Technical School, in the western suburbs of Melbourne. I was flat out.

Of all the work I had been involved in over the previous couple of years, I felt most comfortable with the things I had done for publishers, including a set of creative drama broadsheets done in collaboration with Peter Pavey and Claire Dobbin. Claire lectured in drama at Melbourne State College, was a prominent figure in the emerging alternative theatre scene in Melbourne which centred around the Pram Factory in the early 1970s, and was deeply engaged in the whole Vietnam debate and anti-conscription movement. Astonishingly knowledgeable about all sorts of things, highly articulate, with loads of street smarts, Claire was intimidating but a lot of fun too. In a highly charged environment at the time, politically and creatively, she was hoping our sheets would help kids put together all sorts of socially engaged theatrical productions, whether in schools or on the streets.

Cassell was the publisher, and this was the first time I worked with Bob Sessions who, as editor, was responsible for seeing our little folly all the way through. I say 'folly' because although Peter and I enjoyed the whole experience, we probably didn't clear two shillings and sixpence on the whole exercise. Bob probably couldn't quite believe what he was getting for his money.

One of the greatest pleasures of this project was working with Peter. I had known him only slightly at Swinburne before I left for RMIT. When I saw his final-year folio three years later, I was stunned by his incredibly bold design, snappy typography and amazingly inventive illustration. He pushed the visual presentation of the ideas in the drama sheets far beyond anything that I could have done working alone.

Perhaps typical of an early 1970s share house in inner Melbourne, we had a shifting population at Coventry Street – mostly people who had known one another from art school or teachers college. Peter had the smallest bedroom at about 2.5 metres square, but with his characteristic ingenuity he made sure that everything within it (bed, desk, chair, light) was designed, arranged and built so as to accommodate the most important thing in his life – his ever-growing collection of contemporary picture books from around the world. So the bed went up close to the ceiling, became a loft; a ladder got you up there, and between the legs to the loft were shelves, shelves and then more shelves for all his books. He had been buying picture books for years already; he was passionate about them. It was Peter who introduced me to the work of artists from Italy, France, Germany, Japan and America. He introduced me to the work of Maurice Sendak, Edward Gorey, Arnold Lobel and Tomi Ungerer. He also introduced me to Melbourne's first specialist children's bookshop, the Little Bookroom, and to its owner, Albert Ullin, who enthusiastically introduced us to the work of yet more illustrators, yet more books, new and old, from all round the world. We would drop in there all the time. Peter almost lived in Albert's shop.

Teachers college (the mushroom factory) slowly became intolerable for me. The art department was run by a bloke I reckoned to be some kind of misogynist-fascist, who couldn't care less about kids either. I began to go a bit feral in some sort of feeble protest. It was he who dispatched me to Altona. I was not up to the challenge, not in that school anyway. It was my third year out of art school, my first year of teaching, and by the end of second term I was a wreck.

So there I was in Coventry Street, having collapsed backwards out of teaching, a bit exhausted, not enjoying any of the other work I was doing very much either, and wondering where to from here.

Then, out of the blue, an envelope arrived from Pat Thomas, an editor at Macmillan. I had earlier worked with Pat on some Joan Phipson novels, and she had shown me Karl Holmes' illustrations for Jenny Wagner's *The Werewolf Knight*. Jenny was apparently keen to get picture books going in Australia. Pat said she would introduce me, but I hadn't heard anything from her for over a year.

Inside the envelope were three pages of typescript, to which a small yellow post-it sticker was attached, with a bit of scribble in biro: 'Ron, do you think anything could be done with this?' It was *The Bunyip of Berkeley's Creek*.

I read it, and loved it, straight away. I loved the whole central quest of the story – about the search for identity, for self and for recognition, a search we can all identify with.

'What am I?' it kept saying. 'What am I?'
But the night birds were all asleep.
A passing platypus solved the problem.
'You are a bunyip,' he said.

The bunyip wanders along, asking everyone he meets 'What do bunyips look like?'

'Horrible,' said the wallaby. 'They have webbed feet, and feathers.'
'Horrible tails,' said the emu. 'And even more horrible fur.'
The bunyip wandered sadly along the creek.
'Will someone tell me what bunyips look like?' he said, to anyone who would listen.

I loved the writing – the rhythm, the repetitions, the changes of pace, the pauses, the humour. Every little thing.

Further along the creek he met a man.
'Can you please tell me what bunyips look like?'
'Bunyips don't look like anything.'
'Bunyips simply don't exist.'

I especially loved the overall shape of the whole thing – from the small, quiet and private beginning, to setting out into the world with questions, hopes and dreams; finding only confusion and hurt – then moving on to his own new place. And it's not just another creek…

The bunyip walked all day, and just as the sun was setting he came to a quiet, still billabong.

I love the use of the word 'billabong' there, in all its springy musicality. I love the alternating long and short phrases, too.

'This will do,' said the bunyip to himself.
'No one can see me here. I can be as handsome as I like.'

Against all odds, he remains optimistic, and from the trueness of the journey, the faithfulness of the quest, we are optimistic also.

No one saw him and no one spoke to him.
And then…
But late that night, for no particular reason,
something stirred in the black mud at the bottom of the billabong.
The bunyip put his comb down in surprise, and stared.

Something very large and very muddy was sitting on the bank.
'What am I?' it murmured. 'What am I, what am I?'
Then the Bunyip's own billabong brings forth the gift of 'the other'...
'You are a bunyip!' he shouted.
'You look just like me,' said the bunyip happily.
And he lent her his mirror to prove it.'

––––––––––

The Bunyip is a story about the gift of existence, the gift of life itself. Bunyip exists not only in his own reflection (as in the mirror) but is made whole and alive in the perception and recognition of his 'other', outside and beyond himself.

As the Shaker prayer has it:
'Tis a gift to be simple
'Tis a gift to be free
'Tis a gift to come down
Where you're meant to be.

From Jenny Wagner's point of view, I am sure the text was a play on the ideas of the philosopher George Berkeley (1685–1753), who argued that if the senses are the only source of knowledge of physical objects, then 'to know' and 'to perceive' are the same. All that exists is what we experience, what we perceive; to be is to perceive, and to *be* perceived.

That idea was nicely developed by Jenny into a story about life's struggles – about the search for place, for contentment, and about how love might be found.

It is a love story.

I was so excited by this story, so sure of the rightness of it, even as I read the text the very first time, that I could 'see' the style of illustration I thought would be most appropriate – the technique, the linework, the colours, the landscape. I was sure it had the makings of a wonderful picture book. But I had never done anything remotely like that before and wasn't at all sure I was capable of doing it as well as the text deserved. In fact I was quite sure I was not. So I showed the story to Peter, who I knew had been absolutely burning to make picture books for years.

'Here's your chance,' I said. 'It's beautiful. I'd love to do it, but you would do it so much better.' He didn't like it much at all, and said he wasn't interested in doing other people's texts. 'But this is such a beautiful story,' I said. 'You'd do it beautifully, and then go on to make your own.' He still wasn't interested.

I persuaded him to at least come to a meeting with Jenny Wagner to talk it over, think about it, and then make his decision. We went, and Jenny talked and talked and talked. She was as positive about the story as I was. She was really enthusiastic.

'No way,' Peter said on the way home hours later. 'Definitely. There's no way I could cope with all that. She'd be telling me what to draw on every single page.'

I didn't know anybody else I thought could do it and, as I say, I was in a funny old place myself at the time, so I began to focus on the possibility that I could give it a go myself. It was, after all, a real opportunity to head off in a new direction. I certainly needed that, and it was a direction I had been thinking about for a little while. So, I sat down again, with the text.

I read it and re-read it. I still loved it and could still see everything – the style, the colours and the landscape especially. I could see everything, except for one thing. I couldn't see the bunyip at all. I had no idea what he looked like – no idea at all what the main character should look like.

The text itself was of little help. When the bunyip meets all the other characters and confronts each with the question, 'What do I look like?', they all answer with something completely different, until the man finally says, 'Bunyips don't look like anything. Bunyips simply don't exist.' And when I asked Jenny if she could give me some clues, she said she would like him to be just a brown blob, really, changing shape a little from page to page. She wasn't keen for him to have any particular physical characteristics. I didn't think that would work; I felt strongly that I needed to come up with a tangible character that kids would be able to relate to. To me, that was fundamental.

So I sat there and doodled. Not very cleverly, I must say. Nothing original came out – only a multitude of unimaginative variations on koalas, bears, kangaroos and wallabies. I'm not the sort of illustrator to do a lot of research, or to use visual references, but I went to libraries and read early settlers' (sometimes drunken) accounts of so-called sightings or noises in the night, just beyond the campfire, and looked at drawings which could well have been of seals crossed with my wallaboos. I saw Aboriginal drawings of strange creatures they too had never seen before: cows, horses.

I was incredibly frustrated that I couldn't come up with one original character, when Peter's desk seemed to be jumping with them.

For around two months I doodled away, and every now and again, I would take the drawings in to the offices of Childerset – the rather odd photography studio and publishing/packaging house where Jenny worked as Project Director for the owner, one Haworth Bartram. Childerset was going to produce the book, and Mr Bartram needed to see how I was going with the sketches, whether I was coming up with the goods, before he would give me any money.

Haworth was in his fifties, and rich. He lived alone – well, with his mother – on a huge farm, a horse stud, which seemed to take up half the area of Heidelberg, in the north-eastern suburbs of Melbourne. I was under the impression, no doubt encouraged by Jenny's lavish optimism about our prospects, that he also owned most of the buildings in that street, running between King and Spencer Streets, where his offices were.

His mother still packed a cut lunch for him, every day: sandwiches, fruit and biscuits, in a little box. She would call his office each morning to check that he had eaten, and he would say, 'Yes, good morning, Mama. Yes, I've had my morning tea, Mama. It was lovely, thank you, Mama. Yes…I will eat my sandwiches too, I promise. Yes, yes… I will see you later today, Mama. Yes, thank you, Mama. Bye, bye. Yes… Bye-bye.'

He would smile slyly, cheekily, across his desk at me, and with one hand would wave at his sliced-white sandwiches, inviting me to help myself while with the other he scrabbled yet another couple of

Arnott's Scotch Fingers out of a desk drawer, which I am quite sure contained packets and packets of them. 'I love them,' he would chortle. 'They are the only things.' They were certainly the only things I ever saw him eat. And there was a fridge which was meant to be mostly for photographic chemicals, but which was 95 per cent filled with bottles of orange Fanta. New crate-loads of the stuff stood on the side, ready to go.

Perhaps not surprisingly, Haworth was very large physically. Well over six feet tall, with a large equatorial circumference, he resembled nothing so much as a balloon, one of those pear-shaped water balloons you drop from the verandah roof onto some unsuspecting little brother or sister. But huge… and sort of stretching towards the top, towards the head, just as balloons do with the sheer weight down below… bloop, bloop. Not much of a neck to speak of, just this big, soft, pear-shaped thing, with enormous feet. That was another thing – shoe shops didn't stock his size; he had to have them made specially. Ditto the trousers. And because he had no waist, he wore braces – over the shoulders, crossed at the back and clipped to his pants to hold them up.

I would arrive with my drawings (that I knew were no good), feeling nervous, and his secretary would go into Haworth's photography studio to let him know I was there. And I would wait.

Haworth didn't look like anybody I'd ever met before; he also didn't walk like anybody I'd ever met. Waiting there in his office, I wouldn't exactly hear him coming – no actual footsteps as such – it was more as if I could feel him coming, as he slid, brushed, first along this wall, then the other of the narrow passage, gravitating from side to side, contact with the walls giving him some kind of security. Then there was the breathing, almost humming, almost musical, with each exhalation as he approached. And then, finally, as he entered the office, there'd be one last deep breath and a gentle bobbing up and down as he greeted me. There was something oddly childlike about him.

What he always referred to as his 'special, receiving–visitors chair' had also been specially built for him. It was the size, maybe, of a small spaceship – a huge and generously padded bright-red vinyl number, on a single swivelling leg. Haworth would approach it, turn around, then back up, slowly bend, and begin to lower himself…and then let go, and just drop. He reminded me of my grandfather who, when he was very old, used to approach his armchair, and the whole operation of sitting in it in a not dissimilar manner because he too had difficulty bending. Over the years, all the springs in Pop's chair went, and we had to furnish it with extra cushions. Watching Haworth negotiate this manoeuvre, and feeling some sympathy for his chair, I used to wonder how long it would last.

A short digression, if I may, on Haworth… Because I knew he loved to tell stories, and perhaps to distract from the drawings and my self-consciousness about them, once or twice I asked him how or where he got the chair, the shoes, even the trousers made. Haworth would take this as an invitation to launch enthusiastically into stories from his manufacturing and importing days, mostly in and around Asia. 'Ah, you know, Ron, funny things would happen, because, as you know, they have a funny way with English, and [at this point he would laugh, snort, and wheeze somewhat alarmingly] …I have a very funny way with Japanese! Anyway. There was this time I needed to manufacture a very large quantity of a very particular kind of rope.'

Was it five hundred metres, five thousand metres? I can't remember the quantity he needed, but he had just one small piece, maybe forty centimetres, a sample, to show his Japanese manu-facturers. "Ah so. Yes, exac his one, prease. Five housan metres, exac his one. Same. Exac. Yes sir, Mr Brutum. Five housan metres, exac his one here. Same. Exac-ly."

'And do you know what came back in the shipping container five months later? *Fifty thousand metres* of *exactly* the same type of rope, all in nice little pieces, forty centimetres long!'

And he would laugh, and laugh, and laugh, and slap his desk.

'And then there was the time I needed twenty thousand porcelain plates… I had the sample – an old one belonging to my mother – white, with the pattern I wanted on it running around the edge, but I wanted a different base colour. I wanted a very, very pale blue, rather than the white; I wanted to be sure they could get that colour exactly right.

I was also concerned about whether they would be able to duplicate the profile shape exactly, whether they'd have trouble with the mould, and whether they could get the patterned decoration precisely right, because it was essential that it all match perfectly with another range of products I was bringing out. Well, we discussed all these things in great detail and at great length, I can tell you.

'Now, as it happened, this *particular* plate I was showing them to get the profile and pattern from just happened to have a very, very, *very* fine crack in it – barely visible to the naked eye – running from the outer edge into and just through the patterned area. I didn't bother to mention it. Why would I? I was more concerned about the profile, the blue and the pattern. Oh, and the price, too, of course, ha, ha, ha. But these Japanese, you know, Ron, they are *so* clever; they really *can* do absolutely anything…"Ah…we tink maybe we going surprise you, Mr Brutum, wih how perfec what we do. You go home, you res, no worry, you jus wait and see, we tink."

'Yes, well, experience should have made me sit up at that comment, Ron, but it had been a long week – I was tired. Six months later, back came my twenty thousand beautiful pale-blue plates. The blue was *perfect*, the profile *exactly* right, the pattern better, clearer even than on the original. And on all twenty thousand plates – I promise you, Ron, there it was, precision itself – going into and through the patterned strip, *exactly* as it was on my dear old mother's plate! *Barely* visible. The *finest* crack. You could hardly call it a crack, really, it was more like the *finest hairline*, honestly. Just perfect. *Incredible!* You've got to hand it to them, really.'

Haworth greatly enjoyed recounting the seemingly endless tales of misunderstanding, mishap and mayhem from his manufacturing and importing days – embellishing them with each retelling, fully aware that as often as not these stories were at least partly, and in more ways than one, at his own expense. He did realise, to his credit, that he was not entirely competent at dealing with other people.

But all that was in the past. His new passion, his abiding passion now was photography, and his studio was filled with the most extraordinary array of the very latest equipment. There was nothing you couldn't do with today's cameras. Shaking his head sadly at me as he made the pronouncement – he believed that it was regressive to still be trying to make pictures any other way, 'in this day and age, when we have all this technology at our fingertips'. He just could not understand why I would still choose to go to all that inefficient and time-consuming bother of drawing when I could do it all so much faster with a camera. His great new scheme was to publish photographic books. He would be both the photographer and the publisher, thus eliminating the possibility of mishaps. He would have total control at last.

Then he met Jenny Wagner, and was persuaded he needed a project director to help him put all this together. Jenny was full of ideas and very good with words; she would come up with texts for the books he would then take photographs for, and she would help in all the dealings with people, thus enabling Haworth to spend more time in his studio.

Then, somewhere along the line, Jenny wrote with the text for *The Bunyip of Berkeley's Creek*, and she evidently succeeded in persuading him that this particular text could not be illustrated photographically, that it would *need* to be illustrated, with actual illustrations. Done by hand. By an artist. (Jenny confided in me one day that Haworth would later always refer to me as 'that hand-drawn artist'.)

Anyway, there I was in Haworth's office yet again, with more sketches but still no bunyip, not feeling very happy about the whole thing.

Haworth very probably thought Jenny and I were barking up completely the wrong tree. He did however like a good joke, and maybe he felt he would get to watch a good one happen – but my suspicion is that this amusement had gradually changed into something more like *be*musement, then to outright nervousness about whether we had *any clue at all* about what we were doing.

So…I am sitting on (the edge of) my comparatively ordinary chair, and Haworth is now fully berthed in his big red spaceship, but huffing and puffing just a bit, taking big breaths. Having self-consciously riffled through my sketches on the large coffee table between us, not actually picking any of them up, he begins to do what he always does when he feels nervous: he begins to scratch.

Maybe his knee is itchy, the left one. Then his right elbow, then his upper right arm – both upper arms, at the same time. And then his left thigh also. I can almost see the next one coming…it's going to be the right ankle. But Haworth resists. He crosses his legs, tucking the left foot around that right ankle, giving it a bit of a rub with it as he does so. Meanwhile, I can see, nay, almost feel, Haworth's immediate distraction then, from the ankle, by the twitch which has developed suddenly, inexplicably, in his right ear. It is agonising to watch, but hilarious, too. Haworth hesitates. The fingers on his right hand, the whole arm, moves, twitches, starts…then stops. Another pause, then suddenly – I am taken utterly by surprise – his left arm shoots up and around the back of his head, to scratch furiously at the offending ear. He breathes out, heavily. The arm comes back around and down, the hand moves across to rest on, then hold, the right forearm. It moves further around, until the arms, too, are now tightly plaited. And all the while, there is a bit of a swivel going on, from side to side, and a bit of rising and falling in the sitting position, more heavy breathing, and finally, sighing.

Haworth is looking totally perplexed, almost pitiable, as though he is wondering what on earth I am doing here. Why is he doing these funny-looking, old-fashioned hand drawings? Why isn't he taking photographs? As though he wonders, even, what he is doing here. He has no idea what to say. He is looking utterly lost, doesn't know where to look.

Whereas I – suddenly, after two months of messing about in sketchbooks, two months of searching, and countless meetings – I finally know *exactly* what I am looking at. The revelation has at last hit. He was there all along and I hadn't seen him, hadn't recognised him.

Haworth is my bunyip!

I just mumbled something, apparently. As Haworth later explained to Jenny, 'He just gathered up all his stuff, and disappeared!' No one saw him go.

I jumped onto the Spencer Street tram, couldn't wait to get home, back to the desk. I sat down and whipped up a little pen-and-ink sketch of Haworth sitting on the ground, looking a little forlorn. I stuck some fur on him, a few feathers, a tail – bits and pieces mentioned

The very first
sketch of the
Bunyip

in the text itself plus a few extras for good measure – gave him his
bunyip comb and mirror, and a small voice balloon: 'What am I?'

I had him! I knew it. It was fantastic. I was so happy. After all this
time.

But did I rush straight back in to the office with it? (With him?) I did
not. I wasn't game. Because it was quite a good likeness, really. Haworth
was sure to recognise himself, and I wasn't at all confident about how
he would receive that. I waited a few days, and then called Jenny.

'I think I've got him.'

'That's wonderful! Bring him in.'

So Bunyip and I caught our first tram together, me wondering what
Jenny and her assistant Ian Bolger would think about the drawing, and
whether she would like the character.

They both recognised Haworth instantly, and absolutely cracked
up. They laughed and laughed and laughed…and loved him.

'Dear, sweet, old Haworth!' said Jenny. 'How absolutely lovely.'

The BUNYIP *of* BERKELEY'S CREEK   [69]

Then, seeking to reassure, she reminded me that Haworth wouldn't look at it very closely anyway, wouldn't know how to.

'It's not a photograph, Ron, and he certainly wouldn't recognise himself in a pen-and-ink sketch. I'll tell him it's marvellous, that you've got Bunyip perfectly! Don't worry about it. Just get on with it.'

I knew she was right, that I needn't worry about it too much, but I was still a little nervous. I went home, and wondered whether I could change him, just a bit…

I was saved from all this anguish, as it happened, by our brand-new Prime Minister.

If there was one other thing that was occupying a lot of my mind at the time – just as it was for most Australians it was politics. We had a new government, a Labor government for the first time in around a quarter of a century. It felt like a whole new world! And of course we had a new Prime Minister, Gough Whitlam. He had withdrawn Australia from the quagmire of the Vietnam War; he had pardoned conscientious objectors; he was pushing through all sorts of new legislation and opening up all sorts of issues for intelligent and lively debate by the whole community for the very first time, or so it felt. All sorts of things seemed possible now – possible to dream about, possible to do. It seemed to me that what Whitlam had been doing throughout the election campaign, and now that he was in government, was asking, Who are we? What sort of a country, what sort of a people are we? What do we want to be?

I suddenly saw that these were bigger versions of the Bunyip's questions: 'What am I? What do I look like?'

I had found the solution to my problem. I redrew Bunyip, his face less like Haworth's this time, a bit more like Gough's. And therewith also had the full design for the cover of the book, front and back: it would show the Australian coat of arms, with Haworth-Gough in the middle holding his comb and mirror, kangaroo and emu to the sides. Every which way you looked at it, this country was now asking, 'What am I?'

The rest came easy.

———

DRAWN *from the* HEART

Every book is different. For some I have done, the characters were there from the beginning, while the landscape, the setting in which they lived, took longer to find. As I have mentioned, with my very first reading of Bunyip I could see the landscape clearly. It would be landscape I knew well, from my childhood in and around East Gippsland, and more recently, from drawing holidays during art school, around the old gold-mining areas of central Victoria – Blackwood, Daylesford and Castlemaine. I wasn't planning accurate depictions of specific places, but I wanted the drawings to have the forms, colours, textures, and something of the feeling those places have for me.

Looking at Peter's picture-book collection, thinking about the ones I most responded to, I had arrived at some kind of personal 'theory' about the kind of illustration that I felt worked best for children – those that used a lot of linework, pen-and-ink mostly, and cross-hatching, giving the images texture, tooth, and a certain tangible quality of grip on the page. Presence, perhaps. Any illustrations are, of course, only two-dimensional allusions to and illusions of representation, but in my drawings for Bunyip, I wanted to give kids characters, objects, environments and a whole world that they could get hold of, almost feel.

So, the images would have pen-and-ink linework, with a lot of cross-hatching. The black ink I used was homemade to my own recipe, especially formulated so that when I finished all the linework, and it had dried, I could wash over it all with a brush dipped in clean water which would bring out of that linework a thin brown wash (something like the colour of weak black tea), and this would become an under-colour for all the other watercolours to glaze over – mostly deep, earthy browns and greens, with other spot colours. I wanted a certain moodiness to the whole thing.

In all this, I was wrestling with a very particular paradox.

I was excited about the prospect of trying to make a good Australian picture book; I did genuinely want it to reflect something of the flavour of the place, but equally, I didn't want it to be in any way over-the-top Australianarama.

The bunyip myth is peculiar to this country; there are many other native animals referred to in the text, and I was advised to put in even more. I felt there was some pressure to make the book very obviously Australian. But I was absolutely clear in my own mind about not wanting to be excessive in that regard. Much more importantly, it seemed to me, this was a story about the search for identity, for self, for recognition and acceptance. These themes are timeless, and entirely universal to everybody, everywhere. I wanted to make this book not only for Australians, but for anyone, anywhere. I wanted to make it as universal as I possibly could.

After all, the illustration I most liked from other countries, the books I most liked, did not have any particularly striking national characteristics; they were simply wonderful stories, with beautiful artwork, nicely produced; works that in their totality – in their design, illustration and production – worked perfectly with the texts.

I had also been looking at artwork by children from all around the world. I was struck by how very similar the drawings by younger children are, no matter where they come from. Whatever the culture, the background, the environment – there appear to be not only archetypal figures for mothers, fathers, brothers, sisters, but also for trees, hills, valleys, skies. I also found a commonality in the way young children actually *draw*, the type of lines they use, the kinds of marks they make, the way they use colour. I was excited about trying to make this wonderful story as accessible as possible for as many kids as possible, anywhere. So rather than depict specifically native trees, in an obviously Australian landscape, I went for the more archetypal symbols of trees, streams, landscape, sky. I kept it simple, deliberately kept it open.

But, yes, I wanted the book to say something about our landscape also. So, on the endpaper there is the old farmhouse, a smattering of outbuildings, the ubiquitous solitary palm tree, the abandoned ute, the windmill, a bit of rubbish strewn along the creek, the log, the wooden bridge, and something a bit like a forty-spotted pardalote. Throughout the book are a few other icons – the odd bit of post-and-rail fence, the chimney and tank-stand left standing after a bushfire, another old miner's cottage. On just about every page, in those clumps of trees (which could well be European), there is nevertheless always that transparency peculiar to the Australian bush, through which we can always see right to the horizon – which is everywhere in this book, in almost every picture. And of course there are the platypus, the emu and the wallaby (which actually looks more like a kangaroo, I suspect).

The wallaby, by the way, was a *male* in the original text – 'and he finished his drink and hopped off'. I didn't quite register that, and drew a very obviously female one. The 'he' and 'his' were changed to a 'she' and 'her' for subsequent editions. While the text refers to his 'bunyip bag', I have simply a bundle – it could be a large handkerchief, or scarf, not particularly Australian – tied to a stick. But from the end of the stick hangs the quintessential billy in which he will make his tea, adding that single gumleaf (outside the picture, in the text 'frame') to give the tea that distinctive flavour of eucalypt. And the text is hand-lettered inside monotone borders, decorated throughout with gum leaves and gumnuts, in a small salute to some much earlier Australian children's books.

The late 1960s and 1970s was a time of considerable questioning – of challenges to all sorts of perceived hierarchies. Many younger people were questioning whether anyone in the establishment really knew what they were doing; they felt that the institutions, government departments, and the corporations with vested interests and their so-called experts were not to be trusted, that 'developed' societies were losing their essential relationship with nature and, indeed, that we were losing our humanity. Thus we have the image for 'Further along the creek he met a man' – the only image in the whole book (apart from the endpaper), which uses the full double-page frame, right to the edge of the page. There is no man, just a big, bizarre machine, scientific-looking but wacky. It's meant to be an Environment Observation Post, but there is foul smoke belching from a chimney, a rather poisonous-looking stain coming from a drain, and the trees here are at odds with those in the rest of the book, as though they might be some kind of mutants. The clouds here are unlike all others in the book, and the lone duck doesn't look very well either.

Presently a wallaby came by to drink at the creek.

This irresponsibility toward the natural world, this loss of humanity, sympathy and compassion are further reinforced on the following two pages, deliberately designed also to be out of sync with the rest of the book. The slightly myopic-looking man and all the machinery are drawn in a much colder style, and we see Bunyip stretched out on something that looks like a cross between a dentist's chair and a psychiatrist's couch.

'Can you please tell me what bunyips look like?'
'Bunyips don't look like anything…
Bunyips simply don't exist.'

The other inspiration behind these pages was Monty Python – the sheer madness of it all. And the newspaper – a little indulgence with my self-portrait there – has a reference to one of my favourite films at the time, Fellini's *8½*, which seemed also to parallel some of the themes in this story.

Later, when 'something stirs in the black mud at the bottom of the billabong…'

The bunyip put his comb down in surprise, and stared.
Something very large and very muddy was sitting on the bank.
'What am I?' it murmured. 'What am I, what am I?'

…when the Bunyip's own billabong brings forth the gift of 'the other', I loved making the small shifts in the body language. There is more energy in the movements of his hands, his fingers and (for the first time in the whole book) his ears. They are lifting, coming up…

'You are a bunyip!' he shouted.

The gift of perception, the gift of recognition…

'You look just like me,' said the bunyip happily.

Then, to the last line in the book…

And he lent her his mirror to prove it.

I love that *he, her, his.*

His ears are now well and truly up. Mind you, she is not looking quite so sure. That's why his hands, his feet and his fingers are all suddenly much more tender now. He knows (patient, gentle soul that he is) that she will need a little more time yet to come to the same recognition.

And he lent
her his mirror
to prove it.

She meanwhile is looking neither in the mirror, not quite at him, nor quite at us. And she is still muddy, indistinct. Is she, after all, just a figment of his wishful thinking?

Just between you and me – I do think he is on the right track, and knows it. There is something about those lids and lashes, and *her* ear also…even covered, as it is, in mud.

————

All up, *Bunyip* took me about six months to make – two months to find the bunyip himself, a month to make the rough dummy (a page-by-page mock-up) of the whole thing, and then up to eighteen hours a day at the desk for three months to do all the final illustrations and hand-lettering. I delivered the complete work in early 1973.

Haworth had set up Childerset primarily as a vehicle to publish his own photographically illustrated children's books. I contracted with the company, but he never intended to publish *Bunyip* himself. Childerset was only ever going to act as packager and co-publisher on the book. With all the finished artwork now, Jenny and Haworth began showing the project around the various bigger publishing houses. Nobody wanted it; I was told something like seven publishers turned it down. No market. Not Australian enough. There was only one offer, from Collins, and that was conditional upon Jenny rewriting bits of the text and me redoing some of the drawings. Specifically, I remember them saying the double page with the bunyip and the wallaby meeting at the creek would have to be completely re-done, because – unbelievably! – I had failed to show the actual creek. Ditto with the illustration for 'Further along the creek he met a man.' That would absolutely have to go. What on earth had Brooks been thinking? The text says he met a man, but there is no man in the picture. Children will need to see the man. This sort of stuff is fundamental! They were also not at all happy about the could-well-be-oak trees throughout. If Ron Brooks is not prepared to change all those pictures that have oak trees in them (pretty much every damn picture in the book), and draw gum trees instead, at least in some of them – okay, say around half – then there can be no deal.

But if Jenny and Ron can do all that, we'll go ahead and print (maybe) 3000 copies.

Amazing.

Less amazingly, we said thank you – but no thank you.

Then Jenny showed it to Bob Sessions, who was by then working as an editor with Penguin in their Ringwood office. Bob liked it, and he mentioned that Patrick Hardy, who was the children's publisher with Longman Young Books, associated with Penguin in London, was coming out to Australia. He arranged for us to get together over lunch at Lazar's restaurant, in the city.

All this must have taken some months, because by the time Patrick and Bob turned up together in the Childerset office, I had done my second book with Jenny, *Aranea*. We were going to be discussing both books at the same time.

It was such a pleasure meeting Patrick Hardy that first time – he was so dapper and elegant in his charcoal-grey pinstriped suit, and so precise, softly spoken and articulate; I'd never met anyone quite like him. And it was my very first proper publishers' lunch – Patrick and Bob, Haworth, Jenny, Ian Bolger, and me. I hardly knew what was happening. The food was stupendous, but there was also a lot more drinking than I was used to – drinks before, drinks throughout, and drinks to follow. Jenny absolutely loved it. But for me, everything just became foggier and foggier; I think I might have ended up, literally, under the table.

Anyway, when I woke up, we had contracts. For both books. With Penguin, no less.

I think their first print run for *Bunyip* was 20 000. And it sold, sold, sold, in Australia, New Zealand and Great Britain. And was then taken up in America and Germany. God, that felt good.

Twenty-five years later, the Spare Parts Puppet Theatre company of Fremantle staged and toured their own production of the story that was so beautiful it made me weep; and now, almost 40 years after *The Bunyip* was first published, the book is still in print.

Aranea

Aranea stood in the wind, spinning and spinning.

A fine silk thread lifting into the air and hanging there,
caught on the wind.

As I BECAME more and more deeply immersed in doing the finished drawings for *Bunyip*, I slowly wound down most of the other freelance work I had been doing. The book became something of an obsession for me. The long hours at the desk, day after day, week after week, and working with extremely fine mapping pens, was tending to cramp up the hands, fingers and neck, and working at such close range – just me and the paper there on the desk – was putting the rest of the world a little out of focus. But I loved every minute of it.

I remember my brother Ted one day visiting me at Coventry Street, remarking that I seemed to be putting a fair bit of work into it, and asking whether I thought it was worth it. I couldn't believe he could ask such a question; it was a book for kids, for god's sake, and I had at last found what I really wanted to do.

Jenny gave me the text for *Aranea* before I finished all the drawings for *Bunyip* – before I had done any of the hand-lettering for the text, cover and title pages. I was just about blind and totally exhausted by the time I did finish the drawings, and my hand was shaking like a leaf for the week or so it took to do all the lettering. I wasn't at all sure I could go through all that again, especially when there was so little financial reward involved and (bearing in mind that *Bunyip* did not at this stage have a publisher) following the advance on royalties already paid, there might well be no more money forthcoming.

Though *Aranea* is certainly not one of my favourites, I realise, looking back now, that this was the text that was fundamental in locking in my interest in doing picture books. With all the novels, texts and book covers I did prior to *Bunyip*, the job was simply to find and make the images to illustrate the story, fill in the holes, package the product. I was almost indifferent to whether or not the writing was of any particular quality; I was simply paying my rent.

The Bunyip – just three or four pages of typescript – was a leap away from that indifference. For all its implied particularities of place, character and time, the story spoke to universal concerns. Beautifully written, it also had at the heart of it a character I could invest with charm, warmth and appeal for the reader. And it was an easy project in one way, because the bunyip was nowhere objectively described and that left the way open for me to create the sort of character I thought would best carry the story. The setting (again never described) was also wide open for me to do whatever I liked. While the story was suggestive of so many possibilities, it was also completely non-prescriptive.

There were serious challenges for me in all of that of course, challenges in getting the character exactly right, in finding and achieving the style and quality of illustration I wanted, in creating the whole design and what I call architecture of the book, but within that,

First the cross piece, then the frame, then round and round the long spiral, until it was perfect.

there was freedom too; freedom for me to plain down-on-the-farm have a whole lot of fun doing it.

Aranea, however, was a story about a spider (specifically an orb-weaving spider), not a creature associated with warmth, charm, or appeal for very many readers. Moreover, everything within this story – the place, the settings, the actions, the time of day or night, the weather – is specified, named, described. So the difficulties were right there, from the very beginning: the central character was unavoidably one for whom – spider-lovers aside – there was limited appeal, and there would be no choice but to show what was specified in the text. This left me (in comparison with the *Bunyip* text) very little freedom to imagine or interpret. It seemed there might not be much fun to be had in doing this book.

Even Jenny said, 'Sorry about that, Ron, I'm not sure what you are going to be able to do with a spider!' Haworth certainly was totally pessimistic about the project, right from the start. Nevertheless, amazingly, without even waiting for me to do any drawings or any sort of rough dummy for the book, he had gone straight to contract on it, and paid me to get started.

'If you can draw a bunyip, Ron, I don't suppose you'll have too much difficulty with a spider.'

I think they were both expecting I'd do something like I had done with *Bunyip*...

Given the challenges of the text, why did I take it on?

There were two reasons. Read simply, it is a beautifully clear story about a spider weaving its web, living its life, night to day, day to night, putting up with difficulties, setbacks, doing it all again…but it was also, like *Bunyip*, a classic allegory – in essence about the qualities of character, especially the courage and perseverance one might bring to the life lived. And the text did all that (not an inconsiderable feat) with such deceptive simplicity.

> *Aranea stood in the wind, spinning and spinning.*
> *A fine silk thread lifting into the air and hanging there, caught on*
> *   the wind.*
> *The wind lifted it up; Aranea clung to her thread and floated with it.*
> *For a whole day she swung in the wind, swinging and blowing*
> *   wherever it took her.*
> *Then she landed on a lilac bush in somebody's garden.*
> *She crawled into the curl of a leaf and made herself a hiding place,*
> *   and waited.*
> *At dusk she crept out and made her first web.*
> *First the cross piece, then the frame, then round and round the*
> *   long spiral, until it was perfect.*

Perfect indeed. The clarity in this writing is exquisite; the pacing, all those verbs, are so finely judged. Jenny writes with wonderful rhythm always, but particularly so in this text it seems to me. Every word, every pause, every change of pace, every turn in every sentence so perfectly complementing the action and the changes of mood in the story with such unerring sureness that it was almost like dancing – a slow waltz – just to read it. And within that elegance of rhythm (again like music), there was almost some kind of mathematics at work in its patterns, shapes and repetitions. All with a lightness of touch that I found astonishing, and beautiful. As Jenny herself would say: 'Not a word, not a syllable, not a comma out of place.'

And I thought, what a pleasure, what a privilege, to have the opportunity to work with texts like this, to make books for young children who are just beginning to learn what language can do – to put images to those words, to have the chance to design and make the whole book in such a way as to open that text out to as full a reading as possible.

I began to think of the picture-book form as almost some kind of theatre, a theatre in which the reader sits, quietly absorbed, while there before them, within the pages (on the stage), a whole world opens up. If the words and images are wrought with sufficient care so as to connect with the heart and the imagination, then the reader, the child – in the privacy of his or her own imagination – becomes an active participant in the theatre. The child enters the book; the book enters the child. And if you get the mix right between the words, the images and the child, then that world brought to life by the book becomes part of the child's world, part of the child's life, and never leaves them.

The Bunyip was such a good story, about a great character… From that book on, I have only ever agreed to illustrate texts that I loved: 'good stories, well told', stories that reach out and touch the reader.

It was the sheer elegance of the words in *Aranea* that first revealed to me the importance of beauty in the writing itself, almost independent of the story. That was a wonderful discovery, and I thought, what a rich little mix the theatre of the book is – words, images, and the child. And I suddenly knew, I'm going to make books. I want to be part of that theatre. I want to contribute to that mix. I want to add to children's worlds, to children's lives. I want to add something of value, something genuinely sustaining.

Persuaded by the sheer beauty of the writing in *Aranea* – all the earlier difficulties of 'specificity' of the story and the character were swept aside – I decided that rather than feel constricted by the perceived difficulties in the *Aranea* text, I would positively embrace all those limitations and work with them, use them. Most importantly, I would try to find a way in the illustrations, in the design of each page and in the design of the whole book, to tap into the music within the writing, to actively partner and complement its rhythms.

The first decision I made was to do all the illustrations in very fine cross-hatching, in pen and ink, and in black-and-white only. I took the cue for that decision from the apparent colourlessness and fineness of spiderwebs themselves; I wanted my pictures to be as much like spiderwebs as I could make them – very fine and light, with no colour at all.

I went with the cross-hatching because it seemed the perfect technique to create the areas of graduated and contrasting tones I wanted, from black all the way through the greys to white, because of the grip you could achieve on the page with hatching, and for the engagement kids seem to feel in response to images built in that way.

Secondly, I opted to stay with the same size and square format that I had used for *Bunyip*, even though everybody from Childerset to booksellers counselled against it, just as they had with the earlier book. It was more expensive to produce because it was not a standard size or shape, was an inefficient use of paper, and it wouldn't readily fit into standard display racks in the shops. But I liked it, and the square format, having the circle implied within it, seemed to me to allow all sorts of opportunities for visual reinforcement of the idea of the cycle that was so central to both texts. I also simply liked the fact that I knew of no other book in the same format. So I stuck with it.

I should next have done a dummy of the whole book, just to be sure that I knew what I was doing, and to get Jenny and Haworth's responses. But I was excited about having a second book to do already, and after the long haul of *Bunyip* I was impatient to do this one more quickly. I suspect, now, that I thought I knew what I was doing.

In neglecting to do a dummy of the whole book before I started the final illustrations, in failing to work out exactly what I was going to do on all 32 pages – the normal number, the economical number of pages for a standard picture book – I overran to 36 pages. This was a major blunder on my part, and a serious mistake from a publisher's point of view, because of the effect it would have on production costs. But changing it would have meant re-jigging the whole thing – it wouldn't be a matter of just re-doing three or four illustrations, it would have entailed a complete redesign, and who knows how many new illustrations as a result.

Fortunately, no one ever asked me to do it. Perhaps because it was black-and-white, just a one-colour print job, rather than the usual full colour, Penguin decided they were able to wear the extra expense.

Instead of doing a proper dummy, I had done only a rough break-up of the text into separate lines and blocks for each page, and then set about doing the finished drawings for each. It seemed simple enough, on the surface anyway. Just black-and-white, hatching, no colour…

I wanted my pictures to stay right there with the words – with everything Aranea was going through, as described in the text. I wanted the layout of each page, the size and subject matter of each illustration to follow the patterns, the moods and rhythm in the text itself. I wanted the whole visual presentation to not exactly mirror the text, but to be a partner to it, as in a dance. I didn't want the illustrations to compete with the words, simply to partner and support them. I quite deliberately went for understatement, for an almost diagrammatic simplicity, allowing the words to float, hang, weave and swing… The words were beauty enough.

For the most part I think I managed to do that. Looking at the book now, I almost cannot believe how quiet it is, how restrained. If I had my chance at this text again I would certainly take a few more risks, loosen the whole thing up just a little; but, interestingly, the weakest pages are those where the text was more descriptively straightforward, and where I *did* try to add something:

Sometimes, very early, when the boys were going to school, they
saw it.
And they swished sticks through it and broke it.

Sometimes when their mother was hanging out the clothes
she felt the fine silk threads on her face, and said, 'Ugh! A spider's
web!'

On these two double-page spreads I saw the chance – thought there was a need – to flesh the text out with more fulsome visual offerings. Perhaps not a bad idea in itself, but the draughtsmanship, the actual drawing, is awful, much too tight, too self-conscious (I was trying too hard).

My decision to illustrate the whole book in black-and-white met with some concern from both Jenny and Haworth. Everybody else I mentioned it to thought I was wasting my time, that nobody would publish it. The general perception was that picture books needed to be highly coloured for young children's interest to be engaged; they plain would not respond to black-and-white drawings. I did not accept those arguments. I hung in there with my conviction that the job of the designer and illustrator of a picture book is to find the approach he or she feels is most appropriate for the text, most responsive to its inherent qualities.

As I've already mentioned, the initial cue for black-and-white was simply the nature of a spider-web itself; I was also deeply impressed that a story about such an apparently unappealing creature as a spider could be so evocative, so absolutely engaging. I decided to not 'dress it up' in any way, to be as brave as Jenny had been in her writing, and just stay there with the inescapable fact that this is a story about a spider. Let the text work its own magic on the reader. If that meant taking the back seat with the illustrations, doing nothing at all flash, and sticking to black and white, no matter what the publishers and booksellers thought about its marketability, then so be it.

In a nutshell, I think I did this book not so much for the illustrations, but for the children to get some sort of feeling, some sort of understanding of what language can do. That is why I opted to typeset the text, rather than hand-letter it as I did with many later books. I wanted each and every word to be absolutely clear, either in black on a totally white background, or in white reversed out of a solid black. I wanted no interference at all between writer and reader.

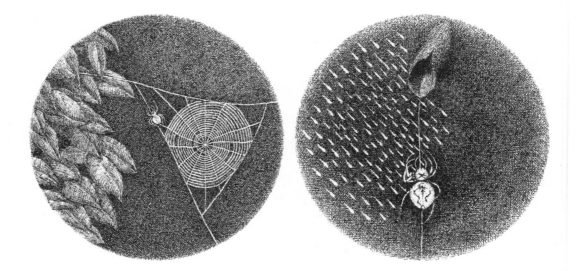

But no one ever saw Aranea. Until one night near the end of summer.

Aranea ran for her leaf, but the rain blocked her way.

Every once in a while I would take drawings in to show Jenny and Haworth. Their reservations about the lack of any colour were not allayed at all, until I reached this section of the text:

But no one ever saw Aranea.

Until one night near the end of summer.

Those two lines are centred below a finely hatched illustration within a circle, in the middle of an otherwise totally white left-hand page.

The facing right-hand page is totally black, and has a lot of text. Here's only the second paragraph:

The sky turned black, but no stars came out.
There was no moon.
Everything was very still and very quiet.
Presently a wind came up and Aranea felt the line sway beneath
her feet.
The wind grew stronger,
and a piece of the frame came loose.
Aranea tried to mend it,
but the wind tore it away.
The lilac bush shook,
and the trees in the garden rattled and hissed.

I reversed all the text out in white, with no illustration at all.

I thought, what illustration could possibly add anything to these words, let alone do the job better? Having only the words left it to the reader to do all the imaginative work – come up with their own images, become even more engaged with what those words are doing.

On the next double page, we read:

Then all at once the sky cracked open.
It split from top to bottom, like a rotten orange thrown against a
* wall.*

This beneath a wall-to-wall illustration of massive dark clouds, heavily laden and billowing; the whole image being split, cracked open, jagged, by lightning.

With these drawings, Jenny was persuaded. She could see what I was doing, the extent to which I was drawing attention to her writing.

As I write this, I wonder whether you might be thinking, 'Oh dear…is he saying he thinks this is the perfect picture book?'

I am not. Alas, and (most definitively) alack…it is absolutely not. A very long way from it. However, I do think it's worth noting that a book that went from being 'unpublishable' in 1973 to being published in Australia, England and New Zealand in 1975, in Japan in 1979, and has been in print in Australia ever since, turned out to be some sort of modest success. Librarians and teachers tell me that the book has always been a quiet favourite with all sorts of children; it's not a book they rave about, but simply a 'keep it to themselves' kind of book that some of them go back to again and again.

Those same teachers and librarians, bless them, have never gone on to explain to me that they believe it might be more because of the story, because of the quality of the writing. They don't need to. I already know it. I always knew that would be the case. And I am totally happy with that. That is, after all, exactly what I hoped to achieve.

Postscript
The very last drawing I did for *Aranea* – a large, full-frame, double-page illustration that I intended for the endpapers – was not used.

The rejected endpaper for *Aranea*

DRAWN *from the* HEART

By the time I had finished the rest of the book, I was so exhausted by the constrictions under which I had forced myself to work, so impatient to let rip on something, that when I came to the endpaper, I think I simply succumbed to complete self-indulgence…

Patrick Hardy had already seen all the artwork for *Aranea*, including this picture for the endpaper, on the day we went to lunch about *Bunyip*.

As we exchanged our farewells with Patrick and Bob, me feeling a wee bit glazed from the effects of the lunch, and very pleasantly dazed by the realisation that Penguin was taking both books, Patrick turned to me and, offering his congratulations, added, 'Oh, just one more thing before we go, Ron, regarding your endpaper drawing for *Aranea* – it is a quite extraordinary piece of work of course, I do like it very much indeed…but, um, it doesn't appear to have a very great deal to do, *really*, with the story itself or, indeed, with *anything at all* in the rest of the book…so, umm, I don't think, my dear Ron, really, that it will detract at all from the book if we leave that one out; I do hope you won't mind – well, not too much, anyway.'

I've put all that in quotation marks because they are the only words I remember from anybody – from that entire meeting. And because, even in the state I was in at the time, I thought, what an amazing sentence! I've never forgotten it.

What none of us knew was that some months later – maybe a year – Jenny would deliver a story that had been triggered by that drawing: *John Brown, Rose and the Midnight Cat*. So it hadn't gone entirely to waste.

Annie's Rainbow

Annie had always wanted to have her own rainbow.
Whenever she saw one she would run to catch it, or jump to reach it.

WHENEVER I VISIT schools to talk with kids about my work, or to do workshops, there is one question I am invariably asked: 'Which is your favourite book?'

For years, the answer I gave was that I did not have one.

I suppose that was a bit naughty of me (they are only wanting to know, after all). But I believe the question deserves something more than a simple answer.

The concern I have is that giving the simple answer implies I am happy with the work I did for that book. And I don't feel that way about any book I have done, and moreover, I know different children will like different books I have done – each for his or her own reasons – and I wouldn't want to interfere with, or discredit, any of that.

Sometimes, depending on the group, I might mention a couple of my favourite kids' books by other people: *Where the Wild Things Are*, by Maurice Sendak; *Owl Babies*, by Martin Waddell and Patrick Benson; *Goodnight Moon*, by Margaret Wise Brown and Clement Hurd; a whole bunch of Rosemary Wells' books, the peerless *Pooh* books, by A. A. Milne and Ernest Shepard; *Wind in the Willows*, by Kenneth Grahame and Shepard (again). Or, again depending on reading and interest levels, I'll tell them which adult writers I love and am reading at the moment. I love all these books, I say, much more than anything I have done.

Pressed, I will say that from time to time I might like one of my books more than another, that one book works reasonably well in one way, while another works more effectively in some other; that I might have a soft spot for one, but know that another is a far better piece of work…

The truth about my own books is that I don't believe any of them is as good as it should or could have been; if only I'd been a little more up to the task at the time. In each of them there is something – more often than not several things – that I wish I had done better, or altogether differently.

'But I'm working on it,' I will say. I am still hoping that one day I will manage to make a book that I really do think is okay, maybe even pretty good. 'Wouldn't that be a good feeling? I'm hanging out for that.

'I'll keep on trying.'

Much more rarely will someone ask me (and when they do, it's usually rather cheekily, with undisguised anticipatory relish), 'Which is your least favourite book?'

This always comes as a shock, bringing with it, as it does, the pain of remembering. But at least it gives me the opportunity to be totally honest about a failure.

Always, by the time I have finished the hard slog of doing the final illustrations for a book – having assembled the artwork and the overlays of lettering and instructions for the printer, having packed it all up and sent it off to my publisher – I am both hugely relieved and excited to be finished at last, and totally exhausted by the concentrated weeks and months at the desk. I feel absolutely drained. I send it all off, then pace around in circles for days, wondering what I'm meant to be doing. There will be discussions, conversations with my editor and publisher about this and that before they send it all on to the printer; but essentially I now have nothing to do, suddenly. I am lost.

The really dreadful thing that tends to sneak up on me while I'm in this state, hideously, is that I begin to fear the work I have just done, the book I have just made, is no good at all. I become convinced that it is probably actually horrible, for any number of reasons. And I wish I could bring it back, scrap it, and start all over again.

Slowly, bit by bit, I find new bearings – a new project, long-neglected chores which now need to be done around the garden and house. I get going again. I begin to forget all about the book, forget that I've even done it. It disappears! Every now and again over the next few weeks or months it will pop back into my consciousness, and slowly I will become excited about seeing it come back from the printer, increasingly hopeful that it might be okay. I become impatient, eager, to see the finished book.

And then, when the big yellow envelope, padded bag or box does arrive at long last, I sometimes cannot open it for a few hours, or days; because I am suddenly sure (again) that I won't like it, that it will be no good.

But I will eventually get round to it, and it has almost always given me a thrill to hold the finished, printed book in my hands at last; to be able to flick through its pages, to be able to savour the odd bit…

In one way or another, every book has given me some sort of surprise. The printed, assembled and bound book is of course always different to the pile of rough sketches, original illustrations or paintings that I have been surrounded by, buried in, for months. Printed and bound together in book form, with the text in place… those images now work together in a totally different way, and there is always something about that I have not quite anticipated or foreseen.

Together those illustrations have become a different thing, a new creature altogether – to such an extent that it is possible almost to see it anew, almost as though it were done by someone else, as a separate being finally – not necessarily quite the one I was expecting – with its own life just about to begin.

This moment will always be loaded. Sometimes it will turn out (just) okay. Theoretically, it can even be wonderful. With a few of my books, I am glad to say, it has been.

With *Annie's Rainbow*, it most definitely was not.

––––––––––

Having decided I wanted to focus on making picture books, I had ceased all my freelance illustration and design work, apart from Staggers, Saba, and the odd book cover, and moved out of South Melbourne. Peter Pavey and Jay and Miche and I were now sharing a house in Warrandyte. Peter and I earned our bread and butter by working as milkmen for his father at the Ringwood Dairy, where Peter had grown up among beautiful big Clydesdales and the heavy old carts they would draw around the streets, laden with crates of milk in glass bottles. The early morning clip-clopping (and the plopping), the tinkling of bottles and harness through the sleepy streets was part of his childhood. By 1974, however, we were using trucks.

Having the strength of a Clydesdale himself, Peter worked a longer shift than me, loading a large truck with crates full of bottles stacked high, then delivering the orders to homes all around the area from around 11 p.m. or midnight to about 7 or 8 a.m. Then he'd drive back to Warrandyte and sleep till the middle of the day. Meanwhile, I would have gone off to start loading my smaller truck at 3 or 4 a.m., then drive around Ringwood and neighbouring suburbs delivering orders to all the shops and schools. I loved it.

I would then drive home, breakfast, and go to my desk.

Miche, half Israeli with a deep olive complexion and jet-black hair – so black the highlights were blue – had a best friend living next door, Shelley, milky pale with pink cheeks and flyaway platinum-blonde hair. They were inseparable, always running back and forth between one another's houses, playing for hours at a time in cubbyhouses, bouncing on Shelley's trampoline in her back garden, feeding Peter's horse Mystery in ours, and running around at kindergarten together, just down the bottom of the hill.

On the last school day of one year, just before Christmas, dressed as Santa Claus, with two pillows stuffed down my front, I rode down on Mystery to give out presents to the children. Unlike Peter, I'm no horseman, not any kind of a rider, and Mystery was a very big – nay, huge – horse. Santa duties complete, I went to make an appropriately dignified departure. Much to the amusement of the kids watching through the windows, I had a lot of trouble getting back on, pillow-bouncing off every time I attempted to swing myself up onto Mystery's very high and very broad back. I eventually had to climb the fence and leap across from there, while all the kids (outside now, and shouting various bits of useful advice), were absolutely falling about. As was my costume and the pillows, I suspect.

In the heat of summer we'd all swim in the smoother stretches of the Yarra River, between the rapids at Pound Bend – just upstream from the tunnel the early gold miners had put through the hill to divert the river. Or we'd picnic among the white gums on the riverbank. I remember the intense, almost opaque cobalt blue of the sky – behind and between the trees, behind and between every trunk, every branch, every twig – insisting on its space; the transparency of the bush; the constant din of the cicadas, equally insistent, equally inescapable; the swallows dashing in and out the mouth of the tunnel. We took long walks through the bush, following the river around the Reserve, or back the other way to the bridge and the village. These walks were pleasant at any time of the year, but they were somehow especially enjoyable in winter when we were rugged up with raincoats, scarves and umbrellas, and the whole valley, misty with rain, could close in under cloud and dampness, everything dripping, closer together.

And then, in all the grey-green dampness, looking down along the river – we'd be taken by surprise every time – the sun would somewhere come through and the whole valley and everything in it would be glazed with those impossibly luminescent seven colours, lighting everything up from within. A great, big, glowing, soft and sumptuous rainbow right there in the back yards of the whole neighbourhood, just down from our house...this veritable feast for the senses would happen time and again.

Shelley had lived all her life in that house next door, but she never took these beautiful rainbows for granted. She loved them. They lit up her world, just as the endless pictures she painted of them lit up the walls of her bedroom. Miche's life, thus far, had been very different. Too many moves, too many changes, often very difficult. There had been too much unhappiness, and there was sadness, still. But as with everything else in their day-to-day lives, Miche and Shelley shared their wonder at the rainbows.

Somewhere in there I did a trip to Canberra with Miche, and driving back via Cooma, winding down Brown Mountain in the middle of the day, under a dark grey sky closed like a cast-iron lid above us, we rounded a bend and the sun found a gap. The valley below was suddenly lit up by the most perfectly complete and incomparably intense rainbow I had ever seen. It was stunning.

If she saw one when they were driving in the car
Annie would ask her father to go faster.

Rather than accidentally drive off the road – that one particularly, with its precipitous drops – we pulled over, got out of the car and just stood, transfixed by the sight. A rainbow is normally seen from below, arcing across the sky. On that day, we stood high on our mountain, both in and under darkness, and there below us, it seemed miles below – the most astonishing rainbow illuminated the land – milk and honey as far as the eye could see. It was all my favourite Renaissance, Neo-Ancient and Romantic paintings rolled into one. Beautiful.

And if she couldn't see her rainbow anywhere she would search
*   for it,*
or wait in hiding, hoping it would come.

An hour or two later, at Merimbula, we dropped in for afternoon tea with my Aunty Shat, my mother's eldest sister. Tiny, bright and as busy as a wren, she greeted us at the front door. It was the first time they'd met, and Miche took to Shat instantly, and to the magic of her lounge room, the exquisite furniture, the knick-knacks crowding every surface, the vases filled with beautiful flowers from her garden.

Annie left notes in secret places
asking the rainbow to wait for her.

Sitting in a late-Georgian rocker, eating biscuits and looking around, Miche announced, 'I found a rainbow the other day.'

'Did you, my dear?' responded Aunty Shat.

'I broke a piece off, and put it in a drawer...'

'Goodness me, darling! How very wonderful. What happened?'

'It melted.'

I attempted to marry all this in my story with something of the classic fairytale where the protagonist must finally confront the fear, the self, and enter that dark place in order to be able to find whatever it is they are looking for. For transformation to take place, fear must be transcended.

Annie had never gone into the garden before because it looked so
  dark.
But the rainbow she wanted so much was in there –
Annie knew she had to follow.

Annie comes to a fountain in the centre of the garden, which is bathed in all the colours of her rainbow.

She felt as though she were standing right inside the rainbow.
Annie reached out to touch the colours
But they just seemed to melt around her hands.

Annie wished she never had to leave this beautiful place. Then she meets an old man. 'It's almost as difficult to paint,' he said, 'as it is to catch it in your hands.' He takes her to a painting set up on an easel.

On the last page in the book, we see the painting hanging on the wall back in Annie's own bedroom.

––––––––––

I still am not sure how well I managed to bring the impulses, the various pieces of inspiration and references into the story itself – but certainly in the design and illustration of it, I half-baked the whole thing dreadfully.

The deeper she went into the garden, the darker it became.

When the book was printed, and the parcel was due to arrive – perhaps because it was the first time I had designed and illustrated a book to my own text – I was more than usually excited and anxious. It took me days to work up the courage to open the parcel, and when finally I did, I was devastated by what I found.

Appallingly designed, with all the single-page illustrations the same size, all the double-page illustrations also, and all occupying exactly the same area of every single spread – and with everything at roughly the same middle distance from the viewer – the book had no structural or dynamic strength at all. The cover and title pages were typographically twee; the *whole thing* was twee. The drawing throughout, especially of the figures, was wooden and dead – tight, dreadful – and the rainbows were amazingly badly painted, completely ridiculous. Everything was equally tight, lacking in imagination, clichéd, cloying and sentimental, sugary sweet and ultimately entirely banal. The pencil linework and the way in which I had used the bottled watercolour totally lacked any richness or depth.

The whole thing was without bone, without muscle. Absolutely bloodless. A pale, poor, weak creature, barely able to breathe… Sadly for me, the book had (already) died at birth. And it was all my own fault.

I put the book back in the envelope and didn't look at it again for months. I couldn't. I disliked it so much. I was so ashamed at having done such an unforgivably poor job of it.

How did it happen?

First, I think the approach I took with *Aranea* had the unfortunate effect of tightening me up. I found it hard then to loosen the way I was seeing things, let alone loosen my wrist enough to change the way I might be able to make marks on paper. I somehow froze and lost the sheer pleasure of drawing, of exploratory, fallible mark-making.

The problem went further. Perhaps it had something to do with this being my first text, but I was starting to take the responsibility of making books for kids – books that might have an influence and might (with a bit of luck) stay around for years – too seriously. Fearful that I wasn't up to the task (which I clearly wasn't!), I lost the courage to take the necessary risks, and ended up doing drawings dripping in timidity.

I didn't know or understand anywhere near enough about what made good texts, illustrations or books really work. I had not had enough to do with them.

With *Bunyip*, I didn't know how much I didn't know, so I just crashed on in, and through. Come the time of *Annie*, I was beginning to get an inkling, and faltered.

The work I did on *Bunyip* and to a lesser extent *Aranea*' was largely done on instinct, intuitively. Applying a more conscious intelligence to my bookmaking has been a much longer, harder road for me. Juggling impulses, inspiration, intuition and instinct with a critical detachment is an ongoing and constant challenge in the creation of any artwork. With *Annie* I possessed not anywhere near enough of the latter and, knowing that, I lost any grip I might once have had on the former. With extremely unhappy results.

It was almost 20 years, honest to god, before I could even look at the book again.

Visiting a school, I had been asked that question, 'Which is your least favourite book?' and, admitting my unhappiness about *Annie's Rainbow*, I went on to explain, a bit thoughtlessly, that the reason I hated it was because the drawing was so bad, the colours so weak, and please could we talk about something else now? Afterwards, during lunch, I was taken aside by the Head of the primary school. He had covered my plate with smoked salmon, delicious cheeses and salad, and plied me with home-cooked muffins, chocolate cake and freshly brewed coffee, and now, sitting across the table from me, told me that he felt I had made a mistake in saying those things about *Annie's Rainbow*.

'We have used that book a great deal, over very many years,' he said. 'It has played a central role in all sorts of projects with both the teachers and the students; it is considered one of our library's more special books.' Their few remaining old copies, held together with sticky-tape, were looking a little worse for all the wear. 'All this,' as he pointed out, 'in a boys school.' I had always thought, if *Annie* appealed to anyone, it would be to girls, more than boys.

'You are quite wrong,' he said, 'and you should think a little more carefully, if you don't mind me saying, about how you speak of that book with children.'

A number of other teachers sitting around at this extraordinarily generous lunch agreed with him.

I felt ill placed to argue the point.

Thinking about their comments later, I realised they were right. I had overdone it with *Annie;* I had forgotten my own rule about never discrediting a child's enthusiasm for any book, even if it is one of my own.

––––––––––

I love going to schools to talk with kids; I love to give them as much insight as I can into how I go about designing a book and creating the illustrations, love to share as much information as I can about everything involved in the whole process, from beginning to end, of making books. And because I am serious about the art form of the picture book, and about what those books might do for the kids who read them, I resist the temptation to simplify the process in any way.

In speaking at schools, I hope to enable children to become more critical, more discerning about books. And much more importantly, I do positively think it is important to talk about the failures, as well as the so-called successes; by being pretty honest about my own work, I very much hope to spark correspondingly deeper insights into their own ways of working, thinking and feeling, whatever their particular interests.

When Van Morrison was asked about the secret of his success one time – how come this concert, that recording, (in short, how come he) was so great? – he replied, 'It's because I don't worry about failin', man. Don't have any kind of hang-up about it at all. It's all *about* failure, man! About being prepared to.'

I would add that when you do fail, it's important to be able to see it, important that you try to figure out why you failed, where you went wrong. And then, especially if you are talking with kids, be honest about it. That way, you'll all learn something.

You, and the kids.

John Brown, Rose and
the Midnight Cat

Rose's husband died a long time ago.
Now she lived with her dog.
His name was John Brown.

JOHN BROWN TOOK me two years. At the time, 1974, Jenny Wagner
was living in a large rambling house in Essendon with her family,
a couple of dogs and several cats. Jenny was very fond of her cats,
many of whom (it seemed to me) were blow-ins who knew a good
thing when they saw it. I remember one evening, attempting to help
prepare and serve dinner, being somewhat distracted by the cats
walking among the dishes on the kitchen benches and dining table –
pausing by this plate, leaning in closer to that, as calm as you like,

noses busy assessing, testing… Jenny, plainly used to this but noticing my distraction, would half-heartedly shoo one of them along a bit, explaining – laughing as she did so – that they were simply looking out for the guests' interests, that they knew what a lousy cook she was; they were the quality control monitors. Another might be curled up next to the warm toaster perhaps, or the electric casserole, while outside, another could be seen sitting on the top of the paling fence just beyond the window – totally still, just watching, waiting. The two big dogs – black, long-haired Labradors – owned the couch (and the evidence was all over it).

The drawing I had done for the *Aranea* endpaper, the one Patrick Hardy had decided we shouldn't use, looked from within a room at an oldish woman sitting by the window. She was wearing a lace shawl, there were lace curtains in the window (causing cramps in the drawing hand), and pigeons outside. The woman had one good eye, one bad… and a tear. Also in the picture was a faithful Labrador dog, with a pipe, dressed in the late husband's vest, with head and front paws in his mistress's ample lap. All a little surreal. The window overlooked an inner-city square (maybe Macarthur Place in Carlton), with a figure looking out from a window opposite, lots of trees, millions of tiny leaves (more cramps) and a large sculpture – Monty-Pythonish (again), atop a pedestal in the park – of one huge hand holding a magnifying glass, with the leaves behind looming appropriately large. Crawling under the edge of one of those leaves, about to disappear, was a spider.

Jenny liked the drawing, and it brewed, apparently. Some time later, when I was living in Warrandyte, Bob Sessions called me from Penguin to say he had two new stories by her, and sent them across.

At first reading I preferred *The Machine at the Heart of the World*, primarily because I felt it could be much more interesting visually, but Bob explained that both he and Patrick thought *John Brown, Rose and the Midnight Cat* the better text, adding that British author Leon Garfield – a bit of hero of mine at the time – who had been in Bob's office when the texts came in, had voted very strongly for *John Brown* also. I allowed myself to be persuaded, and signed a contract to do the illustrations.

So, in the beginning there was the image – the rejected endpaper for *Aranea*. But Jenny's words were much, *much* better. There was the sheer loveliness of the rhythm in Jenny's sentences again, and so many levels, layers, interpretations, all done with such subtlety.

John Brown loved Rose,
and he looked after her in every way he could.

But as with *Bunyip*, I wasn't at all sure I was up to the task. Perhaps I was intimidated by the subtlety, thought that I might not be able to find sufficiently dynamic imagery – enough dramatic change from page to page – to make a picture book that would be satisfying to kids.

In summer he sat under the pear tree with her.
In winter he watched as she dozed by the fire.
All year round he kept her company.

For months the manuscript lurked in a drawer, while I brooded. A couple of chats with Jenny and many, many readings later, a single thread began to emerge more strongly than others. Ominous, dark, it was the thread that Jenny herself seemed most interested in: Death, and the waiting for it. I made a first, very rough, small dummy. It was very dark, and redolent of the work of the American illustrator Edward Gorey, but without *any* of his wit. The front endpaper was a cemetery (can you believe it?), and it only got drearier from there. I don't think I even bothered to show it to Bob. I showed him the still slightly odd second dummy. He found it a little disquieting but, ever reasonable and trusting, he said go ahead, hoping I understood his expressed reservations.

I fell horribly behind schedule; there was no way I could meet the deadline. I became difficult to find, and neurosis set in. I attempted to create an environment with at least some semblance of calm – getting friends to answer the phone and so on. It didn't work. There were always the wolves and the bailiff at the door – or the people from Taxation, who had firmly stuck in their collective cranium the laughable notion that I'd been a roaringly successful one-man show ever since I left college. Then there were the parking fines. Jay used to (try to) placate the local policeman with cups of coffee; our place became a sort of home away from home for him.

Bit by bit, I worked my way into the finished drawings. I showed a few to Bob. He said he liked them; he guided, but never pressed, was prepared to wait. And I kept him at it, the waiting, for another six months, finally turning up with the whole thing completed. Very unfair.

The work I then proudly handed over was what I have come to refer to as the 'first edition' of *John Brown*.

At the time I thought it was the best thing I had ever done. On one level, it was very simple – almost a series of stage sets. But the dark thread had become the whole thing: John Brown began as a common, garden-variety dog, a Labrador, Rose as a sad old woman, so we had dog and mistress, companions. The two or three rooms are cosy, domestic. Always there's a door about to (or already half-) open, or a darkened window, suggesting waiting. With each page, John Brown becomes slowly more human, more like the deceased husband in the photos on the mantelpiece and the bedside table. He dons the late husband's vest, smokes his pipe, reads his books, stands up on two legs, protective, possessive. Rose, no longer the mistress, is herself on all fours now. She sees something at the window and is fascinated, drawn, vulnerable. The roles they play shift back and forth, and John Brown switches from tactic to tactic, all to no avail. Rose offers him an impossible choice: either let the cat in, or – impossible because the result is going to be the same either way – allow her to die. She has made her decision; all that remains is the formality, the gesture to John Brown, who wants the two of them to continue. He lets the cat in.

Rose is not seen again, and John Brown is just a dog, alone.

This is all rather gloomy-sounding, I suppose, and it was…but it does have its lighter moments. In fact, when I leafed through the dummy just recently, I still found it – in places – very funny (albeit in a slightly bent sort of way).

My recollection is that when I took all the finished illustrations across to Bob at the Penguin offices in Ringwood, he was pleased. I recall even having celebratory drinks and sandwiches. From the in-house, company cafeteria – I should have known immediately what that meant. My impression was that he was pleased not only to receive

The drawings from
the first version of
John Brown

it at last, but pleased with the work itself. He was going to send it off in the overnight bag to Patrick in London, *tonight*. He would call me as soon as he had heard back.

Whatever the truth of that recollection, something else altogether must have been going on, at least in my head, because by the time I had driven back across to Warrandyte, I knew the book I had delivered was all wrong, horrible… I'd have to go back to the drawing board.

This was before the time of faxes (let alone emails). I didn't hear anything. A week went by, two weeks, three. And then Bob called me across to Ringwood, and showed me the telex from Patrick. I can still see it: 'Oh dear, I'm afraid Ron has done just exactly what we would much rather he had not… Of course, if he feels unable, after all this, to think about having another look at it, we would understand entirely.'

This must have been a tricky moment for Bob, so I was very happy to be able to tell him that I was not surprised, and that I totally agreed; I had already decided to start all over. But it might take some time…

This was 1974 or 1975. There was a lot going on. I was doing the last few pictures for *Annie's Rainbow*, and Peter and I were still working at the Ringwood Dairy. Somewhere along the line a publisher sent me Olaf Ruhen's story *The Day of the Diprotodon* to look at. I liked it, and showed it to Peter, who still wanted desperately to be making picture books.

'Do it,' I said. 'It's not your own text, but it's good. Do it. It will get your foot in the door, get you started.'

We talked about a style for the illustrations, and I called the publisher to say Peter would do a beautiful job of it. Peter did a couple of drawings, and the publisher agreed. So there we were, me finishing *Annie* and trying to figure out *John Brown*, and Peter working on *Diprotodon* while also fiddling with yet another story about a dragon – this one was having a dream, driving milk trucks around, delivering milk.

Meanwhile, *Bunyip* was out in the shops, doing well, and I was being asked to speak all over the place. One such place was the then Preston Institute of Technology. I spoke to the senior art and design students, and invited them to show me their folios. Though he had only a couple of pieces there with him, I was very impressed with the work of one particular student, Jeffrey Fisher, and no less by the bloke himself – very subtle, very wry. Mentioning that he had a lot more stuff at home that he hadn't bothered to bring in, he invited me to come round some time to have a look.

He shared a large bedroom with his brother Ken. There was a bed at each end, and a full size table-tennis table that doubled as his desk in between. The rest of his work was just as impressive as his table tennis. It was fantastic. So was his girlfriend, Margaret Perversi, who was studying at Coburg Teachers College. We all became great friends.

Margaret later told me that *Bunyip* had been the very first picture book she ever bought, shortly after it was first published in 1973.

It was a busy time. Full. Complicated. There was the bewildering, on-again, off-again relationship with Jay, the ongoing freelance work, illustrations for a couple of novels, book covers and a big screen print A1 calendar (which Jeffrey helped me print) for Morry Schwartz at Outback Press, for whom I also started a picture book, *The Dance Palace,* that I later abandoned. Jeffrey had meanwhile finished at Preston, emerging with a folio full of stunning illustrations; we were spending a lot of time together, and I was introducing him around to publishers and art directors at various advertising agencies and design studios. He did a cover or two for Morry at Outback and slowly picked up a few other things, but it was hard going for a while; people found him a little difficult, simply because he was so quiet.

Peter finished *Diprotodon* and was starting to feel his way into the illustrations for *One Dragon's Dream.* Happily spending time trying to help with that, I was slowly getting into my mess with *John Brown*, and a bit else besides. And Miche and I had an accident in Peter's car.

Christmas 1975, without a car to get to work, Peter moved back to live at the Ringwood Dairy, and Jay, Miche and I disappeared to South Gippsland in search of simplicity, space and a lower rent. I wrote the first draft for *Timothy and Gramps* while we were there, but the simple life lasted just three months – and all the time I was plagued by the dreaded *John Brown*. Occasionally Bob would call, but he never harassed. And somewhere in there, slowly, a new *John Brown* began to stir.

And then things fell apart. Jay and I finally separated – messily, painfully, permanently, without any elegance at all, and we all moved back to Melbourne. And Margaret Perversi and I got together. It was not a pleasant or easy time for any of us – not for Jay and Miche, not for Jeffrey, not for anybody, really.

Margaret and I moved (with a college mate of Margaret's) into a vast penthouse apartment above the Lucky Candy Company nut factory just by the Auburn railway station in Hawthorn. It was an amazing living space, eccentrically laid out, with the long central living area big enough to play cricket in (which we did); the front room, where I set up my desk, was maybe twenty metres by ten. There were huge sliding glass doors out onto enormous patios, the one off the front room twenty by twenty metres, with a three-metre-high brick wall all round. The only view was of sky. Absolutely fantastic for parties.

With the move into the Nut Factory, I got back into yet another dummy for *John Brown*, my fourth. This dummy alone consumed about four months, with lots of meetings with Bob, lots of rethinks, backtracking and attempts at different directions, until I found ways of putting images together that I hoped would open out the many layers in Jenny's text, and develop them in a way which would make the story more dynamic and more readily accessible for children.

My illustrations for the 'first edition', I had come to realise, were a slightly wacky interpretation of just one of the many possible readings of the text – the reading Jenny seemed to talk most about: Rose's waiting for death, and John Brown's resistance to that. I came to see that the story had a lot to say about many things – about different kinds of love, about conflicting loyalties, about possessiveness. It was perhaps not so much about jealousy as about the wish to protect what one has, or to regain what has been lost. I was hoping to open up these themes in the new dummy, to make connections between them, and to do this in such a way that would enrich any reading of the text.

At first the idea of having to go back to scratch and think it all through again was more than a little daunting, but the challenge became increasingly exciting. Those four months – working on the final dummy during 1976, were the high point of the whole project for me. But I should say that there's a part of me that wonders whether I would ever have completed the final set of twenty-three finished illustrations if it hadn't been for Bob Sessions. He gave me space, but kept me at it when my own reserves flagged, which they did indeed, on many occasions. His eye (and he himself would acknowledge having learnt at least something from Patrick Hardy) was invaluable. It was a genuine pleasure and a privilege to work with him.

And Margaret also, who was teaching full-time, and to whom I shall remain forever grateful, supported me all the way through that dummy, and all the way through the making of the final book. I was determined to complete all the finished illustrations before our planned wedding in December. I didn't quite make it, but the wedding did – in the Nut Factory – and it was a lot of fun. There was lots of music, and Hugh McSpedden's projections out on the patio, and friends dancing under the stars.

The complete set of illustrations, as they now appear in the published book, took me another four months. For me it is often something of a comedown when I reach this stage. The work becomes more predictable, simply the hard slog of finishing the whole project off, not as exciting or interesting as the earlier, more elastic stages of working on the dummy. It is satisfying to see all the strands tying up at last, of course, but there are fewer surprises; mostly it's just a matter of seeing out the distance, all the way through to the end. It's a marathon. Afterwards, there's nothing but relief and exhaustion. And at that stage I have absolutely no idea whether it's any good or not. I almost couldn't care less; the further I can get away from it the better.

So we did. When I had finally finished the book, Margaret and I went to Kangaroo Island. And it was heaven.

———————

Not long after we returned, Patrick Hardy was in town, visiting from London, and Bob invited us to dinner at his place in South Yarra.

Over drinks after an exquisite dinner prepared by Bob's wife, Dianne, Patrick leant forward and said, 'You know, Ron, this really is a very good book, and I do think it would be a jolly good idea if you came across to the Bologna Book Fair in a couple of months, so we can introduce you to all your international publishers. Because there will be quite a few, I may say, who should be interested. It would be *very* good for you, you understand, to meet them.'

'Well, that would be absolutely marvellous, Patrick, but there is no way I could possibly afford it.'

'Oh, my dear Ron!' Chuckle, chuckle. 'I do mean, *of course*, that we, Penguin, would pay for everything. Airfares, hotel, everything. And let me tell you, Ron, that in Bologna – which even the Italians refer to as La Cucina d'Italia – there is food, there are restaurants such as you would not be able to imagine… You'll be taken out to meals, absolutely wonderful meals, and all at your aforementioned international publishers' expense. You really would be rather silly, in fact – if you don't mind me saying so – to say no.'

At this point, Margaret – half-Italian, very fond of her food, keen on the sound of Bologna, very cheeky, and a vivacious young woman with whom all three blokes in the room were, quite understandably, a little bit in love – leant sideways on the couch she was sharing with Patrick (quite possibly placing one hand on his knee), and suggested quietly, 'I think double or nothing, Patrick.'

'Ah, now, Margaret.' He gave a very English chuckle, interspersed with snorts, near chokings, and much facial reddening, 'I'm really not sure that, um…you know – it's actually rather a lot of money, really.'

'Now, now, Patrick, double or nothing.'

And they did.

Margaret and I were flown to Italy; and waiting for us on the dressing table of Room 128 of the Garden Hotel in Bologna was the biggest bunch of the most magnificent tulips either of us had ever seen. All those friendly, generous, so-damned-clever London Penguin people – Dorothy Wood, Felicity Trottman, Tony Lacey, Ruth Petrie & co. – were there to greet us. It was absolutely wonderful.

Sadly though, not Patrick. He had had to stay in London. He was in the early stages of what turned out to be a long struggle with a brain tumour. But meet with all those international publishers to whom Patrick had shown *John Brown* we did. I think something like eight or ten of the very best children's publishers from around the world – in all the major territories – took the book straight away. And they *all* took us, Margaret and me, to breakfast, lunch and dinner, every day, for the whole week, and to suppers and drinks into *all* the nights. So many Campari aranciatas!

As they (do indeed) tend to say in publishing – we met so many interesting, fabulous people. One of our favourites was Raymond Briggs, in his inevitable snot-green duffle coat, with the old army bag over the shoulder, bewildering the sophisticated Garden Hotel bartenders late into the night, when everybody else was spending a fortune on their publishers' expense accounts, with his insistence, always, on milk. 'Why can't I get a plain glass of milk anywhere around here?' He was in his immediate post-*Father Christmas Goes on Holiday* phase, constantly 'grumpy', side-splittingly funny.

The whole week was magnificent – from the spectacular opening banquet in the Palazzo Maggiore, with windows open over the piazza, and hundreds of publishers, authors, editors and artists from all over the world, standing about talking, eating, drinking and – almost unbelievable now – smoking and leaning against the walls between the Carraccis and Caravaggios, under the frescoed ceilings. It was wonderful. And Bologna itself was *so* beautiful. Everything, everybody, every day, was absolutely fantastic; we could not believe how lucky we were.

After the Fair, when all the publishers had gone back to their respective countries – taking their respective expense accounts with them of course – we checked out of the Garden, into accommodation and smaller family-run trattorias, much more appropriate to our own budget. We stayed on in Bologna for a few more days, and for a further three weeks in Italy; travelling up to Venice, across to Florence, down to Rome, Naples, Sorrento, the Amalfi coast, and over to Capri…total heaven. Then through Milan to Zurich, where we visited my German-language publisher Artemis in their beautiful thirteenth-century building, right on the waterfront. We stayed in their upstairs apartment which was lined wall to wall, floor to ceiling with bookshelves bursting with everything Goethe had ever done – Artemis being the principal Goethe publisher. Then we went across into France for a week in Paris to soak up Cezanne, Degas, Toulouse-Lautrec, Manet, Monet, Picasso, Pissarro – and just drank it all in…

Then to London, to another incredibly warm welcome from all the Kestrel and Puffin people, and catching up finally with Patrick, so changed from when we had last seen him. We met the legendary Kate Webb, who had set up Puffin and who seemed to have worked with absolutely everybody, and all those extraordinarily bright Penguin editors and publishers, who were all so friendly, helpful and generous with their time. I was keenly aware, in this company, of the relative poverty of my own education; it was a little intimidating, but also hugely exciting, stimulating. There was so much good conversation, so much enthusiasm for ideas, such an energetic engagement with, and love of, language.

After the colour and light of Italy and France, however, Margaret and I both felt the need to escape from the greyness and heaviness of London, and thanks to Kestrel's Art Director, the formidable Treld Bicknell and her architect husband Julian, we were able to escape to Dorset. It was while living at Springhead in Fontmell Magna, nestled in the gentle hills of that beautiful countryside, that I rewrote the text and did the final illustrations for *Timothy and Gramps*, the story I had begun with Miche's attendance at Leongatha South Primary School. And waited nervously for the first proofs of *John Brown*…

———————

The first proofs were a little too red, but knowing that would be corrected in the final print run, I was otherwise happy with the result. There were some drawings I'd like to have done a little better, or differently, but I guess that will always be the case. For the most part, I felt I had managed to pull together all the elements I thought necessary: the clear, central thread of the (main) story that would appeal to children, and the other layers which would give it a greater 'roominess of meaning', open it out to a wider range of interpretations, and a wider readership.

As with any picture book, on the first level there is the text itself, the basic requirements it calls for. A thread has to be picked out, and clearly followed through in images. Once that framework is set up, all the other layers can then be built in and developed through. Some of the 'indications' for those other layers will come from the text itself, its words, its suggestions, its spaces; others from the characters – their personalities, appearance and body language; some from the situations, the settings and environments, or from other sources altogether, quite removed from and outside the text itself.

A great deal of the imagery in *John Brown* is drawn from my grandparents' house in Paynesville, Gippsland – an old Victorian weatherboard, with a verandah across the front and down one side, the front door opening to a passage down the middle, lounge and bedrooms off to each side, dining room, kitchen, bathroom and laundry at the back. Pop's work-shed was at the back corner of the house nearest the kitchen, and the woodheap was behind that, under the big oak tree. There were flowerbeds all around the house, leading out through fruit trees to the clothesline and the chookyard, and a path led through and beyond the vegetable garden to the classic old weatherboard dunny down by the back fence.

Nanna and Pop were poor but almost totally self-sufficient. They grew their own vegetables, preserved the fruit from their orchard and the chooks provided meat and eggs. Both were good cooks. Nanna's cakes, bread, fruit slices, biscuits and scones – all whipped up with the minimum of fuss on the only available horizontal surface in the kitchen, one small, well-worn table – were in constant supply and always mouth-wateringly delicious. Everything was cooked in or on the old cast-iron wood stove. Hot water was supplied from a big urn sitting permanently on top of the stove beside the kettle.

Most of the stumps were gone from under the floorboards, so the floor undulated gently throughout the house – up into the dining room, down into the lounge – and the internal walls were lined with hessian, simply papered over and whitewashed. Although they had a cat and a resident blue-tongue lizard living under the floor (not to mention the odd red-bellied black snake), there was no way they could keep on top of the mouse population…

'We are all right, John Brown,' said Rose.

'Just the two of us, you and me.'

Sitting in the lounge room at night – Nanna in her chair, Pop reading in his, and me on the couch, and each of us with our evening glass of sherry (Nanna's, though she was continually sipping away, seemed never to run out) – most nights Nanna and I would play Scrabble on a folding card table. Apart from the pleasant crackle and hiss of the open fire, it would be totally quiet.

I had to play by the rules but Nanna, totally focused, did not like to lose, so the criteria for admissibility would bend a little for her, her words becoming increasingly creative in their spelling as the game wore on, and I would allow my attention to wander to following the small sounds of a mouse scurrying about inside the walls. It would come to a stop at a particular point behind the wallpaper, which I would then watch, carefully. And sure enough, the concentrated scratching would start, and, eventually, a very busy little pink nose would pop through – sniffing, twitching.

One night Rose looked out of the window

And saw something move in the garden.

And I would say, 'There's another mouse-hole, Nanna.' The nose would of course immediately disappear, and the offence would pass to me.

'Yes, yes,' she would huff. 'Are you playing, or not?'

'What's that in the garden, John Brown?' she said.

John Brown would not look.

Nanna did have the most wonderful solution to these incursions. She would wait until there was a sufficient number of new holes to justify the effort, and then she'd mix up a batch of paste using flour and water (the same recipe we used for our incredibly heavy home-made newspaper kites back in Mallacoota), go to the sideboard and get out the pictures. She had a drawer full of them, cut from magazines. She would set everything up on the dining table – the paste, the

One night Rose looked out of the window and saw something move in the garden.

pictures – and get me to locate all the holes; I was to let her know how many there were in the hall, how many in the lounge, how many in which of the two bedrooms, how many in the kitchen. She would sort through, lay all the pictures out, make her selections, and then go around pasting them up. Eccentric, I know, but it worked, sort of. The holes were covered, and so were the walls, throughout the entire house, with thousands of pictures. Wall-to-wall decoupage through the whole house. I thought it was beautiful. So did the mice. All that fresh flour paste – delicious! Mouse heaven. So of course they'd

be back. It was constant. No wonder Bluey, the cat and the snakes couldn't keep pace.

I loved living there, in that house, with Nanna and Pop, and when I realised their house was the perfect setting for *John Brown*, I was thrilled.

Of course I didn't draw all those hundreds of pasted magazine pictures on the walls into the book, but pretty much everything else in the illustrations – with minor variations – is exactly as it was: the house itself, everything outside and most things inside – the kitchen, dining room, lounge room, bedroom, and all the furniture, vases, ornaments, the old telephone (the first I'd ever seen on a childhood visit from Mallacoota) on the wall in the hall, with the bakelite mouth- and ear-pieces, and the handle to wind. I've simplified it all just a bit, and had to rearrange the geography of the rooms to make it work for the text, but apart from that it's all pretty faithful to the original.

A big part of that book, both the doing of it and the finished thing itself, is simply a thank-you for the time I spent with Nanna and Pop in that house. I only wish I'd had the opportunity to make the book earlier, or that they were still alive, so that we could sit down again now and have a few good old hearties about some of the jokes in there. So it goes.

I revisited those memories again years later when I was making another book – *Old Pig* – not so much for the house itself that time, more the spirit of Nanna and Pop themselves.

It is in the synthesis of all these various references and layers that I sometimes find a personal satisfaction beyond that of simply trying to make a good book for kids. But there is a danger in this: I'm always tempted to put more and more in, and I have to be careful not to overdo it. The challenge is to achieve the layering while preserving overall simplicity. It is possible to put *too* much in, I believe, crowding and cluttering an image with detail to a point where it becomes barely accessible any more, leaving no openings, nowhere for the viewer to get in. Similarly, in the actual technique and style of the work, I think it is possible for an illustration to be too 'clever,' too finished, too polished and smooth, creating a visual tightness and hardness to the surface of the image, to the page itself, that it becomes hard for the eye to pass through and gain access to the insides of the image. It becomes uninteresting to even try.

For example, in the double-page illustration for '*One night Rose looked out the window and saw something move in the garden*', instead of having only a few framed pictures on the floral wallpaper, I could have drawn Nanna's hundreds of pasted magazine pictures (of hundreds of different sorts of flowers), dozens and dozens of them crowded together and overlapping one another, all over the walls; but that extra level of detail would have required an altogether different, much finer and tighter technique. I certainly wanted the room to look and feel like Nanna and Pop's lounge room, but I also wanted to keep the image and the page simpler than that. So I put the illustration of Nanna and Pop's lounge room together rather as one would build a stage set, evocative of the original and retaining the most important, bigger elements – the two armchairs, the fireplace, the window, the door and the bookshelves – and keeping a few smaller items in there: three framed pictures on the walls, the clock on the mantelpiece, the small brass chest next to it, Pop's smoking-stand by one of the armchairs. All these items have a source, a reference back to the myriad details of the actual room, but collectively they have been simplified in such a way as to keep the focus on the main characters in the story – John Brown, and Rose.

I could also have been tempted to try to reproduce all the details of the original nineteenth-century steel engraving from above the mantelpiece back in the lounge room in Mallacoota that inspired the image for

John Brown thought.
He thought all through lunch time and when supper time came,
he was still thinking.

Folds of embroidered drapery, a glimpse of the detailed carving on an old piece of furniture, a patterned rug on the floor – I could have taken the viewer's distance from the subject out a little bit, and included all that as some sort of salute to the original, but I didn't. I stayed in close with just John Brown, his nose and paw resting on Rose's slipper, stayed in close to what I felt to be the heart of the moment.

I think it is important for the image to somehow remain simple enough, open enough, and for the actual technique of the illustration to remain rough enough, almost unfinished enough, as to allow easy entry into the image, and movement within; leaving plenty for the kids themselves to imagine – for the reader, the viewer, to do.

An hour past supper time he went back to Rose, and woke her
gently.
'Will the midnight cat make you better?' he asked.
'Oh, yes!' said Rose. 'That's just what I want.'

John Brown thought. He thought all through lunch time and when supper time came,
he was still thinking.

I sometimes think of myself as some kind of glazier. I don't knock as many holes (unlike the mice) in as many walls as I'd like to, but I do try to make windows – extensions of the text, windows to other possibilities. And I try to make each of those windows in such a way that they will not confront us with complete and final statements, leaving nothing for the readers themselves to do, but rather be invitations to wonder and explore. I make suggestions in the illustrations, provide starting points, things to fiddle with and speculate about, but leave open the possibilities

so that each viewer can find their own connections, and use them in their own way.

It is important to maintain that openness throughout all the images for any text, but in *John Brown*, with all the subtlety of its text, with all the layers of possible meanings and interpretations, it was especially important – otherwise I'd be doing the text a serious disservice. The ending in particular called out for this kind of openness.

John Brown went out to the kitchen and opened the door, and the
    midnight cat came in.

Then Rose got up and sat by the fire, for a while.
(Note, and think about, that comma.)
And the midnight cat sat on the arm of the chair…
We see all three, sitting by the fire. It's almost cosy: Rose is in her armchair, and on the arm of the other chair (usually occupied by John Brown) the midnight cat looks across at her. John Brown is on the floor.

To open out the possible readings, I put the last two words of the text, after that ellipsis, by themselves on the very last page.
and purred.
We see the midnight cat, still on the arm of John Brown's chair, alone, and looking directly at us.

————

I enjoy the paradox that I have control over the making of the initial image, of what I put into it, but none whatsoever over how it will be used or interpreted.

The English (ever democratic) reviews of *John Brown* pointed out endless possibilities in the book, story and pictures. Among the more interesting was Margery Fisher's observation that Queen Victoria also had a friend called John Brown, and that the relationship there was very similar indeed. (And Brian Alderson offered his observation that it was 'probably the best book never to win the Kate Greenaway Medal'.)

The Germans (who take their children's books very seriously) suggested that *John Brown* was a sensitive study of the problems sometimes involved with a first child coming to terms with the impending arrival of a second, and that 'parents in this situation may well find the book helpful'.

The Americans, on whom one can always count for – shall we say – a certain clarity of vision, seemed mostly to think *John Brown* was 'a lovely book about an old woman, a dog, and a cat'.

Timothy and Gramps

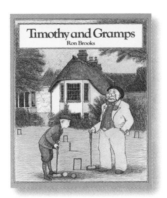

*Gramps always took Timothy to school in the mornings,
and home again in the afternoons.*

*Timothy didn't like school much. He had no brothers or sisters,
and he had no special friends,
except for Gramps.*

DURING THE TIME when Miche, Jay and I lived in South Gippsland, and I was struggling with *John Brown*, Miche attended Leongatha South Primary School, which served the mostly dairying community on the flatlands between Leongatha and Inverloch. There were maybe forty or fifty children, from Prep to Grade 6, divided between two rooms, with two teachers. The school had only minimal facilities, inside and out, but it was relaxed, friendly and welcoming. Many of

Pages from the dummy for *Timothy and Gramps*

Gramps always took Timothy to school,

and home again in the afternoons.

the children walked to school, with brothers, sisters, friends, doing the sorts of things country kids do on such jaunts – jump gutters, push one another towards potholes and puddles, throw stones at power poles and the odd cow, or just yarn about the weekend.

I remember the Monday morning I first saw an old man and a girl walking along holding hands to the school and, on arrival, staying a little apart from the other chatting groups, talking quietly together, before the girl went in. I could not help but see the closeness, the affection that was so evident between them. I also could not help but notice the subtle, somehow extra, respect they were shown by other children as they passed by.

Intrigued, I asked the teacher about them the next day. He told me Ellie had no brothers or sisters, was a thoughtful girl, quiet, a little shy perhaps, and lived with her grandfather, who was clearly her best friend also. There was no one else.

They went on walks together.

Gramps told Timothy stories, and Timothy told Gramps stories.

But at school Timothy played mostly by himself.

'We start every week, first thing every Monday morning with a big Show and Tell session,' he explained. 'Other children will bring in pet lizards, dogs, frogs, whatever…or stand up the front and tell us about some adventure they had, perhaps with friends or family on the weekend, you know, all the usual wonderful things. But Ellie doesn't have any of that.'

But at school,
Timothy played mostly by himself.

Or sometimes they just brought something they had found, and talked about that.

Timothy never talked about Gramps; he just showed him.

Or sometimes they just brought something they had found... Timothy never talked about Gramps; he just showed him.

But Timothy had no pet of his own and he could never seem to find anything special enough to bring and show.

'And it's not that it seems to be a particular problem for her; she'll sit back and enjoy the sessions with all the rest of the children. But, every now and again – evidently only when she feels some sort of need – Ellie will bring her grandfather in. She doesn't talk about him, she just kind of shows him, introduces him. And he doesn't say much either, mostly he just says "Good morning boys and girls," and just stands there, while the children all look at him for a while.'

What happens then? I wondered.

'I know it sounds a little odd, but the children seem perfectly happy with the whole arrangement, and when everyone seems content he simply says, "I will let you all get on with your day now," and leaves.

'They really are rather a special pair,' he said. 'And the others can see that.'

Beautiful, I thought. But also sad, somehow.

'But there have been a few days when Ellie sits at her desk, along with all the other children at theirs, and he stands up at the front of the class and tells us all a story. And he has some beauties, I can tell you; he's had quite a life!

'Yesterday was one of those days. Absolutely marvellous! Everybody gets a big clap of course when they've finished their presentation, but, I have to say, Grandfather gets that, *plus* some…and then he leaves. That's it.

'All the children love him.'

Really beautiful, I thought.

I returned home and found I could not get Ellie and her grandfather out of my head.

Then one night when I was at my desk wrestling with *John Brown*, the story was suddenly simply *there*, and I wrote it down. Next day I sent it to Anne Ingram at Collins who had published *Annie's Rainbow* and was keen to have another book to follow. She liked it, made a few suggestions, gave me a contract, and I rewrote, and rewrote, and rewrote it…somewhere along the way changing Ellie to Timothy (after a young neighbour in Warrandyte who did seem a slightly lonely little fellow), only because I didn't want two books in a row, from the one publisher, about a little girl.

Meanwhile, my personal life was in upheaval. I was no longer with Jay and Miche, but with Margaret Perversi, back in Melbourne – and I was still embroiled with *John Brown*. I was unable to get the text for *Timothy* right, unable to 'see' the illustrations, or where to set the story. The book went to the bottom drawer.

Working my way through and finishing the final dummy for *John Brown* became the priority, as did Margaret…then the finished illustrations for *John Brown*, the trip to Bologna, other parts of Italy, Paris, London, Dorset and finally to the village of Fontmell Magna.

Invited by Treld Bicknell, Kestrel's art director, to spend a weekend with her family at their cottage in Fontmell, Margaret and I strolled together up the hedgerow lane to Springhead, more or less the manor house to the village and mostly hidden from view by hedges, high stone walls covered in ivy, and dense copses of mature elms. Walking through the gateway, we fell instantly in love with the place. Once upon a time a mill-house with attached workers' cottages, it was now one big rambling house set in six acres of beautiful gardens, with huge mature trees, its own private lake fed by springs, extensive vegetable gardens, outlying fields and cottages (one of which was the Bicknells'), all forming part of the estate running down the valley to the village.

The whole shebang was presided over by the indomitably erect Marabel Gardiner, who promptly took us off on a guided tour of her beloved garden, pointing out all her special treasures as we went around: the vast Albertine rose on a wall of the East Wing, water lilies in the front pond, tiny wild strawberries growing up the stone steps and – along one side of the lake, and running along its full length – enormous beds of rare roses, lush herbaceous borders to the broad, beautifully maintained lawns and wide grassed paths; lobelia, lavender, and bulbs of every description were scattered everywhere, not to mention spectacular tulips, and lilies like tropical birds suddenly surprising us among all the green. Further on, into the 'wood', were beeches, elms, liquidambars, maples, oaks, and a small wooden bridge crossing over the small, spring-fed stream. There was less colour on the other side of the lake – the contralto to the other side's soprano – with big elms along the wall, and smaller, more intimate lawns between magnificent yew hedges, a splendid weeping mulberry, massive rhododendrons and an Italian folly on a peninsula running out into the lake; another, larger lawn curved around the northern end of the lake and swept back to the house.

Even where there was a little less sun – between the house and the hedged lane – we saw a scattering of late crocuses, all colours, and around the base of a Chinese oak a crowd of miniature cyclamens, white. We couldn't have chosen a better time to visit – it was springtime, the garden was at its most glorious; the whole tour had been a sumptuous feast for *all* the senses.

Marabel was joyous and proud to show us her domain, sweeping us now into the first of the thatched-roof cottages, the one closest to the gate – two up, two down with thick stone walls, rendered and whitewashed, deep-set windows, and low doorways even I had to bend a little to clear. And then she took us at a brisk trot through the labyrinth of what had once been four or five two-storey workers' cottages but were later opened up to one another to serve as the Gardiners' family home, and now looked more like a living museum. There were gorgeous wallpapers everywhere, and upstairs, set deep into the sloping roofline, lovely dormer windows peered out under the deep thatch to the gardens below; every room stuffed full with antique furniture, beautiful rugs everywhere, and exquisitely quilted bed-covers, an ancient rocking–horse, a very impressive piano, a violin or two, and a huge, multi-storeyed Victorian dolls house – a *total* treasure, itself similarly filled with incredibly finely crafted and painted miniature furniture, including impossibly tiny sets of hand-painted porcelain on the dresser shelves.

The whole thing was like a dream.

We were whisked much too quickly through all this to Marabel's own area of the whole spread – a more recent addition to the building (linking the mill with the cottages), and similarly crowded with beautiful furniture, rugs and (coffee plantations and Egyptologists in the ancestry) all sorts of memorabilia and artefacts from Africa and Egypt. From there we moved on to the western wing, to what had originally been the mill-house – just one great big room, maybe twenty or thirty metres long by ten or twelve wide, with a high 'cathedral' ceiling, and windows all along both sides looking out into the gardens. A *beautiful* grand piano presided, and troops of music stands stood assembled, waiting.

We'd never seen such a place before, Margaret and I; I don't believe I'd ever even *imagined* such a place – so beautiful, and so rich, in every way.

'*Tea*,' Marabel announced, 'after our little gallop? I shouldn't wonder if there weren't even some biscuits in the kitchen…you could come through and help me, if you like.'

The kitchen was another thing altogether. The whole room looked as though it didn't much interest the mistress of the house, and knew it. Originally just a passage, it was dark and narrow and painted a rather strange green a *very* long time ago, and was less than clean throughout. This reluctantly acknowledged utility was a dark clutter of the barest necessities.

Title-page spread, *Timothy and Gramps*

Marabel put the kettle on the old gas stove, and rummaged through the cupboards (and the sink) to find three reasonably clean cups and three saucers, and plonked some broken biscuits on a plate.

Imperious and a little intimidating (and, as we later found out, fluent in something like seven languages), Marabel was absolutely no-nonsense. Sitting down to tea back in her sitting room, with a clear pecking order to the seating arrangements, she said, 'So, you come from Orrrstralia, the colonies, all those convicts and the like – any in either of your families, would you know?'

'Well, all that was quite a while ago, but I suppose there's always the possibility...'

'Quite right,' she said, 'but let's hope that's all *well* and truly behind us. *Now* – just what *are* you doing here? Treld tells me something about books.'

'Well, yes, I've written a story which I'd like to illustrate while I'm here.'

'A book? Good heavens! *Do* books actually *get* published in Orrrstralia?'

'A couple,' I said, 'from time to time.'

'Well, jolly good. And what sort of a book, exactly?'

'A children's picture book. I've written the story, but I'm sort of looking around for the right place, to do the illustrations.'

'Yes, yes, you're repeating yourself, you have already mentioned you had written it – just exactly what sort of a place do you think you are looking for?'

'Well, actually...*this* place, Springhead, the village, all around here would be better than perfect.'

'In that case, perhaps we could come to some sort of arrangement – Treld and Julian assure me you are perfectly respectable; what would you say to living in that first cottage I showed you, and you could do your drawings while you are working for me in the garden? You would have to prove yourself reliable, of course – show that you know the *difference* between plants and weeds. I wouldn't want you to be just wandering about digging everything up!'

So we came to an arrangement, and beautiful Springhead became our home for the spring and summer of 1977. It was heaven.

I got back into the story for *Timothy and Gramps.*

I worked a few hours every week in the garden, and spent most of the rest of the days drawing. Occasionally we'd set off on excursions through the villages of Wiltshire to Salisbury (King Arthur country), Stonehenge and those vast chalk 'drawings' on the downs, but mostly we pottered around Dorset – Thomas Hardy country, and re-read all his books in the evenings. One evening, in neighbouring Shaftesbury, we even got to attend a marvellous lecture by Lord David Cecil, about Hardy's poetry.

The name Fontmell Magna goes back to Roman times, and the now softly rounded forms of the strip lynchets dating back to at least that period are still there on the hillside immediately next to Springhead, as are the remains of even older earthwork fortifications further to the south. Fontmell itself is one of those archetypal English country villages – all pretty little stone cottages with thatched roofs, streets and roads all winding around, some lanes with such massive hedgerows that they are almost tunnels, with wooden gates through to fields on either side. We walked for miles in every direction around the village, through the lanes, along the footpaths, and across the fields, white daisies floating in the twilight, seemingly detached from their long stems in that light, and the occasional pheasant exploding out of the long grasses just in front of us. Looking back down over the whole valley, across to Compton Abbas, walking through avenues of majestic beeches, alongside old stone walls. It was like entering a childhood dream.

The few books I *had* seen as a boy had all been English, with pictures of places just like this, and that image of England, for me, had become some sort of a dreamscape; I certainly hadn't believed I'd ever stand there, in among all that picture-postcard beauty, and find that it really was so, still.

I had found where I would do all the illustrations for *Timothy and Gramps*, and found the last few lines for the story.

I walked and wandered about all these beautiful places with my pens and ink, my brushes, watercolour pencils, paper pads and a small

But Timothy had no pet of his own and he could never seem to find anything special enough to bring and show.

DRAWN *from the* HEART

folding canvas stool. I even had a big old beach umbrella for when it rained. I looked like some sort of peripatetic garden gnome, I'm sure, as I squatted here and there, plein-air, to do my drawings, completing some of them back at the desk, in the cottage. And when I'd finished, I packed it all off to Collins.

———

The book was not particularly successful in Australia. I don't think anybody liked the fact that I'd set a book in England, and they probably thought it a bit *too* cute. And I agreed with them, it was.

My whole conception of the book and all the illustrations were far too timid, with nowhere near enough creativity, no genuinely original vision of my own. While the story had its impulse and heart in the right place – in showing the affection and closeness between Ellie and her grandfather, their having to, and then being able to, *let go* – I didn't manage to do anywhere near enough with that in the writing.

Letting go, albeit softly, was the theme of the story; with my drawings of all that loveliness of small English villages and countryside I was hoping to do something of the reverse – offer some sort of small salute and thank-you for the illusions lasting. Alas, I wasn't any kind of a writer, and as an illustrator I wasn't able to let go at all. I was altogether too seduced by the loveliness of the subject, and far too deferential to the work of a few predecessors also, without remotely understanding what *really* made their images work.

Various books by Shepard, Ardizzone and Burningham were in the back of my mind as I began work on the drawings for *Timothy*, but I failed to see how brave all three of these illustrators are *on the page* – all of them alive, *in the moment*, as they make those marks on the paper; they all make small mistakes, but they all allow the wrong lines to stay. Shepard draws beautifully, of course, as does Ardizzone, and they each might have made another, stronger line next to the wrong one, but sometimes they don't even bother with that – they simply leave the wrong line where it is, leave the drawing as it is, because it *feels* right anyway. Burningham does not draw anywhere near as well as Shepard or Ardizzone, and some of his images look almost inept (even just technically), but with him none of this matters at all – he leaves whole awkward sections and passages, or simply patches another bit of paper over the top of the failed area, and does that bit again with all the re-workings entirely visible, as rough as guts at times…and it very often works, *wonderfully*.

In contrast, with *Timothy and Gramps* I was so worried about doing a single clumsy line, so nervous about simply letting a line stand, letting it go, so terrified of making a single wrong mark, that I made *thousands* of them.

I had retreated right back into my childhood dreamscape of England, into sentimental nostalgia, forgotten all about what I thought I had learnt from Fred Williams, the Impressionists, Post-Impressionists, Picasso, Braque, et al., and had instead done a whole lot of pretty little pictures of lovely English countryside. And all the figure drawing throughout the entire book is uniformly *appalling*, dreadful, dead. Thousands of cowardly, meaningless lines, with no personality whatsoever to any of the characters. Embarrassing.

There are some individual pictures in there that I can't help feeling a fondness for: a couple of pieces of landscape, a village lane, a lovely old house, some trees, which is more than I can say for *Annie*. And I had moved the sizes of the individual illustrations around a lot more in this book than I had in *Annie's Rainbow*, but there is a weakness of colour and tonal contrast throughout, a flatness and general uniformity that again makes the book lifeless, gutless and altogether too sentimental. I began to fear as much, but only when it was too late; it was already off at the printers.

So it was a bit of an improvement, but in other ways the whole experience was horribly reminiscent of the earlier book. So much so, in fact, that notwithstanding all the brouhaha happening at the time – it was 1978, *John Brown* was receiving critical acclaim (I was the golden boy) and winning awards – I had the sneaking suspicion that I didn't *really* know what I was doing.

It was five or six years before I published another book.

From the Big Apple
to the Apple Isle

I HAD TRIED to do another couple of books. While still living in London I had begun working on a retelling of the old Indian story, *The Blind Men and the Elephant*; I had written and rewritten it many times, and finally, (half) satisfied with the text, showed it to Patrick Hardy, who signed it up immediately. I spent three or four months working up first one dummy then another to take to the fair at Bologna with Kestrel in 1977, several publishers expressed interest, and I continued working on it back in London (and on Ted Greenwood's *Pochetto Coat* while holidaying in the Greek Islands), before flying back to Australia.

Visiting a bookshop in Sydney, I saw a retelling of the same Indian story, a picture book by the American illustrator Stephen Kellogg. It had only recently been published, and because I quite liked his work at the time, and liked what he had done with the story, I felt the wind taken from my sails on the spot. I didn't believe there was room for two versions of the one story, and decided to drop the whole project.

Patrick Hardy wasn't too happy about it, tried (unsuccessfully) to persuade me the Kellogg book wouldn't be a problem; but some little time later he sent me the *Longneck and Thunderfoot* text by Helen

Piers. I liked the story – a metaphor for the whole Cold War, the whole America/Russia thing – and felt guilty about Patrick, and put together a dummy and did several finished illustrations for it but, not liking the ending of the story, about halfway through I asked Patrick if Helen could look at that 'because, really Patrick, I think this story could be very good, very strong, but the sheer *obviousness* of that ending is just corny, too sweet, silly.'

He didn't, he wouldn't…

'My dear Ron, no, I don't think I can. Really, this is *Helen Piers* we are talking about. She is a very good writer, a *very* good writer, with a strong reputation and following. You must understand you are quite fortunate to have this text, really.'

One of the paintings from around this time, *Keilor Earthwork*. Acrylic and mixed media on canvas

Tent.
Acrylic on
canvas

I lost heart, and could not continue with the project. Patrick was of course not happy and, after all he had done for me, I felt terrible. But later, when I looked again at the illustrations I had done for the book, I was relieved. They were awful.

Later still, when I heard the book was published and had won the Greenaway, I had a look and yep, there it was, medal attached, text unchanged, and the whole thing sweetened still further by Michael Foreman – a (very) minor variation on his earlier *Dinosaurs and All That Rubbish.* I (almost) laughed in disbelief.

I just about stopped then and there, but I continued looking around for ideas, and remembered Jenny Wagner's *The Machine at the Heart of the World*, the story Penguin and I had earlier set aside in favour of

John Brown. I had always liked the story, found it in a bottom drawer, read it again, and found I still liked it – a lot. But then I thought of Jeff Fisher – he was doing spectacularly good work, but mostly in the advertising and graphic design worlds; we were living next door to one another just off St Kilda Road, were good mates again, and he wanted passionately to do something with books. So I called Penguin and suggested they let him have a go at it. They were stunned (so was I) with the first couple of drawings he did, and signed it up. Jeffrey was thrilled, and worked solidly away at his desk for months on it, producing his own particular brand of amazingly inventive, witty images, and the book was eventually published in 1983.

Meanwhile, I stumbled across a lovely old song by Rodgers and Hammerstein, *The Lady and the Ape.* I loved the lyrics, and thought it would make a great little book, very funny. I put together another dummy and (weirdly, now that I think of it) flew to Germany to show it to Patrick at the Frankfurt Book Fair. He barely looked at it, or didn't like it, or had lost patience with me, or something. Anyway, he didn't respond.

I stopped trying to make books. I returned to freelancing as a designer and illustrator, fiddling about in a fairly half-hearted way on the edge of the design and advertising world in Melbourne. I did a couple of designs for the Victorian Tapestry Workshop; began teaching drawing and illustration at Chisholm Institute of Technology; and did a few book covers for various publishers. One of the more interesting of these was the Blanche d'Alpuget biography of Bob Hawke. Not exactly a kids' book, but an interesting project...

One of the next jobs I took on – my first bunch of book illustrations in years – was for Don Watson's *Story of Australia*, in 1984. I loved doing the pictures for that book. I liked the text – the whole thrust of it – and I liked the pictorial research involved. I enjoyed working with Don, and with Di Gribble and Hilary McPhee. Visiting them in their sprawling Cecil Street spread, in Fitzroy, with coffee and biscuits in constant supply (and those big old comfy couches around the coffee table), was always a pleasure. It was so damn friendly, with people coming and going always, like a big extended family. The whole experience got me thinking about making books again.

Then Mitsumasa Anno, the great Japanese picture book artist, asked me to contribute illustrations for his upcoming *All in a Day* book, which I did (not very well, unfortunately), and I meanwhile continued freelancing around doing all sorts of things for all sorts of people, including Australian Children's Television Foundation – I came up with names, did illustrations, designed logos and documents for several series of films – *Touch the Sun, Figments, Winners*, and *Round the Twist* – until Rosalind Price (then a packager of books for various publishing houses) asked me if I'd be interested in working on an anthology she was putting together for Macquarie Library. She and Walter McVitty would be the editors.

Rosalind began sending me pieces, some of which I liked, some of which I didn't, until it became a collection of about seventy pieces – *The Macquarie Bedtime Story Book*, containing stories and poems by about 30 writers. I began work – decided on the format, explored different internal layouts for the whole book, tried various fonts for the text and titles, read and re-read all the stories, thought about the illustrations and where they would all go into the text, got all the final typesetting done, and then pasted it all up into position, printer-ready, with all the 'holes' in the right places, ready for the illustrations.

They paid me a very nice lump sum by way of advance, and I had an idea for another project based in Manhattan. I thought, why don't we go and live in New York while I do this book? I could do the research for the Manhattan project at the same time. So, off we went – Margaret, our children Sam and Adelaide, and me. It was 1986. Sam was three and a half, Adelaide was just over twelve months old. We spent a month or so with Jeff and Christine Fisher in London on the way through, and looked up old friends from our earlier time there. Dorothy Wood, once with Kestrel and Puffin, then with Hippo, offered me a lovely little story, which I liked and took with me to New York.

––––––––

Before we left Melbourne, thinking (ridiculously) that it would take only a couple of days to find an apartment in New York, I had booked in advance a few nights in the Olcott Hotel on West 72nd Street.

It was July or August, the weather *extremely* hot and sticky when we arrived, and while Margaret and the kids cooled off by the lakes in Central Park, I began looking for an apartment the very next day.

There was a realtor office in the same building as the Olcott. 'You're in a good area. You're lucky. Dere's a okay, smallish studio apartment in de buildin dat Mia Farrow and alla kids live in, just up de street; nuttin straight across from her in the Dakota, unfortunately, where Yoko Ono lives, and, you know, John, once. She now owns most of it, ya know dat?'

'That's okay – probably a little beyond our price range, anyway,' I said.

Dressed in jeans, open sandals and a white singlet, he drove me around the upper west side looking at apartments, starting with a very nice one belonging to Harry Belafonte's sister or daughter, or something. Harry himself lived, or had done, downstairs. Then there was one that had something to do with James Cagney, another linked with Art Garfunkel, and another with 'some folks say anyway – Al Capone. Or maybe it was George Raft. Or his mother, I dunno.'

Capone's, or Raft's?

'It's dat kind of area,' he explained, driving me round for half the day. 'Always somebody.'

'Still just a little too expensive,' I didn't elaborate.

'Yeah, well, *hey!* Dis is *Noo York! Upper West Side! Nice.* Waddya-spect?' An' y'wantin' sumpin' in jussa *cuppla*days, *I mean…!*'

I tried another realtor, and another; and booked another couple of nights at the hotel. A week altogether. That was all they had. I had to look for another hotel. I found a suite at the Royalton, on West 44th Street, the sister hotel to the Algonquin. This was before the Royalton had had its makeover, but we were still pretty impressed to bump into Leonard Cohen in the lobby one evening, walking straight toward us, looking incredibly like – well, like Leonard Cohen, and smiling right at us (mostly at Margaret, I suspect). I swear he was on his way to the photo shoot for the cover of *I'm Your Man.* Wearing the same suit anyway. We were later told, 'Yeah, Mr Cohen – he's got a whole suite on the floor directly above you folks.'

Having by now been told that people allowed themselves twelve, maybe eighteen months to find an apartment in New York, 'Ya can't just turn up, with a wife an' two kids, an' spec to find sumthin' juz like dat! Speshly not on Manhaddan', I bought the papers, went through all the ads, and hit the phones, day and night, for two weeks. And finally found a top-floor walk-up in a brownstone in Carroll Gardens, just across the East River, in Brooklyn. Nice. The whole area was very Italian, apparently the oldest Italian area in all of New York, if not the whole country. We found little cafés, coffee and pasta shops, wine merchants, and laundries around every corner. Everybody seemed to be called Vinnie.

I had a few introductions to people in the design and publishing worlds of New York and, having spent far too much money on the hotels already, hoping to pick up some work, I started calling around immediately, and carting my folio about with me. Me and five thousand other illustrators...

I would phone, trying to get appointments at *New York* magazine, the *New York Times Book Review,* the *New Yorker* and various design studios. 'Yes, of course, Mr Brooks, we'd love to see your work.' And mostly it was, 'We have drops on the third Thursday, every second month.' Folio drops, where you simply drop your folio off in the morning with your card and contact details, and went and picked it up later in the day or the next morning. They'd had one in July. It was August. That meant I'd get to at least drop off my stuff just five weeks from now...

Nevertheless, along the way I met some good people and, amazingly enough, began to pick up work almost immediately.

People were astonished, when I gave them my card, to see where we were living.

'*Carroll Gardens!* How did you get in *there?*'

'Well, you know, I called.'

'People hang out for *years* to get into Carroll Gardens. It's a *really* good area, so *safe*.'

'How do you mean?'

'Well, it's totally Italian, controlled by the Mafia.'

'The *Mafia*?'

'Well, nothing happens that *shouldn't* happen. No blacks *doing stuff* in the streets, anywhere in the whole neighbourhood. I mean, other stuff might happen, but, you know – it's all controlled. Italian. Nothing random. It's all just business. You're very lucky. You won't have any trouble there at all.' And 'other stuff' did indeed happen, twice while we were there: one time, a bloke's legs were seen sticking out of a garbage bag down by the canal early one morning, and a couple of months later, another bloke was 'filled full of daylight' while he was parked in his car by the local playground.

I rigged up a table, shelves and light, and set to work. The *Macquarie* was going to need about 150 drawings – a bit of a job – so I began instead with the text Dorothy had given me in London, *Go Ducks Go!* by Maurice Burns. It was a simple but lovely little bit of writing for very young children, and I used it as a sort of warm-up for the *Macquarie*. I did the whole of *Go Ducks Go!* – the dummy, design and all the illustrations – in about ten days, and sent it off to London.

Then I started picking up the odd bit of freelance work in New York.

Somewhere in there, Bob Sessions sent me Jenny Wagner's *Motor Bill and the Lovely Caroline*. I loved it, but there were things about the story, and things about the main character that puzzled me. I didn't really have the time to think about it, so I said no and went on with what was on the desk already.

After three or four months in Carroll Gardens, Margaret and I thought, 'Have we come all the way to New York just to live in Brooklyn?' and took up an offer of an apartment on Manhattan on St Mark's Place in the East Village, between 2nd and 3rd Avenues. Two apartments, actually – the back apartment to live in and the ex-dental surgery fronting directly onto the street as my studio.

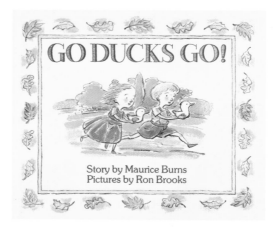

GO DUCKS GO!

Story by Maurice Burns
Pictures by Ron Brooks

If people were amazed at our getting a place in Carroll Gardens, they plain could not *believe* St Mark's Place.

'New York, New York – madness capital of the entire planet; the East Village – the heart of madness in New York; St Mark's Place – the main street in the heart of madness, the very *epicentre* of madness. And you've moved there from *Australia* – into St Mark's Place, for god's sake – with *two young kids*?!'

There was a lot of truth to that, but we loved the 'madness', all those extreme characters wandering or just hanging about in the streets, the slight shabbiness of it all, the wackiness of some of the shops, the graffiti, the art, the Jewish bakery, the Polish delicatessen, the Ukrainian butcher, the Italian pizza joint, the theatre just around the corner – we loved the mix, the sheer intensity of it all. We were just a stroll away from Greenwich Village with all its bookshops and cafés, and Washington Square with its sandpit and playground for the kids and all those amazing musicians and buskers; and Central Park – 843 acres of expansive meadows, gardens, bush, lakes, restaurants, cafés, playgrounds, a zoo, and with the Metropolitan Museum of Art backing into it from 5th Avenue – was an easy train ride away.

Just being able to walk the streets and avenues of Manhattan, filled with the most breathtakingly beautiful architecture, was heaven. As part of the research for my other NY project, I planned to walk and explore the entire island – it's only about 20 kilometres long, and narrow, so I figured it would only take a few days. But every square metre of it is so tightly packed, there is *so* much to look at, so much to see, I'd be exhausted after only a few blocks trying to take it all in. And of course there were galleries and museums everywhere.

And I had to get to work on *The Macquarie Bedtime Story Book*. With my desk set up in a small room on the ground floor facing directly onto St Mark's Place, I began slogging away at it, encumbered by all the usual self-doubts about my abilities. I was behind schedule, we were on a six-month visa, and time was running out. Trying to get an extension to the visa, being referred to and treated as 'Foreign Aliens' and borderline criminals by the US Immigration Department was exhausting, but we got another six months and I kept slogging. It was even harder work for Margaret, knee-deep in snow in a New York winter with two young children in a double stroller, and then a New York summer, when anybody who can afford it leaves town because it is so damned hot and sticky that everybody goes even more insane than usual. And she did all this with little assistance from me, while I sat in my little room.

It was so odd sitting there, in that 'epicentre', with all the bizarre goings-on happening just outside my window all hours of the day and night, trying to come up with the illustrations for all those stories and poems – most of them set in Australia, most of them in some sort of country setting, most of them gentle and reflective. But despite all my usual self-doubts about whether I was capable of doing the work anywhere near well enough, I slowly, very slowly, worked my way through the illustrations for *The Macquarie*. I had loved the exercise of designing the whole thing – the cover, title pages, and the layout and typography for it all – before I left Melbourne, and I was happy with that part of it, but now there were about 150 illustrations to do, around half in colour, half in black-and-white. I thought I'd *never* complete it. But I was reasonably happy with most of the illustrations by the time I had finished. At some point I showed it to a number of publishers in New York. I even took it to the American Book Fair in Washington, showing it to everybody and anybody I thought might be interested in doing an American edition. They loved it, they said, would *love* to

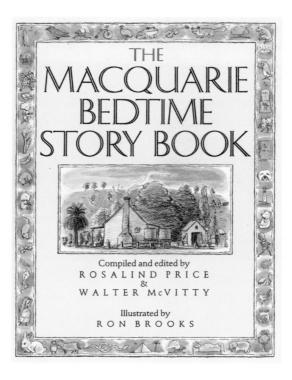

do it. It 'looks like a classic', they all said over breakfasts, lunches and endless drinks. But maybe they were just being American – friendly – or maybe Jim Bebbington, the managing director of Macquarie, didn't get round to following up on all the names and leads I gave him.

I sent all the drawings off to Rosalind in Sydney. Nothing ever happened with it in the US.

———

The NY project was going to be a huge treasure-island map of Manhattan, showing all my favourite buildings, and all the galleries, museums, bookshops, cafés, delicatessens, markets, the docks, the rivers, the bridges; everything that I loved about New York. I was going to print it as a very big poster, maybe a couple of metres high.

We'd been in New York for close on a year, and were rapidly coming up to the time when our second visa would run out. I'd given up the battle with the Immigration Department to extend our visa

THE MACQUARIE BEDTIME STORY BOOK

Compiled and edited by
R O S A L I N D   P R I C E
&
W A L T E R   M c V I T T Y

Illustrated by
R O N   B R O O K S

THE MACQUARIE LIBRARY

yet again – it was all too hard. So I had to gather a lot of material together in just the last few weeks remaining. I walked for miles and miles, took hundreds of photographs, made notes, bought maps, aerial photographs, books, postcards, everything.

We then hired a car to drive to Boston and back *en famille*, spending our last couple of weeks in America exploring as much of that north-east corner as we could, and just taking it easy.

As soon as we crossed the Washington Bridge and headed north, upstate alongside the Hudson, just minutes out of Manhattan, we were all astounded by the beauty of the countryside. We'd been up into Connecticut and Vermont the year before, in October, which was glorious, especially with all the autumn colours, but this time we made it only as far as Woodstock. We just stumbled across it, and found that little town, and all the woods and streams around there so damn beautiful, we just stayed put in a nice little 'woodsy' place with a pool, poked about in the town, took long walks in the woods, and generally

An illustration for
'Elephant's Lunch',
by Kate Walker

enjoyed ourselves. Then we went back, packed all our stuff and headed for home, taking in two very relaxed weeks in Fiji on the way, which – after the intensity of New York – was fantastic.

We arrived back in Melbourne after a year away, and I had to think about what I wanted to do, yet again…

Something about the whole New York experience – or something about the 1980s – had exhausted me. I loathed the obsession with money (not only in New York) that seemed to grip everybody throughout that decade; I found it appalling and depressing. And though I loved the idea for the New York map, wanting it to celebrate all that beauty, nevertheless I had a sneaking suspicion that my main motive was to make a bit of money. Maybe quite a bit. I began to feel a bit grubby about the whole thing, and dropped it. But having to start up the whole freelance thing once again in Melbourne, take the folio around, was a dreary prospect. I knew I had to make a change.

Then a friend called from the University of Tasmania's art school in Hobart, wanting to know what I was planning to do. They needed a new lecturer in the graphic design department. Initially I said no, but eventually allowed myself to be persuaded to at least go and have a look…and then decided that both the art school and Hobart were among Australia's best-kept secrets. But I was plagued by indecision, and faffed around for another six months in Melbourne, impressing nobody, especially myself, until finally Margaret said, 'Let's go.'

We went, in mid-1988, the plan being that I would teach, fiddle about with a couple of books, perhaps do some painting, all with no financial pressure attached for a change, and meanwhile think about what I *really* wanted to do, in all that time off that teachers are meant to have…

The Macquarie Bedtime Story Book had by now been published. I liked some of the illustrations at the time. Possibly for reasons more to do with nostalgia than the quality of the work, over twenty years later, I still do: the celebration of my family in the title-page illustration; Margaret, Sam and Adelaide reading together on the dedication page; Sam, in his pyjamas in 'Goosey, Goosey Gander'; Margaret, in Margaret Mahy's exquisite 'Witch Poem'; Adelaide as Clara – and the elephant, especially the elephant, in Kate Walker's beautiful 'Elephant's Lunch'. My tree in Mary Robert's 'John's Task' is a salute to Shepard. I like the landscapes in Kath Walker's 'The Bunyip' and Bill Scott's 'How Fire Came', and some of the smaller coloured and black-and-whites also.

It wasn't long at all, though, before I could see that the book was generally speaking a great deal weaker, paler on the page, than I would have wished, and that there was the usual unevenness of quality in the illustrations. While some of the draughtsmanship was okay, in other places the lines and colour lacked conviction and courage.

My design for the book was extremely conservative: the typography and layout was respectably traditional, excessively so. It was timid, too quiet. I had been far too uptight about the seriousness of the whole exercise, too hung up about the importance of every single picture, far too timid in the way I made marks, chose the colours and laid them on the paper. Afraid to fail, I wasn't in the moment, wasn't confidently *right there, on the page*. The result: too many of the illustrations are weak, lacking impact and substance. Again.

This Baby

Story by Julia McClelland
Pictures by Ron Brooks

'Come on…' said his dad, 'tell me what the problem is.'

*'I don't want a baby around. It'll only break my toys
and rip my books and everything.'*

He sniffed again. 'And there's all this stupid fuss over it.'

I THINK IT was in 1991 that Rita Scharf at Oxford University Press in Melbourne sent me Julia McClelland's text for *This Baby*. I had read it a couple of times and was carting it about with me in my briefcase, to and from the art school, so I could have a look at it whenever I wanted to.

It was nagging at me. There was something about it that I liked, but on the other hand I was hesitating about calling Rita back to say I would do it, perhaps because it was simply about a straight mother, father and child. All a bit too normal. I wasn't sure I could do very much with it.

Margaret had picked me up from the art school. Sam and Adelaide (eight and six) were both in shitty moods, sniping at one another in the back of the car, and the three of us waited while Margaret took the opportunity to escape and do some shopping.

'Tell him to stop it, Dad!'

'What am I doing? I'm not doing anything!'

'Oh, come on, you guys. This is *sooo* boring!'

'*Sam* is being boring. *I'm* not doing *anything!*'

'Oh, *yeah* – you're not doing anything! *As usual!*'

'Oh, for god's sake!'

It had obviously been going on for quite some time, and Margaret would very probably be taking the opportunity to be gone for another while yet…

I had a thought.

'Would you like me to read you a story?'

No response. I could see them in the mirror, glowering and shoving at each other.

Lacking a better idea, I took the manuscript from my case and climbed into the back, between them. They both moved as far away from me as they could (in such a confined space), turned away, and looked studiously out the window.

I began reading.

One day when Andrew went to sit on his mother's lap as usual, he
noticed a strange thing. There was no longer any lap to sit on!

'*Where has your lap gone, Mum?*' *he demanded.*

His mother patted her large tummy.

'*It will be back as soon as this baby is born – don't worry.*'

'*But I* always *sit on your lap before bedtime,*' *said Andrew.* '*This*
baby has taken my *seat!*'

I'm not sure how long it took to read – maybe twelve or fourteen minutes, and (this is the truth), *as I was reading it*, I felt Sam and Adelaide change. The quibbling stopped, their bodies relaxed, and they both eased into it, into the story.

They came away from their windows, they both slowly leaned against me, and relaxed. By the time I'd finished, by the time (later still) Margaret came back, they were both as quiet as lambs. Margaret couldn't believe it.

'What on earth did you do?' she asked me later. 'They've been so horrible all afternoon. Driving me crazy!'

There was something so simply *true* about that text that it had cut right through the rubbish and reached them. Stopped the rot, just like that.

I decided I would call Rita and say yes.

What appealed most to me about this story was not so much the quality of the writing, as the universality of the situation – a new child coming into a family. The story was so straight and honest about the challenges that change brings and represents. Especially to the first (and thus far *only*) child, and hence to the parents. Everything about the way Andrew reacts to the news, and how the parents deal with him, is totally credible. And this is *all* done through the dialogue: the story is entirely dialogue-driven.

*At kindergarten,
the children were
asked to paint a
picture
of their families.*

*'No, I'm not,'
said Andrew.*

*'Stupid baby
– go away!'*

'But a baby is worth fussing over,' said his father.
'I bet you never fussed over me like that,' said Andrew.
'We made even more fuss getting ready for you, Andrew. 'You
    were our first baby. You are extra special.'
'I don't remember you making any fuss over me,' said Andrew.
'That's because you weren't born then,' reminded his father.
'Oh, yeah,' said Andrew.

There was the paradox: I liked the story for its straightness, for its universality, I wanted to explore and salute all that; but I felt that if I drew three *specific* humans, Mum, Dad and Andrew, we'd lose the universality of the text. I decided to make the characters animal – that way they could be equally true for anybody, everybody, anywhere.

There are many classic models for this approach, of course. Think especially of Shepard's drawings for *Winnie-the-Pooh* and *The House at Pooh Corner.* How entirely, archetypically true and real are Eeyore, Piglet, Tigger, Kanga, Roo, Rabbit and Owl. They are all real characters, real people we know. They speak to us all. We feel with them; we feel for them. In all their eccentricities, foibles and fantasies, *they are us.* I believe it is simply not possible to achieve that archetypal depth with illustrated human characters.

But for *This Baby*, I have to admit, the models I had in mind were the Frances books by Russell Hoban, with illustrations by Lillian Hoban and Garth Williams. The texts are glorious, beautifully written, and *so* funny, *so* true. As with Milne's Pooh books, you can read them over and over, and *never* tire of them. Successive generations go back to *A Bargain for Frances, A Baby Sister for Frances, Best Friends for Frances, A Birthday for Frances* and *Bread and Jam for Frances* again and again and again. Though the books are very ordinary pieces of design and production, they have become classics; I doubt they'll ever go out of print.

Why? Well, primarily because they are such lovely stories of course, and *very* funny, but more than that – there is *such* subtlety of observation, they are masterpieces of observation about the world of the child, about children. And all done with the lightest touch. However, there is less to get excited about in the illustrations. There is nothing much in the way of settings; the characters aren't well drawn. In fact, though they are utterly believable, they are awkwardly done and clumsy. That's about it. There is no sophistication about the books visually. The design and layout are about as rudimentary as you can get; and the printing was atrocious too, at least in some runs. I have one very old and worn-out paperback edition of *Bread and Jam* in which the registration of colours is so bad that Frances looks as if she has three pairs of eyes! But it doesn't matter at all. She is *still* believable!

So that was my model for *This Baby*. I wanted that degree of simplicity for the book; I hoped to achieve that kind of charm and that kind of authenticity for Andrew and his parents. Unlike my previous books, which always had a lot of background detail, I decided to put all the emphasis in the illustrations for *This Baby* onto the characters themselves. Have almost no landscape, no setting – just a few key objects as props. This represented quite a challenge for me, because it meant paring the visual story right back to the bones, and I'd always been a bit of a sucker for detail – found it hard, in fact, to draw simply.

I wanted to tell the whole story through the body language of the characters.

I did a lot of sketches until I arrived at a character that was a cross between a bear and a wombat – a wombear. Then I put together my usual hand-made dummy – 32 pages and cover, stapled together, of sketches done with a charcoal pencil, quite quickly, and roughly, including lots of wrong lines here and there – and posted it to Rita Scharf, who sent it on to Julia McClelland.

They were both a bit amazed at the change from garden-variety humans to my slightly odd wombears, but they both liked it.

———————

For the finished illustrations, rather than continue with the thick charcoal pencil, I used a big old dip pen and black ink with watercolour. To achieve the looseness of line I wanted, I gave myself some 'elbow room' and did all the drawings quite large. That was my first mistake. When the drawings were reduced to the finished page size – to about half the size of the originals – the linework of course tightened up, became sharper; it became colder and hardened somehow. And that, combined with the 'prettiness' of the colour, more evident in some pages than in others, made the finished images and the whole book just a bit too tight and thin – and, especially given that this family lives most of the time underground, *much* too clean. It would have been more appropriate to use a much thicker,

'Imagine how
the poor thing
must feel…'

softer, even 'hairy' line for the characters, and to have employed an altogether earthier palette. If I had used a soft, fat charcoal stick for the linework, rather than the metal pen, the characters would have had more warmth, more 'body', more weight, and if the whole thing had been a little grubbier, rougher, less finished – more like my dummy, in fact – it would have been a better book. As it is, it's all a bit too 'nice'. Again.

Mind you, for all its faults, it was published in quite a few countries – in Denmark, the Netherlands, Sweden, Korea, Japan, China, and throughout all the English-speaking territories.

And sometimes when I look at it, there *are* a few bits and pieces that I find myself liking quite a lot…

I like the opening drawing for *'But I* always *sit on your lap before bedtime,' said Andrew. 'This baby has taken* my *seat!'*. It sets the whole

scene – the family, their characters and relationships are all there in the body language; the comfiness of the furniture, their home.

'I don't think it's much fun being a baby,' he said.

Over the next two pages, over breakfast the next day, Andrew sits there, arms folded, angry and defiant, the cereal box transformed into Ned Kelly's helmet on his head, and says, *'Is it a girl or a boy? Will it have any teeth?... Let's call it Gummy Face, then... Will it have any hair?... Well, what about Baldy Head?'*

Especially considering that kindergarten rooms are often fairly cluttered places, I like the spareness of the following two pages, when Andrew is with his teacher. She has asked the children to paint a picture of their families, and says to Andrew, *'I'll bet you're looking forward to seeing the new little member of your family.'* And Andrew says, *'No, I'm not.'*

When his mother comes to pick him up from school, Andrew asks,

'Will this baby be able to play chasey with me?' 'Not for a couple of years,' says his mother. 'Babies have to learn to walk before they can run.' Andrew is showing how much more clever and interesting *he* is – tightrope-walking along the top of a fence. 'Babies sound boring.'

His mother tells him to go to his room and stay there. 'All right, I will!' Andrew bellows at his mother. 'I'll stay in there forever! I'll never come out! I'll die *in there and then you'll be sorry!*'

A couple of pages further on are my favourite drawings in the whole book. On facing pages, we see the three of them – Mum, Dad and Andrew just sitting together on Andrew's bed. The two pictures are almost identical, except for the changed body language from one page to the other, which says everything about the change that takes place in those few quiet moments together.

On the left-hand page Dad has one hand on Andrew's shoulder, and is leaning back a little after the cuddle they have all just had; Mum is still a little tense, leaning forward, both hands on Andrew's shoulders, trying to explain; Andrew is listening, but closed in on himself, head and eyes down, hands tightly clasped, feet together.

On the right-hand page, the text reads:

He tried to imagine what it would be like to be a baby. What if you couldn't walk and couldn't talk and couldn't feed yourself when you were hungry?... He imagined... a small, helpless version of himself, lying in the cradle. Maybe this baby felt as angry and as bored as he did sometimes.

In the illustration on this page, Andrew's whole body has relaxed and opened up; he is leaning back *into* his dad, one hand resting comfortably on his dad's leg; he's looking upward at his mum, and reaching the other hand out to her while she, also more relaxed now, holds his hand in hers. '*I don't think it's much fun being a baby,*' he said.

When his mother goes to the hospital to have the baby, Andrew's Auntie Robyn comes to collect him from kindergarten. She is standing on one toe, Sylph-like atop a tree stump, framed from behind by the only fully drawn tree in the entire book – life, nature, growth. There's a generous bunch of flowers at her feet, and she's offering a rose to Andrew.

Andrew has a painting he has done for the new baby rolled up under his arm, which he shows to Auntie Robyn. They set off in the rowboat, crossing to a new life, the water gently rippling, with the glorious bouquet like a living figurehead in the bow.

A couple of openings later, at the hospital, there's a close-up picture of the new baby on the right-hand page, nothing else. On the left, this text floats in space on the page:

Her eyes were screwed up, her cheeks were bright red and her nose was squashed flat.

Andrew felt sorry for anyone who came into the world looking like that.

The baby *is* beautiful. I *loved* doing this simple little drawing, leaving so much air around it that the new baby in its nest of soft, golden blanket floats like a gift on the page. This is probably the gentlest pair of facing pages I have ever done in a book.

On the next page we are closer in. Mum, Dad, the baby and Andrew are framed by flowers, soft curtains around a light-filled window and soft fabrics. Andrew stands on a chair to look more closely, holding the rolled-up painting behind his back, and notices that the baby is wearing a tag on her wrist.

'What's that?' he asked his mum.

'It's a message – for you,' said his mum.

'For me!' said Andrew. 'What does it say?'

Andrew's dad looked at the tag and pointed to the words as he read them out. 'Hi, Andrew. My name is Jane.'

Then he turned the tag over and read the other side...

And we turn over to read, on the left-hand page,

'But you can call me Learnalot.'

On the right, Andrew holds up the painting he has done for his new sister. It's a picture of the whole family, Mum, Dad, Andrew and the baby, all holding hands. This painting of Andrew's is my favourite image in the book. I am right-handed. I did this one (on Andrew's behalf) using my left hand, not with a metal-tipped pen but with a soft, fat brush. Much better.

On the very last page, with no text at all, we see Learnalot in her cradle with its new moon above her sleeping head, Andrew's favourite old blanket tucked around her, and on the wall behind her, Andrew's painting of his – and her – family.

Strange, now that I go through the book again, looking closely at the drawings, thinking about why I drew this rather than that, I find the work I did in this book is better than I thought.

But I know for sure it is *nowhere near* up there with *Pooh* and *Frances*, and nowhere near close to staying in print forever, alas.

Closing the book now, turning it over, I see the drawing on the back cover. Andrew is sitting in the big, comfy floral armchair, with his baby sister on his lap, wrapped in his old blanket. She is awake now, interested, looking a bit cheeky, gazing up at her big brother – and reaching up with one hand, sticking it in his mouth. The toy bear we saw in the garden earlier, sitting in for 'this baby' in the pull-cart, is now perched, slightly to the side, on one arm of the chair.

I do like that one, *that* picture. Well, I like what is *in* there – what is happening between the characters.

But, it's like the whole book, isn't it? It's just a pity it's so damn *pretty*.

Motor Bill and the Lovely Caroline

Bill had a car. He was the only person in his street who did. And because he didn't go to work, and spent all day playing in his garden, and because he couldn't tie a bow, nobody believed his car was real. That's why they called him Motor Bill.

WHAT A WONDERFUL opening paragraph, beginning with that first sentence of just four single-syllable words: 'Bill had a car'. The second, longer sentence seems similarly unambiguous at first glance, but somehow raises questions about Bill. The third suddenly rolls out to four phrases end on end, painting a pretty full picture not only of Bill and how he spends his days but of the whole neighbourhood's perception of him also. The last sentence, back down to just seven words, nods with a similar sort of affection to those kinds of Australians who give the nickname 'Blue' to a best mate with bright orange hair, or 'Shorty' to another who is well over six feet. The wry humour of that opening is so characteristic of Jenny Wagner, and so economical; in just four lines the whole scene is set.

But perhaps the cleverest touch is the phrase 'and because he couldn't tie a bow', half-hidden as that third sentence builds up to its finale. Subconsciously the reader is taken aback, just a little – it doesn't seem to fit. When you think about it, isn't it odd that someone has a car, must surely be an adult, yet can't tie a bow? At the same time, the audience for the book has just been defined quite clearly, yet by implication only. And this is part of what propels us forward into the story, curious to find out more. Also, when you think about it, the first sentence says flatly that he has a car, the second as strongly confirms it – and yet people don't accept that he has. What's going on?

As I've said earlier, Bob Sessions sent me *Motor Bill* when we were living in Brooklyn, in 1986. He had only recently set up a new publishing company under his own imprint. It was ten years since I had worked with him on *John Brown*, and I liked the idea of doing another book with Bob. At the time the envelope arrived, however, I was busy trying to drum up a bit of freelance work to help us survive in New York, and I already had *Go Ducks Go!* and *The Macquarie Bedtime Story Book* on my desk.

Also in the envelope was a copy of Graeme Base's *Animalia*, which Bob had just published, or was about to. I suppose he included it thinking I would like it, that it would show me the sort of quality he was aiming for with his new imprint, that it would help persuade me to say yes to *Motor Bill.* It had the reverse effect. I could see that a lot of people would love it, of course, and that it would probably do very well, but I didn't like it at all, and gave it to the landlord's kids, who absolutely *loved* it.

But the bigger problem with *Motor Bill*, for me, lay in the text itself. As always with Jenny Wagner's writing, I loved the elegance, the ease with which the words and phrases flowed, the musicality of it; I loved the characters, the subtle humour and the strangeness. The story was extraordinarily open to different readings, but, equally, it was a little obscure.

It is a story about Bill, who lives in a village, out in the country. He has something of the 'village idiot' about him. Only Caroline believes, almost, that he has a car. She will stop and talk with him, and walk with him. But there is also a general affection for Bill in the town, and when he has a special idea, neighbours are happy to help, and give him flowers, fruit, titbits and toffees. Bill wraps it all up, and goes to visit Caroline. He invites her to come for a picnic in his car. Together they go off to the country, where they eat currant buns, oranges and plums and drink ginger beer beside a creek. The grass is short and soft, and they spend the rest of the day there, coming home after sunset.

In the dusk, with no one to see, Caroline found herself believing completely.

The day has, just possibly, transformed their lives.

Bill never forgets how he learnt to tie a bow, and neither does Caroline.

When I was first looking at the story in New York, there were a couple of things I didn't quite understand. I couldn't make up my mind about Bill, about who or what he was, and I had no idea what to do about his car. Did he *really* have a car? Was it some sort of a model, a toy, or just an old steering wheel, perhaps? I couldn't quite make up my mind which reading I was more interested in, which made it difficult for me to put images to it.

But I didn't have time to even think about it. I didn't want to simply keep Bob waiting, so I wrote back to say I couldn't take it on, got on with my other stuff, and forgot about it.

Seven years later, in 1993, when we were living in Hobart, I rediscovered it. I was going through my filing cabinet trying to sort out my tax, trying to find all the paperwork, and there in a shoebox in the bottom drawer, in among a whole mess of things from the year in New York, was an unmarked envelope. Inside it was the text for *Motor Bill and the Lovely Caroline*. I read it, and was stunned. After seven years, I got it.

This was the line that did it:

When they got to the country they found a place where the grass
    was short and soft,
beside a creek where they could cool their feet.

Why didn't I get that before? Suddenly I knew *exactly* what to
do with the car. Simple. The car would be a box, a bit like an old fish
box, the sort we used to make billycarts out of when we were kids,
but without a bottom, and Motor Bill and Caroline would run in it,
Flintstone-style.

I read the story again, and again, and loved it more each time.

Bob was by then back with Penguin. I had a very full load with
my teaching at the art school, didn't really know how I was going to
find the time to do the book, but I was so excited I wanted to ring
him straight away to ask if they had already done it. Seven years. I
was a little embarrassed ... surely they would have, I thought. I called
Penguin's Art Director, George Dale.

'Oh god, Ron, I honestly don't know. I know we tried, but I'm not
absolutely sure. Let me check, and I'll call you back.'

Two hours later, he did. 'We certainly showed it to other illustrators,
but I don't think anybody else could figure out what to do with it
either, so Bob got to thinking the problem was with the text and asked
Jenny to have another go at it. He's excited to hear you're interested
and says that it's still available, and that I should send you her second
version. It's much better.'

'I like the original. It's beautiful,' I said.

'Yeah, okay, Ron, but I'll send the second for you to have a look
at also', which he did, and I didn't like it at all. All the strangeness, the
range of possible readings was gone. Everything was completely spelt
out, simplified, clarified – it was a far less interesting piece of writing.

I called Bob. 'I'm not at all interested in the second version. I want
to do the original. I love it.'

But I was still unsure about the character of Motor Bill himself; so
unsure in fact, that at one stage I even asked Jenny to tell me how she
saw him – something I would never ordinarily do with any author.

'Well, Ron, I'm very glad you ask, because different people have
suggested all sorts of things. And the fact is, he is between sixteen and

twenty-four years old, and intellectually challenged. And that's exactly how I'd like you to draw him in the book.'

Just for interest, I asked Bob also.

'I'd say he's possibly around six, maybe seven – anyway, just a little late going to school. But definitely *not* anywhere near between sixteen and twenty-four, and definitely *not* intellectually challenged. I want you to draw a boy, round about seven who, for whatever reason, I'd like it to stay open – maybe he lives way out in the country or something, I don't know – is simply a little late going to school.'

I wasn't interested in either suggestion.

Certainly the story was about 'difference', but it could have been about any old sort of difference as far as I was concerned. Of course it might be that Bill is intellectually disadvantaged in some way, it might also be simply that he wears odd-coloured socks, or doesn't follow Australian Rules football, is poor or rich, black, white, brown or brindle…or, god forbid, that the poor bugger might actually be a bit *sensitive*, is a poet, a bit girly, maybe even gay, or some kind of artist.

The trouble with what both Jenny and Bob were saying was that they were each speaking about only one possible reading of who or what Bill might be. His *simpleness*. I felt that if we focused on only that one way of reading Bill, we confined the interpretation of the story to being essentially about acceptance of only that particular sort of difference. It would make a narrow reading of the text inevitable.

I *never* saw Bill as simple. Special, yes – *very* special; but not at all as in 'special needs'. Special only as in *different*, for *whatever* reason.

We are all different, for god's sake, aren't we? Or certainly feel ourselves to be.

But how to show that? If I wasn't going to follow either Jenny's or Bob's suggestions, how was I going to make Motor Bill different? By making him hairier than everybody else, totally bald, skinnier, fatter, blacker, whiter? By somehow simply dressing him differently? Making him the only one wearing, or *not* wearing, a hat, perhaps?

I didn't see Bill as necessarily being even eccentric. What I *did* always see about him was some sort of innocence and simplicity – not born out of any kind of handicap, but rather from being unusually *unspoilt*, uncorrupted. He was unusually clear, pure, quite simply and wonderful*ly*, *himself*. Special.

Kind of like a donkey, actually, I remember thinking. Have you ever seen a donkey simply standing out in the middle of a field, a small yard? On a warm sunny day, when there's nothing much going on. Perhaps there are idiots roaring around on trail bikes in the paddock next door, or it's raining cats and dogs and corrugated iron...and the donkey is just standing there, in its own world, thinking its own thoughts. I love the way donkeys can do that.

And then I stumbled across a book by Emma Chichester Clark, *Myrtle, Tertle and Gertle*, a picture book about three young women, they may be sisters, and the various adventures they have when they go on a summer holiday together, taking a sea voyage among the islands of the Mediterranean. All the other people – the crew and fellow passengers and the people on the islands – are drawn as straight, garden-variety people, but Myrtle, Tertle and Gertle are donkeys. It is such a good little book, so fresh, such good fun, and totally believable. The fact that our three protagonists are so different from everybody else only makes them all the more attractive, intuitively, all the easier to identify with. More than anything, it was these three gentle characters who persuaded me to make Motor Bill a donkey.

Later still, I thought about the young donkey accompanying Christ entering into the bedlam of Jerusalem. He could have chosen an older, mature donkey, or a horse, train or plane. He could have captained the lead ship of a caravan of camels, or walked, by himself; he could have had himself carried, like some sort of a king, after all, but he chose a young donkey. Innocence.

So I made Bill a donkey and modelled my characterisation of him mostly upon an old friend, Noel Crombie, who has a bit of a thing about cars (not to mention topiary), and also put something of Patrick Hardy into him – the physical smallness and grace, and the gentleness. Patrick had been so influential in bringing *Bunyip*, *Aranea* and *John Brown* into the world. I wanted to thank him. Albeit too late for him to know.

And how should I represent the Lovely Caroline? Because she is

different too – different from all the other townspeople in that she is
the only one who 'believed him, almost'. But she is unlike Bill, too,
and just as special. Caroline is just a little more knowing, a little more
worldly than Bill, and she has pluck, cheek and courage enough to be
able to cross that fence. What animal is more likely to do that – what
better to make her? – than a goat?

The Lovely Caroline's character I modelled on another old friend,
the beautiful Sally-Anne Mill, who has spent a *lot* of time in drapery
shops, is very clever indeed with fabrics and just about everything else,
is married to the aforementioned Noel Crombie and, yes, shares his
love of old cars and gardening.

Motor Bill is a story not just about the acceptance of 'difference' in
another, especially not merely a story only about accepting somebody
else who has 'special needs'. It is an extraordinarily tender story about
openness and generosity, about love and trust; an exquisitely written
text about *recognition* – about recognising genuine specialness of any
kind in another, embracing, celebrating and sharing in it.

But above all, it is primarily a story about *imagination* – the making
power, the creative power, of love and imagination.

Early that afternoon he went to visit Caroline.

And after the picnic,
with the piece of ribbon he had brought,
Caroline showed Bill how to tie a bow.

Like *The Bunyip of Berkeley's Creek*, the first book Jenny and I did together, *Motor Bill* has as its central motif recognition of the other, but it goes further than *Bunyip* did. It is about how *something new becomes possible* as a result of that shared recognition. Something that was not quite there before is created, something that is greater than the sum of its parts.

Unlike *Bunyip*, in which our restless hero goes searching, and finds, finally, another bunyip, Motor Bill is quite content to spend all day 'playing in his garden'. It is the Lovely Caroline who makes everything possible by accepting an invitation from Bill. She steps out

When Bill got older he still played with his car every day.

of the ordinary, the everyday, and crosses the boundary into a realm of imaginative possibility.

So off they go, donkey and goat, Bill and Caroline, and so persuasive are they together, that 'everyone honked and cheered them on'. And together they make something that was not there before.

————

My pictures of the village Bill and Caroline live in are based primarily upon Ross in the Tasmanian Midlands, with its church on the ridge above the township, the bridge over the small stream, and with echoes of the countryside and coast around Cremorne, and of Daylesford in central Victoria.

I did two dummies for this book – a small one, then a larger, more detailed one – and while many of the images didn't change much, a few key images did. For example, the endpaper of the first small dummy showed pretty much just the church on the hill. In the second, the church had moved to the background, Bill's mother's house into the foreground, with a caravan next to the shed in the back yard. Though it is not said in the text, in my mind Bill lives not in his mother's house but in the caravan. In the finished book the church has disappeared from the endpaper altogether. One of the most important changes was in the spread 'Early that afternoon

When Bill got older he still played with his car every day...
second dummy (first version)

OPPOSITE: *Early that afternoon he went to visit Caroline.*

And after the picnic, with the piece of ribbon he had brought, Caroline showed Bill how to tie a bow.
both from second dummy (first version)

Early that afternoon he went to visit Caroline.

DRAWN *from the* HEART

MOTOR BILL *and the* LOVELY CAROLINE   [179]

he went to visit Caroline'. In the dummy, Bill is floating, flying in the air. In the finished book, I have brought in the stump from *This Baby*, and Bill is up, not unlike Auntie Robyn, on one leg – in pure faith offering the flowers.

Alongside the lines 'When Bill got older he still played with his car every day. But he never forgot how he learnt to tie a bow', he was shown in my first dummy standing in his garden, hammer in hand, gazing out over the model village he has built. In the second version, the model village has all but gone. Bill is holding clippers, and there is a topiary car in the middle of an intersection. In the final book, it is just Bill, standing on a stool, happily clipping at his topiary car.

I wish now that I had stayed with the first version, keeping the whole village, but including the topiary car in there somewhere.

In the original dummy, the last line 'Neither did Caroline' showed Bill and Caroline standing by Bill's workbench. Caroline is holding in her arms a baby goat-donkey with a big bow around its neck and Bill is giving her a small wooden model of a car wrapped in another big bow. The final image in the book for that last line 'Neither did Caroline' has Bill and Caroline driving away together. There's a big ribbon tied in a huge celebratory bow on the back of their dream car: a 1955 Citroën, a Light 15. I used to have one – beautiful – but theirs is a convertible, which would have been *my* dream.

Essentially, though, it was all pretty much there in the second dummy, the one I first showed Penguin. To my amazement, both Bob Sessions and Julie Watts, the children's publisher, liked it and were enthusiastic about my representations of Bill and Caroline. So was Jenny Wagner. Penguin signed the book up.

I then did all the finished illustrations in an inspired burst of about four non-stop weeks, in the middle of 1993, just after we had moved to the Huon Valley. We were in a gorgeous little house, overlooking the Huon River, the valley and the mountains, surrounded by all this beautiful landscape, early-morning mists and fog over the river and exquisite evening light, and it all fed directly into the final illustrations.

I loved doing all the pictures for this book – I poured love into all these drawings, but I have two favourite double-page spreads. The

Neither did Caroline.

first illustrates the line 'Early that afternoon he went to visit Caroline.' Motor Bill is up on the stump against the expanse of blue sky, his head and heart in the clouds, with the landscape around Ross and the bridge and church in the background, all in warm summer greens and yellows. Love in a good climate – spring coming into summer – I've never used so much green and yellow in my life.

My other favourite is the drawing I originally did for 'And after the picnic, with the piece of ribbon he had brought, Caroline showed Bill how to tie a bow.' That picture, which showed an aerial view of the church on the hill, overlooking the bridge and river, was there with that line right up to page-proof stage. Bob became nervous about it. He worried about what people would think might be happening there, when Bill and Caroline are nowhere to be seen. I sketched in a rug, with bits and pieces of the picnic visible, but still no sign of Bill and Caroline themselves. Bob was still nervous, and requested that I do an alternative illustration. The original worrisome image went onto the back endpaper of the book.

The image that appears in the book for that piece of text is a close-up of Bill and Caroline's heads and shoulders against the sky and clouds;

They drove home after sunset. In the dusk, with no one to see,
Caroline found herself believing completely.

MOTOR BILL *and the* LOVELY CAROLINE   [183]

their noses are almost touching, and Caroline is tying a bow around Bill's neck. Personally, I would much rather that they had had that very special moment to themselves. I certainly hadn't been thinking about any 'nooky' going on the bushes... Rather, I imagined that both Bill and Caroline had stepped beyond their former boundaries; a quite wonderful transformation had taken place, there had been an imaginative transcendence. I wanted an image that would show something of *their* new point of view. In short, I much prefer the original.

The printer's first proof of *Motor Bill* was spot on; the colours in the hand-bound advance copies that Penguin forwarded to me were perfect, so I signed them off and said go ahead. But then something went wrong and the printing of the whole first run was dreadful, much too pale; about a 20 per cent drop across all colours. After a difficult discussion, Bob agreed to a complete reprint, which I was extremely grateful for.

But for that final printing, across the top of the imprint page, Penguin had typeset an additional acknowledgement which Jenny obviously wanted: 'With very special thanks to the children of the Maryborough Special School in Queensland.' I was not happy. I disliked the political correctness of it, but much more importantly I believed that the reference to a 'Special School' right at the beginning of the book would lead to a narrow reading of Bill, and to a correspondingly narrow reading of the entire text – causing a near-complete shutdown of all that 'roominess of meaning' and scope for interpretation in Jenny's wonderful writing, thus killing the book for a wider audience. I felt it had, indeed, *already* killed the book. But it was too late. It was done. And there was no way Bob would or could have reprinted the whole thing yet again...

And the book did bomb. It didn't do very well here or in New Zealand, and it was barely noticed in the UK or in America, the only other countries where it was published. It deserved better. The text is exquisite, it is still one of my favourites.

Even the illustrations... I believe they are among the best I've ever done.

But there you go.

Old Pig

Old Pig and Granddaughter had lived together for a long, long time.
They shared everything, including the chores.
Every day, Granddaughter chopped the wood,
while Old Pig cleaned out the fire grate.
Granddaughter swept, while Old Pig dusted.
Old Pig made the beds, while Granddaughter hung up the washing.
Granddaughter made porridge, tea and toast for breakfast.
Old Pig diced carrots and turnips for lunch.
And together Old Pig and Granddaughter prepared
their dinner of corn and oats.

IT WAS EARLY 1994 when Rosalind Price, children's books publisher at Allen & Unwin, phoned me about *Old Pig*. I was at the University, in the middle of a class. She said, 'I have a very nice little story that I'd like to send you, by Margaret Wild.'

I said, 'I don't like *nice little stories*, Rosalind, you know that.'

'Oh dear,' she said. 'That's a pity, because we all think it's really very sweet, and were hoping you'd be interested.'

I said, 'I *very* definitely don't like very sweet either, Rosalind, really.'

The conversation went on, but I had to get back to my class, so I said, 'Thanks for calling, Rosalind, I do appreciate you thinking of me, but I'm really far too busy right now – god knows when I'd even be able to look at it. I think you should offer it to somebody else.'

'Are you sure?' she said.

'Absolutely.'

'Well, maybe it's just as well – and perhaps you shouldn't after all, because in fact it's another one about death.'

'Oh?' I said. 'Really? Then send it along. I'll have a look.'

Rosalind was referring to *John Brown, Rose and the Midnight Cat*, a story I hadn't much liked at first reading, which on one level at least could certainly be read as a story about death.

The story she sent me, *Old Pig*, I completely loved at first reading.

I had wandered down the hill to the letterbox, poked about in the sheds and garden on the way back, and opened the envelope only when I was back at the house, on the verandah.

I began reading, and was in love by the third or fourth sentence, with the writing, and with the characters Old Pig and Granddaughter – I could *see* them, both of them, so clearly, straight away. As clear as bells, as clean as whistles. Two stark naked little pigs. It was as though I'd known them all my life.

'I hate corn and oats,' Granddaughter always said.
And Old Pig always replied, 'Corn and oats are good for you.
While I'm alive, my dear, you'll eat them all up.'
At that, Granddaughter stopped complaining.
She'd eat corn and oats for breakfast, lunch and dinner
if it meant that Old Pig would live forever.

One morning, Old Pig did not get up as usual for breakfast.

I sat down, right there on the floor, with my back against the wall.

'I'm feeling tired,' she said. 'I think I'll have breakfast in bed today.'

'But you never eat in bed!' said Granddaughter.

'You don't like getting crumbs in the sheets.'

'I'm tired,' Old Pig repeated.

And when Granddaughter brought her a tray of porridge, toast and tea,

Old Pig was asleep, and she slept through lunch and dinner too.

While Old Pig slept, Granddaughter chopped the wood, cleaned out the fire grate, swept, dusted, did the washing and made her bed. She tried to whistle while she worked, but all she could manage was a lonely little 'oink'.

That was when my wife Margaret came in from somewhere else in the house, and saw me with a lap full of mail, weeping.

'What's the matter? What's happened?'

'Read this,' I said, and handed her the manuscript.

The next morning Old Pig was still tired, but she made herself get up…

'I have a lot to do today,' she said. 'I must be prepared.'

'Prepared for what?' asked Granddaughter.

Old Pig didn't reply. She didn't have to. Granddaughter already knew the answer and it made her feel like crying inside.

We *both* ended up sitting there on the floor, quietly weeping.

'You've *got* to say yes to this one,' she said.

And of course I did call both Rosalind and Margaret Wild, within a day or two, when I had given myself time to let the story sink in a little.

'I completely love it,' I said. 'I'll do it. I think it's the most beautiful picture-book text I've ever read. So sad, but incredibly beautiful too. And the writing is just wonderful, so beautifully paced, with such lovely rhythms and patterns in the phrasing. Deceptively simple and clear, but subtle, nuanced – so many layers to it.'

Old Pig returned her books to the library – and didn't borrow any more.

*She went to the bank, took out all her money, and closed the
account.*

*Then she went to the grocery store and paid the bill. She also
paid the electricity bill, the greengrocer's bill and the bill for
firewood.*

As Adam Gopnik wrote in his review in the *New Yorker:* 'A
heartbreaking, gentle, perfectly indirect story about the last days on
earth of an elderly pig offers a better introduction to the fact and the
poetry of mortality than many a more studied attempt.'

*When she got home she tucked the rest of her money into
Granddaughter's purse.*

'Keep it safe,' she said, 'and use it wisely.'

*'I will,' said Granddaughter. She tried to smile but her mouth
wobbled, and Old Pig said, 'There, there, no tears.'*

*'I promise,' said Granddaughter, but it was the hardest promise
she'd ever had to make.*

But some people really didn't get the fact and the poetry – or
didn't think children should. Friends I read it to, and one of my
brothers, said, 'Why the hell do you want to make this one into a
kids' book, for heaven's sake? Do you really want to depress them
all *that* much?' Even my agent at the time, though he may have been
joking, said, 'Why you want to make a kids' picture book out of a
story about a *dead old pig* beats me, Ron!' He went on and on, over
the two years or so that I worked on it, about how he guessed it
was because, like him, I must have been fond of a good roast pork
crackling.

Yes, it *is* a story about death, and how to say goodbye to someone
we love, of course it is. But *much* more…it is a story about *life*, and
how we might try to live it. Live it, taste it, celebrate it, share it.

'Now,' said Old Pig, 'I want to feast.'

*'You've got your appetite back?' Granddaughter asked, suddenly
feeling hopeful.*

*'I'm not hungry for food,' Old Pig said, 'I want to take a slow
walk around the town and feast my eyes on the trees, the
flowers, the sky – on everything!'*

It really is the most glorious celebration of life. *That's* why I wanted to do it. But *how* to do it?

The first thing I did, a few months later, was resign from the University. After seven years of running a department and teaching, I was exhausted. I realised that I was in danger of becoming one of those lecturers who only talks about other people's work and no longer does his own – either because he no longer has the time, or because he has forgotten how to.

I *really* wanted to do *Old Pig*, but the text had been sitting on my desk at home for months already. I had to choose. So I resigned.

So Old Pig and Granddaughter went for a slow walk around the town.

Every now and again Old Pig had to stop and rest. But she kept on looking.

Looking and listening, smelling and tasting.

With a lot more time on my hands, I was able to think much more about the text, probably too much. The more I read it, the more I thought about it, the more I discovered in it. It all became a bit too much. I began to doubt that I could do it well enough. And that was before I'd done even a single sketch!

After another four or five months sitting in my studio, staring at the words, I still hadn't managed to do a thing. Why? Because I couldn't see anything. I could see Old Pig and Granddaughter well enough – very clearly, in fact – but nothing at all of where they lived. And with this story particularly, their house, their garden, the landscape where they go on that last long, very special walk together, was of fundamental importance. It would play a huge role in all the images for the book. I couldn't see any of it, so I couldn't get started.

I searched through memories of places, and wandered about looking for possibilities, for months and months, but couldn't find anything which felt right.

I was becoming distressed. I had quit my job at the University, we were up against it financially, and I was beginning to become unwell.

After five months of searching, finally I found the place, the place where Old Pig and Granddaughter lived, quite by accident.

My parents stayed with us in the Huon Valley for a couple of weeks in the autumn of 1994. They were both in their early eighties. We mostly just hung about together, or went out on the odd drive. They were both keen 'rock hounds', members of their local gem club, and really loved any chance to get out and scratch around, to see what they might find.

They had heard about a little place called Drip Beach, known for its agates, somewhere in Tasmania. They wondered whether I'd ever heard of it, or knew where it was. It so happens that it's just a little further down the valley from us, along the winding road that follows the shoreline of Port Cygnet through blink-and-you'll-miss-it Lymington.

So off we went. A track leads off to the left, out to a sheltered little cove and beach, very pretty, looking south-east. Running along the back of it, between the beach and the bush, is a sandy bank about a metre and a half high, all the way along. And in this bank you can see all the various layers of stone, pebbles, sand, topsoil, roots, grasses and gravel, which my mother and father promptly started to dig up! Heads down, bums up, they scratched about with their hands, looking for agates.

I left them to it, and wandered off along the sand, around the lovely shoreline, across the rocks, up over a headland ... and fell in love – with a paddock. With the trees in and around it, the whole lie of the land, the soft roll of the slope coming down from the ridge, the grasses, the remains of an old garden, the light, the position there overlooking the water, the small boatshed, the sky, the clouds... I felt as though I had stumbled, quite by chance, into a holy place.

And do you know what? I was standing there, drinking it all in, the breeze blowing softly through the trees – eucalypts, of course, but also oaks, liquidambars, macrocarpas, Lebanese cedars, poplars, big pines whispering... And it was like music. It was as though the place was speaking to me. 'This is it. You've found us. This is where we live.'

I had found their place.

'Look!' said Old Pig. 'Do you see how the light glitters on the leaves?'

'Look!' said Old Pig.
'Do you see how the light glitters on the leaves?'

I later discovered it was known as Captain Taylor's Paddock. The old garden and ruins I had seen were the remains of a house he built some time in the nineteenth century.

I'm not sure that I would ever have done the book if it hadn't been for that particular little excursion with my parents.

'Look!' said Old Pig. 'Do you see how the clouds gather like
    gossips in the sky?'

After not being able to do a thing on the book – not a single sketch even, for just about a year – I was suddenly able to do the whole dummy in just two days and nights of non-stop drawing.

'Look!' said Old Pig. 'Do you see how the summer house is reflected in the lake?'

It just poured out…

'Do you hear the parrots quarrelling?
Can you smell the warm earth?
Let's taste the rain!'

Then I did two of the finished pictures, and sent them off with the dummy to Rosalind. She loved them, as did a whole lot of other publishers from around the world when she showed them at the Bologna Book Fair.

*'Look!' said
Old Pig.
'Do you see
how the light
glitters on the
leaves?'*

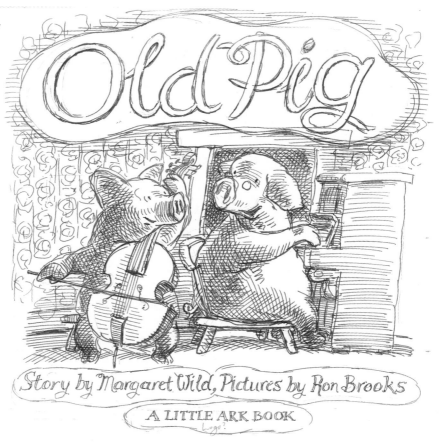

Then I ground to a halt again, partly out of fear that I couldn't draw well enough for the text, partly from fear that I simply couldn't draw.

It was late by the time Old Pig and Granddaughter got home.

Old Pig was so exhausted that Granddaughter helped her straight into bed.

And that went on for another I don't know how many months…

If it hadn't been for the support of my family, the support and inspiration provided by Rosalind Price and by wonderful books and writers – James Hillman, Annie Dillard, May Sarton, Russell Hoban, Shirley Hazzard, Janet Frame and others – and if it hadn't been for Bob Dylan, Van Morrison, Neil Young, John Lennon, Jessye Norman,

Beverly Sills, Maria Callas, Richard Strauss, Schubert, Bach, I would never have got through.

All these people, all their work, helped me get back and into my work.

And though I never found it an easy book to make, on the other hand, what a pleasure it was also. What a privilege it was, to try do justice to this beautiful text, and find the images that might add something to it. What a pleasure it was to be inside the story at last, in there with Old Pig and Granddaughter, both of whom I had fallen totally in love with. Drawing them, Old Pig particularly. Such a sweet old thing, with so much heart; so wise, and so generous. But old, yes, and physically fragile, near her end. It was such a privilege to try to get inside her skin, feel her age and fragility, but her strength also… to try to *become* her, so that I could then draw her, find her body language.

I thought of my own elderly mother, I thought of her mother, I thought of Pop. I watched a little old lady down in Huonville – bent over, leaning her weight into her stick – trying to cross the main street in town; other oldies at the supermarket, shuffling, or trying to reach up to things high on the shelves. And I would come back home, back

Then she climbed into Old Pig's bed.

Then she climbed into Old Pig's bed.
She put her arms around Old Pig, and for the very last time
Old Pig and Granddaughter held each other tight until morning.

to my studio, where there was a big old wardrobe with a full-length mirror, and I would walk or waddle about, turning this way and that, until I found her – and I'd hold her there, *be* her – then turn back to my desk and start drawing.

The lines I used for her needed to be fragile, cobweb-light, fleeting.

I loved drawing Granddaughter too, a child, stronger, just beyond her beginning. More upright, looking up and out more...the lines needed to be a little firmer, with just a bit more spring in them.

Such tenderness between them, so much love and heart.

So much life.

How would Old Pig say goodbye? As Margaret Wild tells us in her text, Old Pig takes Granddaughter on a last long walk around the town – looking, listening, smelling and tasting. Totally beautiful.

Even more importantly – to me anyway – how would Granddaughter be able to say goodbye to Old Pig? When I first read this story, I heard music – cello, mostly, with just a touch of piano. Later, when I first walked into Captain Taylor's Paddock I heard the same music, in among the trees. So even before I began drawing, though I didn't know exactly how, I knew music would play a key part, would be a major thread running throughout the whole book.

Our daughter Adelaide was around eight or nine at the time, and learning to play the cello. She had a natural talent, an easy feel for it, and I loved to listen to her practising in the lounge room, next to the piano, which is what she plays now.

Then I realised – though the text makes no mention of it, Old Pig and Granddaughter play music together! Old Pig plays the piano, Granddaughter plays the cello. *Wonderful!* That's it. Onto the title page they went, right at the very beginning of the book – Old Pig playing the piano, Granddaughter the cello. And I knew that *that* would be how Granddaughter says goodbye. She must play her cello for Old Pig.

I'm going to embarrass myself here. Have you noticed how my cello has six keys rather than only four, as cellos *actually* have? Adelaide, quite rightly, was not very impressed with that.

Old Pig and Granddaughter's cottage is based on an old pickers' hut we have at our place which had been added to over the years to make a slightly larger cottage. The combustion stove is the one we have cooked on for years in the main house, and most of Old Pig and Granddaughter's furniture goes back, again, as did everything in *John Brown, Rose and the Midnight Cat*, to Nanna and Pop's house. So does the rhythm of their life together, the rituals of cooking and cleaning, the simplicity of their days, and their respect for one another.

The other buildings in the book, the town buildings, are based on a cluster of sheds near Captain Taylor's paddock, with a bit of Shaker aesthetic thrown in – in the mix of materials, the proportions, and the spatial relationships between the buildings. The landscape throughout the book is faithful to Captain Taylor's Paddock, except for the view through the window, which is the view across the fields from our pickers' hut.

The lake and the summerhouse, mentioned in the text – but not there in Captain Taylor's paddock – I 'brought in' from England, from Springhead, where Margaret and I lived while I was working on *Timothy and Gramps*.

In the double-page spread where Granddaughter says goodbye, Old Pig is in bed, not yet asleep.

So Granddaughter switched off the lights,
and opened the window to let in the breeze,
and opened the curtains to let in the moon.

But there is light also from Granddaughter, the cello and from Old Pig herself.

This picture is a salute to one of my all-time favourite picture books, *Goodnight Moon*, written by Margaret Wise Brown and illustrated by Clement Hurd – including the picture above the heater of the cow flying over the moon. The other picture within this picture, on the left just above Old Pig's bed, is from Wise Brown and Hurd's *The Runaway Bunny*, another favourite with my own kids when they were young. I love Wise Brown's writing – the elegance and absolutely perfect pitch for young readers, the quality of her voice – but the simplicity of Hurd's artwork in *Goodnight Moon* is extraordinary. The repetition of that room from page to page, with only the light and some small details changing. It is utterly beautiful, despite the clumsiness of his drawing and painting skills. The man could neither draw, nor paint. It's almost unbelievable, particularly in *The Runaway Bunny;* so awkward, *so* crudely done in places, but absolutely better than perfect. I have read both books a million times. I love them. And I don't think either of them has ever gone out of print in America. Certainly not *Goodnight Moon*. As the owner of a little bookshop in Brooklyn told me, 'No decent, self-respecting bookshop anywhere in America would be without it.' And he meant the *hardback*.

It's the same in Japan, by the way. Apart from all those Manga comics, Japanese publishers would hardly dream of publishing books for children in paperback. It's a matter of simple respect. They believe children are worth more than that, as are the books themselves. Huge children's libraries I visited in Tokyo and Osaka didn't have a paperback anywhere to be seen. The zillions of books on the zillions of shelves were all hardbacks – books from all around the world, many of them Japanese-language editions of great English-language classics that I haven't seen in any Australian library for years.

'Why wouldn't you want to keep all these wonderful old things in print?' a librarian in Tokyo said. 'They are too beautiful to lose. And, of course, a well-produced hardback lasts a lot longer than a paperback does.'

Yes indeed. So it pleases me immensely that Allen & Unwin decided to reissue *Old Pig* in hardback fourteen years after its original publication. I'm glad about that.

———

In doing the illustrations for *Old Pig*, I used pencil and watercolour, and worked on hand-made Lana *pur fil* French watercolour paper. Because of the sheer delicacy, the tenderness of the text, wanting to somehow match that, for the linework I used a ordinary 'click pencil', a tool I would normally never draw with. I wanted never to have to stop, once I put the pencil to paper, to sharpen it back to a fine point again. I wanted, once I started to draw, to be able to keep going. I wanted a lightness and an almost continuous flow and consistency in the fineness of the line. With the click pencil I could achieve that, just by turning it, rotating it as I worked, to keep that line, and a 0.7 2B lead, with just a little bit of increased pressure, gave me that bit of extra body, depth and tone to the line where and when I wanted it.

The same was true for the lettering. For the Australian and English editions, all the title and text lettering was done with the same click pencil. I wanted to have the drawing and the lettering as much *of a piece* with the writing voice as possible.

As to the colour, I used a lovely French boxed set with about thirty tiny pans of very concentrated watercolour.

'Look!' said Old Pig. 'Do you see how the light glitters on the leaves?'

Sometimes I would go and sit out there in the paddock, on my small folding stool, and just paint away all day; sometimes I would work at the desk in my studio. Either way, my head was filled with Old Pig and Granddaughter's place now. I was inspired also by the work of Sempé in *The Vacation* and for Patrick Süskind's novella *The Story of Mister Sommer*. Monet, an old hero, was also there – most obviously in the endpaper and the cover, especially as it wraps round to the back.

When searching for the best visual solution for the last lines of the story, I knew only that I didn't want to show them in bed. I wanted to go back outside, into their larger place; I wanted, somehow, to show the leaving – Old Pig's leaving – from *out there*. I even tried a couple of flying pigs, can you believe it, in my original dummy...

While I was struggling to find the right image, I went for a walk down the hill, along the river and across the bridge into town. The idea was to buy a loaf of bread, and a bottle of milk, and clear a few cobwebs at the same time.

From the bridge, looking down onto the river to see if any ducks were about, I spotted a small cream-and-green dinghy, tied up by the shore.

I knew it instantly. That was it.

And I liked the echo of a similar dinghy, though far too clunkily drawn, unfortunately, that I'd put into *This Baby*, when Auntie Robyn comes to take Andrew to the hospital where his new sister has just been born.

Birth and death are closely related – both a kind of crossing from one place, one realm, to another. Anybody who has ever attended the miracle of a baby's birth will know what I am talking about. There is the absolute miracle of new life, but you *know* that death also – at least the possibility of it – *is right there*, in the room.

So of course the boat had to go into the book, not only onto that last spread, where we see the empty dinghy on the lake, the night crossing into sunrise, into day, and a single white bird gliding across, but onto the cover also. The endpapers then had to be simply water, to imply the ferrying, the crossing of the Styx.

Then she climbed into Old Pig's bed.
She put her arms around Old Pig, and for the very last time Old
Pig and Granddaughter held each other tight until morning.

The final illustration is a wall-to-wall double-page image. On the left, Old Pig and Granddaughter's cottage is floating in the darker colours of night, but is held also in the shapes of landscape, trees and clouds, with a cool, restful light from the full moon illuminating it all. Pale smoke rises from the chimney, there are soft white lilies in the foreground – a pencil cypress, soft and full, is leaning to the right, a white bird glides across also…

All the shapes on the right-hand side – of the distant headlands, trees, grassy slopes, and summerhouse, the clouds reflected in the lake, the jetty, the empty boat, the garden – are more open. It is still restful, but there is more energy on this side. The boat is drifting, but it is also crossing the lake, crossing the reflections of the clouds, towards the sun. Everything is illuminated, lit from within and glowing; there are roses in the foreground here, the warm red roof of the summerhouse is a kiss in the glow of a glorious sunrise.

For the next, single page, the last in the book, there is no text. My final version of the illustration for this page shows Granddaughter standing by the summerhouse at the edge of the lake. There is a duck by her side, two parrots hanging in mid-flight above. Granddaughter is holding a basket of flowers, her other hand rests companionably on the duck while she looks up to the right, at the parrots. There has been new planting; we can see a wheelbarrow and a spade, roses in bloom in pots, a climbing rose growing on the side of the summerhouse and a young pencil cypress close by.

–––––––––

Long before I'd done any drawings for this story, I would take the manuscript with me to schools and read it to the kids, some of them groups of wild and raring-to-go boys, streetwise nine- to twelve-year-olds. I swear that by the time I got to the third sentence there was not a sound to be heard – forget 'dropping pins' – I could not hear anybody *breathing*.

So Granddaughter switched off the lights, and opened the window to let in the breeze, and opened the curtains to let in the moon.

There is something so intensely intimate and human about the way this text is written, and the story is so absolutely timeless – true for everyone, everywhere and forever – that it just cuts right through the chaos, slips effortlessly into the hardest heart – allowing each person to respond as they will. Respond they must. It is impossible *not* to be moved by this astonishingly beautiful 'flicker of intense and private humanity'.

In the face of all life's chaos, distractions, idiocy and madness, it is not often we see such clear expression of love, truth and unambiguous generosity as this story represents. It is simultaneously both totally humbling, and enormously inspiring. Cutting directly to the heart, this text somehow allows each of us to feel – *makes* each of us feel, even more intensely – our own fragile humanity. And then the words draw us out of ourselves and we are reconnected with the world, and become quietly strong again.

It really is an extraordinarily beautiful piece of writing, and I hope I've managed to add something to that beauty with my illustrations. It was certainly a privilege to have the opportunity to try.

Henry's Bed & Henry's Bath

Henry is going to sleep in Henry's bed tonight.
Oh, yes!

Henry is going to have a bath today.
Oh, yes!

GOING BACK A few years, I was still teaching at the end of 1991, beginning of 1992, and at the time we were still living in a terrace house in Mary Street, North Hobart. Sam was nine and Adelaide was six and a half when Margaret and I realised we were pregnant, with a third child on the way.

Not expected.

It gave us both a bit of a jolt.

'What do you *mean*? Of *course* I'm sure!' was her response to the obvious question.

To be honest, I wasn't sure that either of us was ready for this. I felt Margaret was having doubts about me, and I was way too busy at the art school. 'I honestly don't think I have the energy required for a brand-new baby now, I don't think I'm *strong* enough.'

'And…' – this was the big one for me – 'I honest to god don't think I'm anywhere near *unselfish* enough any more.'

Nine years earlier, the day before Sam's birth, I had resigned from my teaching position at Chisholm. I hardly did any paid work at all, more or less, for his first couple of years. I just wanted to be there with him and Margaret. And when I did get back to work, it had been as a freelancer, so I was working from home through Adelaide's first three or four years also. I believed in being at home as much as possible for your kids, especially when they're young. I still do.

Neither of us would consider ending the pregnancy, so it meant we needed to adapt, prepare ourselves for it. But I was committed to my job at the university. I was head of the Graphic Design department, teaching too many hours, and directing all the activities of the semi-professional design studio that I had set up within the department. I had no idea how I could possibly even reduce my hours there. Moreover, I had decided I really wanted to get back to painting, after five years of not doing any, and had just got myself organised to start.

The university provided me with my own studio at the art school, and I'd put my etching press in there. I did a series of etchings for the new Parliament House in Canberra, six or seven small images which were used on menus, wine lists, etc. in the members' restaurant. It was a good commission. I enjoyed coming up with the images, was paid very well, and we'd been able to buy our first house as a result, but the studio was too small for the paintings I wanted to do.

What I most loved about that little hole in the wall was that it was right next door to Rodney Glick's studio. We were often the last to leave the building, around midnight, and would then walk home together, via the hot-dog shop, to North Hobart. We became friends.

Rodney Glick is an extraordinarily talented bloke; intelligent, smart and wonderfully crazy in the best possible ways. Totally honest, immensely generous and, when he wasn't partying, he just worked all the time. In 1989–90 he was doing his Masters. I couldn't believe the amount of work he managed to produce in that tiny, three-by-three metres studio. More often than not there'd be a pile of people in there, friends, smoking cigarettes, drinking beer and standing around talking. Rodney would be joining in, listening, laughing his head off, telling stories and dirty jokes, but working all the while. Just sitting there working, always. He was casting thousands – literally, *thousands* – of small, grey concrete objects: palm trees, sewing machines, aeroplanes, picket fences, trains, telephones. The room, his available space, only got smaller and smaller.

Rodney had decided he wanted to set up his Masters submission – a massive assembly of eighty-one groupings, nine to each group, of these small concrete objects – in a vast, dark room with thick sandstone walls, on the top floor of the then totally derelict old Henry Jones building, next door to the art school. The art school administration was not at all happy about the idea, made all sorts of objections, but Rodney – nothing if not persistent and, as I say, smart – invited me to set up a painting space for myself in there with him. He enlisted my help in persuading the city council, who were responsible for the building, to give us the necessary permissions and keys. So, ignoring the unpleasant looks we'd both get from other people who clearly would like to have grabbed the space for themselves, we moved in. We had the whole building to ourselves.

Blacking out the small windows overlooking Hunter Street to make his room even darker, and then carting all his stuff up there over the weeks and months leading up to his presentation at the end of 1990, Rodney began laying it all out on the floor, selecting, assembling, editing and re-assembling. He brought in a whole lot of electrical stuff: power leads and boards, extension cords, wiring – boxes and boxes of stuff.

Meanwhile, whenever I could find the time, I'd be up there in my big open space next to his on the top floor, right up under the skylights, working on my paintings. I didn't want to paint on the usual stretched canvases, so I had advertised in the *Mercury* and managed to fill the place with an assortment of all sorts of second-hand tents. It didn't matter what condition they were in; the worse the better.

The first piece I did was on one of those small tents electrical contractors or Telstra technicians use to keep the weather off an access hole. I hung the tent up on hooks and chains against a wall, and worked directly onto it with enamel paints and bitumen. It got redder and redder, blacker and blacker. It was not a very jolly piece at all. Rodney once said it made him think of the Holocaust; that it *felt* like the Holocaust.

Rodney had been working away in his space for weeks, and finally declared his piece finished. To get to it, you had to enter the building from a small door off Hunter Street, go through the small old manager's cottage within the larger building, up a flight of stairs, through the first floor filled with rubbish, up another flight of increasingly rickety stairs to the top floor, wade through more junk, through my space, and in through a door hung with a heavy black curtain. And you'd be in Rodney's vast, dark cavern...

You would have to pause, and wait for your eyes to adjust to the dark, and then – slowly, it was as though you were coming in over a city at night, in a plane... There were thousands of tiny lights spread out below you in the darkness on the floor, strung out in lines and, in places, clusters. As you came in closer, and walked around, you began to make them out – these 'suburbs and city blocks of buildings'. They were groupings of small grey objects, all lined up, nine to a group: cows, picture-frames, ashtrays, toy trucks, telephones, trains, palm trees... It was like some kind of dream. Like a whole *lot* of dreams. You walked, drifted, a little removed at eye-height above the whole thing, with these 'streets', these little pieces of theatre, laid out below you.

It was extraordinarily beautiful, the whole thing was extraordinarily beautiful. Until you got right round the room, to the last grouping...

Nissen huts – dull grey concrete Nissen huts, each only about eight or ten centimetres in length – were arranged in tight, straight lines, nine times nine of them, I think, with a single light, just slightly larger and brighter than the others, raised on a pole and illuminating them from above. And you were looking down, over all that. Not so much a dream – much more like a nightmare. A slow, dark, nightmare. There was no

sound, but you could feel it. Like a single rifle shot. You didn't actually see or hear it being fired, but it was as though you could. Certainly you could *feel* it, slowly repeating, dulled, like a pulse, into the night.

It felt pretty damn special working next door to Rodney for that period of time, and it was wonderful to be painting seriously again. I would try to get in there at least three or four times during the week, and maybe for a few hours each weekend also.

I had cut up some big old army tents – the roof out of one, the end wall out of another – and had taken the pieces across the docks to the sail makers at Johnston Ship Chandlers, who would sew them up for me into whatever new configuration I wanted. I nailed these stitched-up assemblages to the walls – I thought of them as skins, really – and painted onto them with bitumen, oil and enamels, mostly just black, and red.

If anybody had asked, I would have had to say they were self-portraits.

In the beginning I wasn't doing them to show anybody – I was simply seeing whether I could paint the sort of things I had in my head…whether I could *get* them. Just for myself. But as the work went on, I became quite excited about it and, to my own surprise, I began to think about exhibiting them in a gallery and seeing what other people thought. It would be the first time I had ever 'shown' my paintings. I invited Dick Bett, a Hobart gallery owner, to come in and have a look. He wandered around for a while, commenting on what a great space to work in, what a great building, what a waste that nothing was happening with it, that it wasn't somehow being used; and, eventually, having a look at the paintings themselves, remarked on their size.

'Well…I can see it's stuff you obviously *needed* to do, Ron.'

I kept on painting anyway. I had to keep building more internal plywood walls to nail my 'skins' onto. I also wrapped bits of canvas around rods and circular steel hoops I had made, strung them up, and worked on them.

I very rarely feel about my own work the sort of confidence I felt about these paintings. They felt good.

I worked away up there for a couple of years, getting as much done as I could, until Henry was born in August 1992.

Wrapped Rod.
Oil, enamel and
bitumen
on canvas

The house we lived in was a narrow, double-storey weatherboard terrace overlooking Hobart and the river; we'd been there for almost four years. It was on a very steep block, with a tiny garden that Margaret and I had made in the front. I'd managed to transform the previously basic back yard into a lovely garden with terraced vegetable beds, espaliered apple trees and a three-storey cubbyhouse for the kids. Our back neighbours referred to it as the 'Swiss chalet'. I had built it on four tall poles running up through the old apricot tree; it had stained-glass windows, French doors, a balcony and a loft – the lot. Even a sandpit on the ground floor. Our kids never used it all that much, in fact. There were other houses to visit, skateboards and bikes to ride, and there was always a game of cricket going on in the street. Though only two or three kilometres from the CBD, Mary Street was a very quiet cul-de-sac, and seemed more like a street in a small country town.

Everything was shipshape enough outside, but we had decided it was going to be a home birth, so we had plenty to do inside. Make the necessary space in the lounge room upstairs, move a cot into our room next to our bed, build some new shelves next to that for all the baby clothes, nappies, towels and bedding. We had adapted to the idea, and all of us were now excited at the thought of having a baby.

Meanwhile, Margaret had decided that if the baby was a girl, we'd stay in Hobart; but if a boy, then we'd sell up and move to the country, where we'd have a bit more space.

Time went on, and the baby showed no sign of coming – didn't arrive by the expected date, nor a week later…

Margaret, who had done most of the preparatory work after all, figured that was because *I* wasn't really ready. I kept saying, 'Oh god, not yet, I'm far too busy at school.'

About two weeks beyond the expected date the midwife said, 'If not sometime this weekend, then it will have to be a hospital birth.'

'That's okay,' I said, 'I'm ready.' And I was.

'O–*kay!*' said Margaret. 'This weekend, it will be.'

Nothing happened all day Saturday…but some time during the evening, Sam said, 'I reckon the baby will be born at ten o'clock tomorrow morning.'

'Not at half-past?' I asked, 'or twenty to, or [as I thought] much later, in the afternoon?'

'No. At ten o'clock,' Sam repeated, totally sure. And he was right.

In the lounge room overlooking the city, at exactly 10 a.m. on Sunday 30 August 1992, Henry was born.

Sam and Adelaide were there, of course, and the midwife, and a very good friend from directly across the street, the angel of Mary Street, Robyn Mathison.

As with all successful births, it was amazing. Seeing a brand-new person arrive in the world feels like a miracle. Yet so rudimentary also. So *animal*. And entirely beautiful. We had been through it before, of course, twice – but we prepared, went to the classes and read the books all over again. Still, there always is the possibility of problems, misfortunes, mishaps, tragedy even. The possibility of death is right there, with you, in the room. All the greater, then, the miracle…the blessing, the relief, the thankfulness.

Henry arrived, and began crying at once. We ran a bath and just moved him round gently in there, caressing him all the while, and at last the crying stopped. He relaxed. Everybody relaxed. From that moment on, we felt it. We felt what was different about Henry.

The moment Sam had been born, we sensed, and we could *see*, how entirely self-contained he was. He was relaxed, and still, and simply gazed, in perfect contentment, at Margaret.

Adelaide, from the moment she arrived, was looking around, making eye contact with everybody, and as soon as she 'found' Sam, seemed to say, 'So, *there* you are! O-*kay*, what are we going to do?' We could see her sociability, her gregariousness.

With Henry, whatever our concerns might have been – from the moment he stopped crying and relaxed, none of that mattered; all our concerns simply disappeared. We relaxed with him. And we felt all the energy and strength he had brought with him, the generosity and affection – truckloads of it – and we felt him give all of that, then, to us.

And he just kept on giving. There was no longer any sort of concern about energy levels or selfishness. He arrived and simply *re-fuelled* the lot of us, right there and then. And kept on doing so. A complete and utter blessing.

––––––––––

I didn't go back into my studio in the old Henry Jones building until January 1993. Wanting to paint the laundry at home, I needed to pick up some brushes.

It felt strange after not being in there for four or five months, going back in through that small door off Hunter Street, up the two flights of stairs to the top floor, walking back into my old painting space.

Intent on my errand, I didn't notice any change at first, but I noticed the smell – I remember that – an amalgam of dead fire, dog and filth…

Confused, I stopped and looked around. Where was the glue, the oil, the turps? Only half the brushes were there, and everything seemed in a mess. Everything *was* in a mess. And there *were* things missing.

Then I saw. Half my paintings were slashed to ribbons – just hanging off the walls in strips. Others had had glue or bitumen or something thrown all over them. The two hoop pieces had obviously been set fire to where they hung, one had fallen from its place on the wall, still alight…there was a two-metre hole burnt right through the floor.

I stood there looking around in disbelief. It was only then that I saw the camp fire, the sleeping-bags, the backpacks, the bongs…and the unbelievable filthiness of it all.

It was very strange. I was not angry, not even upset at first. But, as it slowly sank in, I thought, well, it doesn't matter, I can always do more. I'm just going to have to find somewhere else to work.

We started looking for that place in the country, hopefully with a big shed, and moved to the Huon Valley in June 1993, into a place that had a two-bedroom house, a separate studio with a sleeping loft above it, a toolshed, a small cottage, and two big sheds. It was our own little village on about 12 hectares overlooking the Huon River, just outside Huonville.

It was beautiful. Plenty of space for everybody, a wonderful place for the kids, and for Henry to grow up.

At the time of Henry's first birthday I was working on the final illustrations for *Motor Bill and the Lovely Caroline*, as already described, and flat out at the university. My painting just went by the wayside.

Then the Art School, for me, slowly began to fall apart. There was a personal element to that, but I was also becoming fed up with all sorts of things about the way the place worked. I absolutely loved teaching, loved working with the students, but I was feeling utterly burnt out, unable any longer to teach as well as I liked. I'd had enough. And the *Old Pig* text had come early in 1994, and I hadn't managed to make a start on it at all.

So I handed in my resignation, and left just before Henry's second birthday.

I had returned from nine days interstate, meeting with my publishers and talking at schools. It was the first time I'd ever been away from my family for that long. I was feeling a bit displaced, disoriented by the time I got home – too many different places, too many people, too much talk. I badly needed to reconnect, become grounded again.

We had finished dinner, and Margaret said she would put Henry to sleep.

I was a bit put out. I loved taking Henry to bed, cuddling up and reading with him, just as I had done with all of them, pretty much every night, ever since they were babies – maybe just the one book, maybe two or three, and then singing, until they went to sleep. But Margaret felt she and Henry had finally found a bit of a routine together while I was away. She would take Henry to bed while I did the dishes, ensuring a clear and clean kitchen in the morning.

I had brought in some wood for the stove, cleared the table and benches, given the floor a bit of a sweep – simply enjoying being home. I had run the water and was about to start on the dishes when Margaret came back down the stairs.

'It's not working at all,' she said. 'It's exhausting. I think he wants you. Would you mind?'

'Not at all,' I said, 'I'd love to.'

'I'll finish cleaning up,' she said.

I'm not sure how long I was up there with Henry, but when I finally went back downstairs the dishes were still in the sink, exactly as I had left them, and there was no sign of Margaret anywhere.

Then she called me from the sunroom, our improvised office at the time.

'Come and see what I've *done!*'

'Not the dishes, that's for sure.'

She was at her desk, looking very pleased indeed with herself. 'I've written a *story!*'

> HENRY'S BED or: OH, YES!
> *Henry is going to sleep in his* ^{Henry's}*bed tonight*
> *Oh Yes!*
> *Mummy can't sleep in Henry's bed*
> *Oh No!*
> *Daddy can't sleep in Henry's bed*
> *Oh no!*
> *The goat can't sleep in Henry's bed*
> *Oh no!*
> *The cow can't sleep in Henry's bed*
> *Oh no!*
> *The pussy cat can't sleep in Henry's bed*
> *Oh no!*
> *The rooster can't sleep in Henry's bed*
> *Oh no!*
> *The hens can't sleep in Henry's bed*
> *Oh no!*
> *The dog can't sleep in Henry's bed*
> *Oh no!*
> *But Henry can sleep in Henry's bed*
> *Oh Yes!*

She was thrilled! Sitting there with a huge smile from ear to ear.

'Yes,' I said, 'I think it's nice. I like it.' 'Really?' 'Yep, I do,' I said. 'A lot, I think…'

'I think it's *amazing*!' she said with a smile – not one of her high-voltage, thousand-watt, light-up-an-entire-room smiles, more inward, one of your energy-savers; a smile slowly warming from the inside out, the outside in.

'I can't *believe* it,' she said, 'I don't know how it even happened!'

'By not doing the dishes,' I suggested, 'as we agreed?'

'Hah! Very funny.'

She looked so happy with herself, so excited, that I left her sitting there, and just as happily went back to the kitchen. She kept fiddling away in there throughout the evening, and even did some tiny pencil sketches: a hen-house, some animals and a pencil cypress on a hill, with a moon, and a star.

We talked about the story over the next few days. I really liked it, believed it had something very special about it, but also thought it was just a little mono-dimensional, needed something else, but wasn't sure what...

Margaret was still so excited about her first go that she found it a bit difficult to change it at all at first, but continued to fiddle with it over the next three months or so, doing minor variations, making small changes – to a line here, a word there. By November she had changed quite a few things, definitely brought a lot more life to the text, but seemed to have ground to a halt on it. It still needed something more.

With Margaret's permission, I started to fiddle with it myself, not wanting to change its essential wonderful simplicity, its character or voice, but trying to add dimension, layers. I wrote four or five variations over the next few months, and yes, the rest of our lives went on. I was still trying to find my way into *Old Pig*, and Margaret had begun teaching at Tarremah, the Steiner school which Sam and Adelaide attended.

I could fill 30 or 40 pages of this book with all the variations *Henry's Bed* went through. A year went by. Late in 1995, I asked Margaret to read my most recent version. By then I had added another seven lines – only fourteen words in all, but amounting to another seven pages in the book I could see in my head. Those seven lines were a whole second half to the book, which echoed something of the

simplicity and contemplative qualities of Wise Brown's *Goodnight Moon.*

Some time after *Old Pig* was published, I had done the first dummy of *Henry's Bed* and sent it Rita Scharf, who was then at Penguin. Rita and Bob Sessions were enthusiastic, and committed to a contract immediately. But Margaret and I continued to fiddle with the text, albeit in smaller and smaller refinements, occasionally faxing them to Rita for comment, until finally we had this:

> *HENRY'S BED*
> *Henry is going to sleep in Henry's bed tonight.*
> *Oh, yes!*
> *Mama won't sleep in Henry's bed.*
> *Not tonight.*
> *Will Papa sleep in Henry's bed?*
> *I don't think so.*
> *The cat shouldn't sleep in Henry's bed.*
> *Oh, no.*

Mama can't sleep in Henry's bed
Oh, no!

Above and
opposite:
roughs from
Henry's Bed,
first dummy

The dog wouldn't sleep in Henry's bed.
No, sir.
The hens can't sleep in Henry's bed.
Certainly not.
The ducks can't sleep in Henry's bed.
Definitely not.
And what about the goat?
Can the goat sleep in Henry's bed?
No, he cannot!
How about the cow?
Can the cow sleep in Henry's bed?
Nooo!
But Henry can sleep in Henry's bed.
Of course he can.
It's warm
and snuggly
and just the right size.
Goodnight cow
Goodnight goat
Goodnight ducks
Goodnight hens
Goodnight dog

What about the dog? Can she sleep
in Henry's bed?
I don't think so!

But Henry can sleep in Henry's bed
Of course he can!
It's warm and snuggly and just
right size.

Goodnight cat
Goodnight Mama, Goodnight Papa
Goodnight Henry

Margaret became a little self-conscious, embarrassed I suppose,
about the text being no longer entirely hers. But the initial idea, which
I loved, *was*. And I suppose I viewed my tinkering with her text as
not very different, after all, from what I try to do with any text I am
offered and have said yes to, as an illustrator. That is – I try to expand
it out, give it more space, more 'roominess of meaning'.

Mama won't sleep in Henry's bed. Not tonight.

Margaret's original story held in it the possibility of being not only a very nice little going-to-bed story, about a child overcoming a reluctance to go to bed, the fear of going to sleep, going *inside*, but her reference *outward* to all those animals gave it the possibility of going outside the child's self – out into the world, seeing something

about *everything* having its own place – and finding comfort in the realisation of one's own place within all that.

Being able, then, to breathe out, and let go. Relax. And go to sleep knowing – as the Shakers say, ''Tis a gift to come down where you're meant to be.' That is why I added those last seven lines; just fourteen words, no big deal in themselves – most of the work of them would be done by the illustrations – but to me, critical.

Fortunately, Margaret agreed. So it was good.

And then, somewhere along the line Margaret had the idea for another story, again inspired by Henry. He hated bath time, just as I had when I was young. We had tried everything with him: bubble bath; rubber ducks and all sorts of floaty things; other things that sank to the bottom. 'See if you can pick that up, Henry.' Coloured shapes which (when wet) you could stick on the tiles and make pictures with; an

Goodnight cow

extraordinary assortment of boats – little home-made wooden dinghies, bigger painted jobs with paddle-wheels propelled by rubber bands, tin boats with tea-light candles, two or three sailing boats, through to a massive great pirate ship with full crew. At times there seemed barely enough room for Henry in there. We tried anything and everything.

'We could do a *Henry's Bath*,' Margaret said. 'A companion to *Bed.*'

And straight away, I thought, *Wonderful*. We have the breathing

out, the letting go; now we can have the breathing in, the taking hold
of, the embracing.

'Yes,' I said, 'wonderful. We will.'

We decided to use exactly the same format, the same characters,
essentially the same text, simply with a bath instead of a bed. The only
change was to the second section of the book, where we reversed the
order of the characters. Instead of starting, as in *Bed*, with the cow –
the biggest and 'furthest away', and coming back through the goat,
ducks, hens, dog and the cat, to '*Goodnight Henry*' – from those
furthest out, to those closest *in* – we went the other way round, from
the cat out to the cow...

Hey cat
Ho dog
Yay hens
Yo ducks
G'day goat
Howdy cow

And beyond the cow, out to the whole valley, with the one new line in
this text – moving out into his whole world – to all his friends, whom
he invites back in:

Guess what?
I'm having a bath!
And a hair-wash too!

We were thrilled. We had been totally happy with the whole idea
of *Bed*, thinking that it was complete in itself; but with *Bath*, it really
did feel now as though we had found 'the other half'. We had both the
breathing out and the breathing in, the letting go and the taking hold
of; both halves making up the whole of a young child's world.

Penguin was happy also, and signed up the second book.

Through most of the manuscript and earlier dummy stage – I
did four dummies altogether, three for *Bed*, one for *Bath* – we had
worked with Rita Scharf, but she then left Penguin, and the editorial
responsibility for the project was taken over by Erica (then Irving)
Wagner. There wasn't much to do on the text; mostly she simply had
to wait for the finished illustrations to come in.

Title-page illustration from *Henry's Bath*

And they could have taken a very long time, really, because by the time I got round to starting on them Margaret and I were in trouble... I had mucked up, been an idiot, and had hurt her. I had also hurt myself. And neither of us was able to forgive me. There was far too much pain on both sides.

I poured all the energy I had into the *Henry* artwork. I sat at the desk day and night, for months. Working on a heavy, rough watercolour paper, using a thick black conté pencil for the linework, I drew everything up very close, bringing everything right up to the front picture plane, to the front of the stage, the reader in the front row. I'd wash the line with water to bring out grey washes, work over that with repeating layers of watercolour, and glaze over the top with

But Henry can hop in Henry's bath. Of course he can. It's warm and bubbly and ready to go.

shellac, trying to make the whole image surface as warm and tactile as possible. I wanted the very young readers to be able to feel the characters, feel that world. I wanted them to feel that they were part of it and it was part of them.

The cat (Max), the dog (Nickel), the hens, ducks, goat and the cow,

the house (just a little changed) and the landscape – the valley, the hills all around, the trees and the river – they were all parts of Henry's real world. The little trolley, specially made for Henry by friends one Christmas, was not there in any of the dummies. It was the key visual trigger, the motif that gave me the idea for the Bear subplot, which became so important for both books. It was only when that trolley turned up that I was able to begin on the finished illustrations. And the

HENRY'S BED & HENRY'S BATH

bear himself was just one of Henry's considerable collection, most of which were made by Margaret, a dab hand with a needle and thread.

The tricycle and the fireman's helmet in *Henry's Bath* had belonged to Sam initially, then Adelaide, and all the pirate allusions came from Sam, from when he was about three. He loved pirates. We built pirate ships everywhere and anywhere, out of everything and anything, he had a veritable arsenal of swords, and was good at using them too. All of this Henry inherited, and it all went into the book.

I loved doing all those drawings; all of them, all of it. Above all I loved drawing Henry. In *Henry's Bed* particularly; a little guy in his baggy pyjamas. Beautiful. Simply so-damned-nice to draw.

I was drawing it all for Henry, for the texts, and for the kids, but for Margaret too, absolutely, the only author for whom I've ever drawn, even in part. With every other book I have drawn for the text.

I can remember delivering the finished artwork, the lettering, everything, to Penguin. Bob Sessions, whom Margaret and I had known for years, who had been at our wedding, said, 'These are very beautiful books, Ron. We'll do them in hardback and keep them in print forever. They will become classics.' He was extremely positive, to the extent of putting me up in a swanky hotel in Queens Road for a week, so I could personally supervise the printing, which I greatly appreciated.

Robyn Mathison launched the books wonderfully for us at the old Hobart Bookshop in 1997. She read a story by Bill Neidje, who was born along the East Alligator River in about 1911. His *Story about Feeling* is an utterly extraordinary text, told with great simplicity, and was all about what Margaret and I were trying to do with the two *Henry* books, and much more.

Margaret spoke – not for very long at all – about Henry, about the books, about how they came about, and what we tried to do with them.

I then spoke, and read from various favourite writers and books – as always, for far too long. I was going quite mad by then, I suspect, and I think everybody there at the launch could see it. One of my kids – I can't remember whether it was Sam or Adelaide – heard somebody say, outside in the street, 'What do you think is wrong with that fellow? I think he is seriously ill.'

I remember, too, the call from Penguin the next year, when the books failed to be shortlisted for the Children's Book Council of Australia awards. They were both dead in the water as hardbacks, and Penguin would sell them off, remainder them. The books would be reissued in paperback, in the hope that they would find a new life at a lower price.

Several years later, at the instigation of my agent, Margaret Connolly, who always felt Penguin had wasted these books, we retrieved the rights. They were eventually republished as paperbacks by Walker Books in Australia and the UK, in 2007. With punctuation in the second half of both books this time, which Margaret and I decided we could live with.

––––––––––

Postscript

Ten years after the books' original publication, and shortly after I received the artwork back from Walker, I gave it all to Margaret. Except for three pictures: the half-title illustration from *Bed*, which I had already given as a Christmas present to the friends who made that trolley for Henry, the final illustration from *Bed*, which will continue to hang in Henry's room in my house, and the final illustration from *Bath*, which I had given to my father.

I gave it all to her with pleasure. I did do it all for her, after all. And none of it would have happened – neither of the books could or would have been made – without her.

Honey and Bear &
Special Days with Honey and Bear

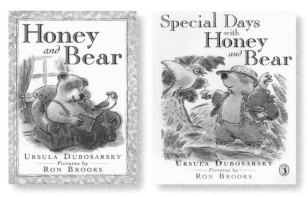

Bear and Honey were going on a visit.
They were going to see Bear's mother, who lived on the other side
of the lake. Bear had not seen his mother for a long time.

Honey and Bear were sitting in the kitchen eating apples.
'Bear,' said Honey, 'today is a very special day.'
'Is it?' said Bear, his mouth full.
'Yes,' said Honey. 'Today is the last day of the year.'
'Oh,' said Bear.

THE FIRST Honey and Bear stories, by Ursula Dubosarsky, came at a time when I was not feeling at all strong. I was falling apart.

I met up with Ursula and Julie Watts (the children's publisher at Penguin) to talk about the stories, and how I was planning to approach the book – the style of illustration, and the overall design and look of it. I talked about how much I loved Ursula's writing, the quietness of it, the tone of voice, the clarity of the phrasing; about how perfect I thought all this was for very young children.

Ursula was glad, thanked me. 'Well, they're just simple little stories,' she said, smiling with the same modesty that I felt in her writing, 'but I'm very happy that you like them.'

I couldn't leave it at that.

'No, no – I *love* your writing here, Ursula,' I said, 'I love these stories. I love them. They're beautiful. I love them for their gentleness.' And promptly began to weep.

Ursula was sitting there so quietly with her big eyes, looking about thirteen, yet at the same time somehow very much older and wiser. She has that look of someone who has always, since infancy, sat just a little to one side – the thoughtful watcher – not exactly taking notes, but certainly thinking a bit more than most, taking everything in; digesting, filing, categorising, for future reference and (very likely) use.

God knows what she thought at the sight of me across the table, dissolving into a blubbering idiot like that…but the good Julie, who may well have the heart of a horse, was very sweet. 'We are so glad you like them so much, Ron. It's wonderful that you feel so deeply about them. That's exactly why we thought of you, knowing that you'd bring your own special insight to the work. We know your drawings will be very special, and you will make a very beautiful book.'

But the fact was that at that stage I had no idea how I was going to approach the illustrations – in which media, or in what sort of style; no idea at all.

These apparently simple stories presented all the day-to-day complexities of the friendship between Honey and Bear – the sharing of things, cooking, co-operation, walks and talks together, all the daily rituals and affections of their living together. Misunderstandings were there also, small misdemeanours, hurts – and then the reconciliations, the coming back together. It was all done with delicacy and nuance, gentleness, and much good humour.

The stories were simply about getting on with each other; about generosity, and forgiveness.

Perhaps I wept because of the contrast between all that and so much of what was going on in my own life at the time. In a way, I think it was only having the drawings for *Honey and Bear* to do, and then, a little later, *Special Days with Honey and Bear*, that kept me this side of insanity.

I told Ursula and Julie that I'd like the book to have something of the feel of Arnold Lobel's Frog and Toad books, maybe a little of Sendak's Little Bear – both very simply drawn, focusing almost entirely on the characters, taking the viewpoint close in, having only a minimum of background detail. I wanted the book to be a small portrait format, similar to the Lobel and Sendak series, but to be spacious in its design. The images sitting comfortably within very clean and clear typography, with a lot of air around and between all the elements. I wanted a classical but warm and old-fashioned feel, gentle, friendly. Absolutely the opposite, in every conceivable way, to what I was thinking I would have to do with another story I had recently taken on, Margaret Wild's *Fox*.

I was also thinking of the charm and simplicity of any number of Rosemary Wells' beautiful books, wanting to achieve something of that warmth. I had tried to find that kind of simple warmth for *This Baby*, but in using pen and ink I had chosen the wrong tools. Switching to conté, watercolour and shellac, I had come a little closer to that warmth for the Henry books, but they were a different kind of creature altogether. With *Honey and Bear* I wanted to get simpler still. And I wasn't at all sure I was capable of doing that.

The very best drawings by any number of the great artists – da Vinci or Raphael, say, or Rembrandt, Holbein, Daumier, Degas, Picasso, Kollwitz – and by far fewer illustrators – Ernest Shepard, Edward Ardizzone or Charlotte Voake – are essentially simple. The vision is clear, and the drawing is not overworked. Having that clarity of vision is rare enough; knowing what *not* to put into a drawing, knowing when to stop, is just about as important, and as rare. Only occasionally have I got anywhere near the clarity of vision I have been after; rarely indeed have I ever managed to achieve anything like the directness or simplicity of execution that I felt was needed. But I came closest, I think, in the Honey and Bear books.

The need for simplicity started with the text itself. There is a spacious elegance and sophistication in the writing – it is beautifully crafted – but there is also a certain down-to-earth-ness in the clarity and directness of the text, the modesty and simplicity of the characters' circumstances, and the clear delineation of the two very different personalities. Honey is a bird, probably small, quick, witty, just a little bit flighty; Bear is a bear, probably big, amiable, comparatively slow, and generous.

I wanted to reflect all that, not only in my choice of media and style for the illustration, but also in my whole design for the book.

I had trouble finding what sort of bird Honey would be, so I began with the design of the book instead, deciding first on size and format, and then thinking about the internal layout. I experimented with different typefaces, Baskerville, Bembo, Century Schoolbook, Garamond, Goudy, Palatino, and with the letter spacing, the line spacing, the margins. I spent ages mulling over it all, revisiting and tweaking particular elements again and again; thinking about what particular passages in the text most seemed to need illustration, and about what was *not* in the text but needed to be illustrated, deciding where to leave holes in the typesetting to drop those illustrations into.

By the time I'd finally decided on all that, and had the complete manuscript typeset in Cochin – so elegant, with its beautiful rounded shapes and long ascending strokes which, especially when combined with extra leading between the lines, gives a lovely spaciousness – I *still* hadn't decided on Honey, still couldn't get started on even the first rough sketches.

When all else fails, go and work in the garden. Mow the lawns maybe or, yes, finally get started on tidying up that ugly bank just behind the house – pulling out the weeds, digging it over, bringing in a few rocks here and there, planting small flowering natives along most of its length, with a rose and a bit of a herb garden towards the kitchen end. Mulch it all in with a combination of straw and manure, hoping to hold moisture in the bank, hoping for lots of worms…

It was hot, and I'd done a very satisfying day's work – disappeared right into it, almost entirely unaware of anything else around me. I'd certainly forgotten all about the book. I stood there in the warmth of the late-afternoon sun, hose in hand, watering it all in with a fine, gentle spray. I was vaguely wondering, standing there, whether I should remove the two silver wattles from the top of the bank; were they taking too much nutrition, would they make it a bit of a struggle for the new plants? I liked their shapes, though, the sweeping lines of the branches, the featheriness of the foliage, and I liked the dappled light and shade they created. On the other hand, they dropped a lot of rubbish into the guttering at the back of the house. Perhaps I should take their tops out… I was standing there, dreaming, watching a rainbow arc through the fine mist of water – watering the freshly planted basil, chives, parsley, oregano and rosemary. Among them there were a few old cream-and-green enamel pots, a colander and saucepans I'd bought at the local market. They were no longer any good for cooking of course, with the enamel chipped and flaking off in places, but perfect to plonk into a kitchen garden.

I was dreaming, and hadn't noticed a small bird, sitting on one of the wattle branches. It dropped suddenly, and swooped down and across onto one of the rocks I'd placed near a callistemon. It hopped and turned – not much bigger than my thumb, with beautiful, soft colouring – this way and that, and flitted across to land with its back to me this time, on an old fork-head I'd dug up and stuck in there among the herbs and pots. It hopped again, turned, looked at me, tilted its head this way, then that – peered into the mulch, looked at the herbs, the pots, the colander, at the mist of water…and then, quick as a flick, flew right through it, to the top of the rose stake. Hop, jump, tilt, turn. Another quick look, another quick decision, a dive – back through the mist, through the rainbow, and up onto her branch again. A bit of a ruffling of the wings, a quick clean of the flight feathers with her beak, this side, then that. Another quick look, a short series of bouncing skips – there was *no weight at all* to her, and all her movements were so quick, and *strong* – along the branch, turning this way and that as she went, before quickly diving down, this time onto the green handle of the pan. The fine mist, the sunshine, danced gently on the surface of the water. Then she made an abrupt, short, vertical flight, up through the rainbow, turning sharply and swooping down onto the edge of the pan with the briefest hesitation, a glance up at me, before hopping into the water, spreading her wings, shaking herself – her whole body, head, wings. And then, suddenly she was up, out, and back onto the head of the fork again, shaking herself all over, like a dog on a beach. Then turning, tilting her incredibly pretty little head at me again. This way, then that. So wonderfully *cheeky*-looking.

And that's when I finally noticed the eyes – those big silver rings around the eyes. She was an eastern silver-eye.

They are not what many people would describe as a spectacular bird, but I love them – very softly coloured, from the ochre head, unusually large in proportion to its body, a bit wren-like, down through the soft grey at the back of the neck to the predominantly ochre and darker grey wings and the faintest blush of rust, with just a hint of grey on the breast. A thin, finely curved and pointy bill, and yes – those large silver rings with a fine black line around the outer edge, right round the eyes. Almost like a drawing already. A bit like a Leunig eye.

She's perfect, I thought. That's her! That's Honey.

We stayed like that, the two of us, for maybe ten or fifteen minutes – me just standing there with the hose, Honey loving the water and the chance of a good bathe after such a long hot day. I watched her flitting from place to place, from pot to fork, from rock to pan, from rose to branch, flying through the spray, through the rainbow, turning and twisting in flight. Flying directly at me, veering away at the very last moment with what looked for all the world like – if not outright laughter then certainly an exuberant joy on her beautiful little face. Dropping, swooping, skimming the surface of the water, up onto her branch again. Fluttering and fluffing out her feathers, turning herself into a soft, round little ball. Tilting her head, looking at me again. Almost asking me, it seemed, 'Have you realised yet? Should I keep going, have you got me, seen enough yet?'

I may well have actually said it out loud: *Thank you.* I'm not sure.

But I was so grateful. Either way, and she had probably bathed enough to last her for a fortnight by then, she seemed to get the message. Providing her own musical accompaniment, a series of quiet little notes in an unchanging key to a few last hops and turns on the branch, she was off across the gully in that distinctive jerky flight, disappearing into the bush on the other side.

————

Bear was different. I mean, there aren't as many choices as with birds – he was simply a bear. So I drew a bear, standing, friendly; and then fiddled about with him – the length of the arms, the legs, the dimension of his girth – always with the aim of trying to make him as warm and friendly as I possibly could. Comfortable in his own skin. Earthed. He became slowly rounder and rounder, and his legs became shorter and shorter. I wanted him to have a low centre of gravity, but I was astounded myself, at how short his legs became. And then, without ever seeing him as the Beau Brummell of the bear world, I began to think about his wardrobe. Would he wear any clothes? If so, what sort of pants might he wear, or would he prefer some sort of overalls? A shirt, vest, jumper, jacket? Short or long sleeves? Would he wear any sort of shoes, boots, or perhaps some sort of sandals? What about gloves? No. Any sort of a hat? Maybe he had a couple of different hats…

And then – what sort of colours? If he had pants, overalls, a vest, a jacket, what colours would they be? What sort of colours would Bear like?

God knows, really… A bloke can fiddle about with, muck about with, waste a whole lot of time on, these sorts of decisions for *weeks.*

Eventually I got there; no Beau Bear he would have be a pretty basic wardrobe, with very few variables: indoor/outdoor, warmer/cooler, that's it.

Looking at him now, more than a decade later, I am surprised at how similar his anatomy is to Bunyip's. Even to the pants, with braces to hold them up. But apart from the rust-brown pants and braces, reddish buttons, he wore nothing much else. A blue jacket and

An early rough

Bear never told anyone at all.

[21]

a wide-brimmed straw hat for outdoors. And a bag, an old-fashioned leather schoolbag to be precise, the sort we all slung over our backs as primary-school kids, way back when, to carry our books and school lunches in. Bear uses his for picnics and excursions.

But how to draw all this? Using pen and ink? What sort of pens? Watercolour? What sort of brushes? Pencils? If so, what kind? And so on, and so on… Oils? Gouache? Acrylics? Collage? All of these tools and media have their own particular qualities and characteristics. There are so many different ways in which you can use those characteristics, it is almost endless.

Then there's the audience. What is the likely audience for this particular story? How best could I reach that audience? Though I had moved away from my earlier theories about what style of illustration worked best for kids, and begun to think a lot more about the text – the tools and media, the technique and style I thought would best serve a particular story, best answer *that* voice, became my uppermost consideration. Irrespective of any ideas about a particular audience.

He poured it all into a tin, and put the
tin in the oven.

Then Bear had the second idea.
'Honey will be home soon. I will cook
her a seedy cake.'
Honey was a bird, and she liked seedy
cakes.
So Bear went back to the kitchen. He
mixed up the flour and the sugar and
the butter and the eggs and lots and lots
of black seeds in a bowl.

[6]

[7]

Above, and on following pages: early sketches and page layouts for *Honey and Bear*

I wanted the whole book and all the images in *Honey and Bear* to be simple, clear and strong. I wanted Honey and Bear themselves, and every other thing – the settings, the house, the rooms, the doors and windows, the furniture, the stove and kitchen utensils, the garden, the landscape all around – to be simple and archetypal. I wanted weight and substance *on the page*, warmth and softness throughout. The stories also needed a lot of air, white space flowing between the images and the typesetting and around the margins.

Pencil and watercolour would be best, I decided, narrowing the choice of pencil down to three types – charcoal, carboncino or conté. I eventually decided on the No. 3 carboncino, because it is a wee bit softer than the 1 or 2, giving a slightly warmer quality of line, and because just that little bit more tone comes out from the line when it is washed over with a brush dipped in clean water, marrying the drawing beautifully into the paper, and giving a deeper foundation of combined line and tone over which to build the washes of watercolour. I tried to do all that strongly, yet *lightly*, simply, using not too many lines – just enough to give it the substance I was after, but with not too much fussing about. No image was to go under or behind any of the typesetting, none would go right to the edge of the page and only a couple of them, if any, would occupy a 'formal' shape – a square, say, or a rectangle. Each image was to be free-formed and 'floating'. Relaxed and easy.

And once I finally got started on them, how I loved making these drawings! Such a pleasure to do. Looking at the drawings now – I realise that, again, they have something of Nanna and Pop's place about them: the big, bulky armchairs, the simplicity of the furnishings, the windows, the curtains. Something of the simplicity of their life…their landscape above the lake. The stove is the same one I put into *Old Pig* – the circa 1950 Rayburn I cooked on at home, and there are elements of

'I know,' said Bear sadly. 'This morning I had an idea. To clean up the kitchen.'

'That was a good idea,' said Honey.

'Then I had a bad idea.' Bear went on. 'To cook you a cake. Now everything is a mess again.'

Honey looked in the oven.

'Oh!' she cried. 'Seedy cake!'

Bear took out the seedy cake and put it on a plate. Bear ate the cake with his big paws, and Honey pecked at it with her beak.

[10]

[11]

Honey came in the front door.

'What is it, Bear?' she asked.

'Oh, nothing!' said Bear, quickly, hiding the empty marble bag.

Honey poured herself a long glass of water. Some of it spilled out of the cup, into the sink.

[16]

That's very strange,' she said. 'The water will not go down the plug hole.'

'Won't it?' said Bear.

'No,' said Honey, peering down. 'There must be something stuck down there.'

'I just remembered,' said Bear, suddenly. 'I must go out into the garden right now to do some digging.'

But Honey did not seem to hear. She was right inside the sink, looking down the plug hole.

[17]

the Huon Valley, of Cathedral Peak and Mount Wellington, in Honey and Bear's place.

Bear has a great deal of my father in him. In fact, one time when my parents were visiting, my father came into the studio where I was working, and he happened to see the drawing on page 17, from 'Bear's Secret'. 'That's *me!*' he said, chuckling. 'That's how Mum makes me feel, most of the time.'

Poor old Dad.

There's another picture of my father, slightly more relaxed, on page 25.

I loved doing all these drawings; as with drawing Old Pig and Granddaughter, it was just such a pleasure to be inside the *Honey and Bear* stories, be right there with these two lovely characters, feeling their affection and warmth, and trying my best to capture all that.

Some drawings gave me particular pleasure – the very last drawing in the book, for instance, of Honey and Bear, reconciled and together now in their armchair, just before Honey falls asleep, snuggled close into Bear's neck. We were initially going to use this image for the cover, but thinking it perhaps just a little *too* cute, I changed my mind.

I am fond of the final cover drawing, showing Bear in that same chair, reading a book by the window, with Honey on the arm of the chair this time, wide awake, chatting. I also like the picture of Bear putting the seedy cake he has decided to bake for Honey into the oven. I simply loved drawing that stove. For many years it was at the very centre, the very heart of our lives – it was what we cooked all our meals on, it was our source of heating, of warmth for the whole house, downstairs and up, for the whole family.

Most of all, I loved doing the opening illustration for 'The Visit', page 29, where Honey and Bear are setting off from home to visit Bear's mother, who lives on the other side of the lake. In the foreground is Bear, fully dressed for the outdoors with jacket and sunhat, backpack

He poured it all into a tin, and put the tin in the oven, from 'Good Idea, Bad Idea'

filled for the picnic they will have on their way. He is standing with his weight on one leg, arms raised, one of them reaching forward in the direction they are about to take, his hand over the water of the lake, just touching the reflections of the tree and hill on the other side – poised in the very same pose that I now realise I have used again and again in my books, when I wish to express a revelation of the rightness of everything. It's on the cover of *This Baby*, and in the internal image of Auntie Robyn bringing Andrew news of the baby's arrival; Motor Bill is in the same pose, standing on a stump, his head among the clouds, holding a bunch of flowers, before he goes to visit the Lovely

Caroline; so is Rosie on the cover of *Rosie and Tortoise*; and it's there on the title page of the original edition of *Henry's Bath*, where Henry stands on his tricycle with sword raised, victor over bear and bath…

This opening image from 'The Visit' was the one image from all the stories in *Honey and Bear*, it seemed to me, in which I had the chance to show not only the specialness of their relationship, but something of their whole place. Honey and Bear have just gone out their front gate – we see the roses, the flowers, the planting along the hedge of their front fence, the verandah, the roof, the chimney, beyond it a tree, a hint of their garden. Behind it all is the lake, reflecting tree and hill, the sky and two clouds. Honey stands alert on Bear's hat, her head right between those two clouds, eagerly anticipating their day ahead…

Bear and Honey were going on a visit, from 'The Visit'

I loved trying to infuse every single object – in every single drawing – each bit of furniture, each tree, each flower, each hill, blade of grass, lake, wave, sky, cloud, with rock-solid 'there-ness'; everything belonging exactly where it was, in its place, *right there.* I wanted to give everything permanence, even the air, the light, the shade, the physical space between things – the *relationship* and connection between every single element so that the viewer felt none of it would, and none of it *could, ever* go away.

————

God knows how, but I did *Special Days with Honey and Bear* after finishing Fox (see two chapters on). We've all heard of writer's block; in my sheer exhaustion immediately after *Fox* – in what I would only years later come to realise was my failure to make my own 'long journey home', and before *Fox* was actually published – I had collapsed with *illustrator's* block. I was unable to draw at all. For quite a long time, I wasn't even able to *read*. But, somewhere in there I did the pictures for Ursula Dubosarsky's second suite of stories about Honey and Bear.

I do remember trying again to capture all that gentleness, affection, good humour and generosity – all the heart, all the love and rightness of it – using the same design approach and techniques I used in the first, the same shapes – the shapes Robyn Mathison, in her launch of the Henry books, referred to so beautifully as 'the shapes of holding, and of letting go'.

In the Henry books I was after a bit more vitality, a bit more drama and zest, commensurate with the drama which is going on inside Henry's head and heart. Henry is at that stage where he is both *imagining* and *constructing* the world, *as* he is discovering his own place in it. Honey and Bear, by contrast, already know themselves; they know one another, and they know their world. Everything has its place, and they know and love, lucky them, their place within it. With all this, they are blessed.

With *Honey and Bear* and then *Special Days*, I was trying to capture all that, trying to suggest that the 'rightness' is already well and truly established.

I loved drawing Bear and Honey themselves, the lines and shapes

DRAWN *from the* HEART

of them, the relationships between them as well, their body language; the closeness, the affection, the good humour between them.

I loved drawing the *things* – the chairs, the table, the window, the curtain, the door – and the relationships between them, the visual dialogue, the conversations between all these things.

I loved bringing the boat from *Old Pig* onto the title page of *Special Days*, showing Bear and Honey setting off, into their life together, into the stories. The boat is there again in the opening story, 'Staying Up Late', moored at the jetty by the shore of the lake, like an invitation. Also in that same first story is the clock, the warm old shape of it, from my childhood.

In this second collection, it is almost the last image of 'Bear Gets Lost' that seemed especially important to me at the time. In 'The Visit',

Bear was glad that Honey had found him, from 'Bear Gets Lost'

'Bear,' cried Honey, 'There you are! Did you get lost?' 'I think I did,' said Bear.

from the first collection, Honey and Bear are together in every image. In 'Bear Gets Lost', from the second, we see only Bear for the first seven illustrations. We don't see Honey until she comes looking for him in the dark with a lantern around her neck, and finds him, the only double-page illustration in the whole book. I *loved* doing that one. It is the next illustration, on page 40 of *Special Days*, that means most to me – the one showing them returning home together. It is an almost-reminder of that opening illustration from 'The Visit', but Honey and Bear are coming from the opposite direction, and at night, with the only light coming from the lantern around Honey's neck. The Pre-Raphaelites are no longer fashionable, but I harboured a soft spot for them in my youth. Holman Hunt's *The Light of the World* was not any particular favourite, nevertheless this illustration is a funny old salute to that image. I chose here to echo some of Hunt's symbols: Christ at the locked door – Honey and Bear together at their gate, about to enter; the untended ivy and weeds outside that closed door – Honey and Bear's garden, the roses; the lantern Christ carries, surely a symbol of love, for those who will open – the lantern/love Honey carries, lighting their way home.

It's certainly not the best illustration in the book, but as with that opening illustration for 'The Visit', it gave me the opportunity to say something essential about the nature of Honey and Bear, about the depth and breadth of their friendship.

The Honey and Bear stories helped me find a way through a difficult passage in my own life, and for that I am enormously grateful. But by contrast with *Fox*, both the Honey and Bear books disappeared almost without a trace in Australia. The books have only slowly been taken up and translated into a very few other languages, most notably into Japanese – where the publishers, bless them, produced both volumes in hardback as per my original design and intention. I welcome the fact that Penguin are at least and at last, roughly ten years later, about to reissue both collections of these beautiful stories in one combined paperback edition.

Rosie and Tortoise

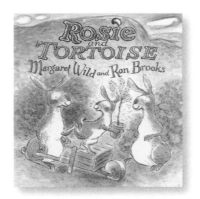

Rosie couldn't wait for her baby brother to be born.
'I'll teach him how to hop, leap and run – just like me!'
she told her mum.
'When is he going to be born, Mum? When?'
'Be patient,' said Mum. 'It'll be a while yet.'
But she was wrong. Bobby was born the very next day.
He was the smallest, weakest little hare ever.

IT IS AN odd thing, memory, isn't it? How does it work? Why do different people very often have conflicting memories of the same events? I'm quite sure some of the people I mention will not recollect events and circumstances in the same way I do. Is it just a matter of perspective, of having divergent ideas about what is important?

This chapter is dedicated to the memory of Felicity Oates: the most beautiful, entirely welcome girl, who so wonderfully showed that inside every painful thing, there is some kind of beauty.

Why do I tend to remember those things about which I feel most embarrassment, guilt, sorrow or shame? It's not as though it is particularly productive. Very often, in fact, it can grind me to a complete halt.

As a friend of mine says: you've just got to turn the page, leave it behind, and get on with it.

I'm not very good at turning the page.

—————

Some time in 1995 or 1996, Rosalind Price called me to say that Margaret Wild had written a sequel to *Old Pig*, and would I like to see it.

'A sequel to *Old Pig*?!' I said. 'How could she write a *sequel*? Why would she *want* to?'

'Dial, the American publisher, suggested it, because they loved *Old Pig* so much. They thought it would be nice, I suppose…'

'Well, I'm sorry, but I'm not remotely interested. I don't *do* sequels anyway, and I can't imagine what sort of a sequel you could do to *Old Pig* that wouldn't somehow undermine the original.'

The fact was that I loved *Old Pig* so much – the bravery and beauty of the text – that I wanted simply to leave it at that. I certainly wasn't interested in any story about how Granddaughter maybe went on to have a lovely life after all.

A second story – not actually a 'sequel', more a variation – on a similar theme came and went, after which I didn't hear anything more for quite some time. Eventually Margaret Wild wrote *Rosie and Tortoise*. It is not a sequel, but is a *very* lovely answer.

Old Pig, among many other things, is a story about how to say 'Goodbye.' *Rosie and Tortoise*, among many other things, is a story about how to say 'Hello.' Or, perhaps, a story about how to say 'Welcome.' But, although 'Welcome' is a very beautiful word, very old and full of respect, nobody uses it very much any more. It's probably seen to be old-fashioned, too formal. But I do like it. There are all sorts of nuances to it.

Welcome. Well come. It is well that you have come. It is well, very good, from my point of view, that you have come. I am glad, that you have come.

Or, inverted: Come well. You have come well. You have come properly, in the correct manner, and with the appropriate respect. Well done.

Either which way, it means, 'I am glad.'

Although I see the book *Rosie and Tortoise* as saying 'Hello', in the text Rosie herself says neither 'hello' nor 'welcome' to her new baby brother. In fact, she doesn't speak to or with him at all, throughout the entire story. Because, for Rosie, he didn't come very well at all; he came too early. And he was 'the smallest, weakest little hare ever'. She thinks he is sickly. 'He's so tiny, it makes me scared,' she whispers.

Indeed, for most of the book Rosie is avoiding Bobby, running away. Not until the very end of the book is she able to touch him:

That night Rosie held her brother for the first time.

She could feel his heart beating against hers.

Not until the very last line of the book does she finally greet him.

'Hey, Bobby', she said, 'hey there, little Tortoise!'

Margaret Wild could well have had Rosie say, 'Welcome' or 'Hello', and indeed, there is something in the story – the simple clarity of the parents' dialogue, or their attempts to leaven Rosie's anxiety, their slightly clunky humour, which she studiously ignores – that leads the reader almost to expect something like this. Instead, Margaret gives Rosie her very own voice: 'Hey, Bobby' (her little brother's proper name), 'hey there, little Tortoise!' (Rosie's own name for him, taken from her dad's re-telling of the old hare and tortoise story). A fresh new voice, totally unlike that of either of her parents, a voice that is totally true to kids *now*. Beautiful.

I loved the whole story – the simply human truth of it. The vulnerability, the tenderness, and the story within the story – but it was really that last line that got me. Rosie has transcended her earlier fears; she finds her own name for her little brother, and is able to greet him at last in her very own voice.

It was precisely because of that line, the sheer surprise of it, that lovely fresh voice, the complete resolution of all the key elements within the story – '*Beautiful*, Margaret,' I thought – that I said *Yes!* to the text.

Hello, *and* welcome.

Very well come indeed, Margaret Wild, yet again.

I said yes. How could I not?

————

All this was happening while I was working on the two Henry books, both of them as complete a celebration of our own third and last child, of *every* child, and the rightness of his place in the world, as I could possibly make them.

It's ironic, and not a little sad, that there I was, working on the Henrys, attempting to celebrate the rightness of everything – of belonging, place and of family – just when my own belonging, my own place and my own family were beginning to fall apart…

The family didn't, quite, just then, come apart. But I very nearly did. By the time I came around to doing the dummy, and certainly then to the final illustrations for *Rosie and Tortoise*, I barely knew what I was doing.

I can't remember who my editor for this book was at Allen & Unwin, or whether I even had one. I have no memory of whether I worked with anybody at all.

How long did I work on the dummy? I have no idea.

How long did the final drawings take? A complete blank. Though, looking back through some diaries, it must have all happened over a twelve- or eighteen-month period.

What I *do* remember is that I was so unhappy throughout the entire making of this book, so unwell, so *not there in my own skin*, so *dis*placed, that I felt I really had no idea at all of how to make a book. I genuinely did not know what I was doing.

I was totally numb. It was horrible.

But I had said yes to the text.

What would I do?

The only thing I felt I *could* do at the time: I did the whole thing by memory.

I was so *not there* – that at each line of text, at each image, at every moment of the making of the book, I had to ask myself, 'What *would* I (once) have done, for this?' I had to somehow *remember* how I *used* to solve these sorts of problems, whether they were to do with design and layout, typography or lettering, the various interpretations of particular lines of text, the various possible images for those words, the style of drawing, painting, the quality of line, what sort of tools, media, what sort of feel, what sort of tone I would best engage with the text...*all* of that. I had to try to remember how I'd once been able to do it.

Because I honest to god had no idea how to do it *now.*

I slowly, very slowly, worked my way into it, slowly worked my way *through* it, and all the time – every day for I don't know how many months, for every single line, for every image – I felt I was never *really there.*

When I stood back from the desk and saw that it was all done, finished – I couldn't believe it. I had no idea where it had come from.

And then, when I finally delivered it to Allen & Unwin, did I take it over to Melbourne myself, did I send it by Express Post? I have no idea. It is almost as though I had nothing to do with it. It's gone.

––––––––––

Oddly, looking closely at the book now, I can deduce certain things about the process I must have gone through – the decisions I made, how I made them, why I made them.

First there was the fact that I read this text as a very beautiful answer to the 'goodbye' of *Old Pig*, and therefore wanted to make this new book exactly the same size. This seems simple enough, but settling on a size for a book, that could well have been any one of perhaps twenty-seven other possible formats, is vital. The size and shape of the book *matters* – that's where I begin: deciding on the size and shape of the thing.

In *Old Pig*, trying to match the tenderness of the storytelling voice, I had used a very fine and floating-away pencil line, barely there in places, and similarly floating washes and glazes of watercolour. Though all four seasons are there, suggesting the fullness of Old Pig and Granddaughter's life together, there is generally an autumnal feel throughout the book. In some spreads – most notably in the four double-pages of their last long walk together – I brought the colours forward, closer to the reader, warmer; but, for the most part I was trying in *Old Pig* for a slightly ethereal, not quite otherworldly, but heading there, quality. There is a drifting, a layering, and a slightly cool palette toward the end, where I began moving the colours further away.

With *Rosie and Tortoise*, I wanted to bring it all much closer, anchor it *in the earth*, in this world. I wanted it to *feel* like birth, soft and warm; like spring, the season of new growth. So I used a black conté pencil, dark and velvety, for the linework, and a very much warmer palette, and deeper tones of colour throughout. With greens, yellows and ochres predominating and a few blues and 'spot' colours here and there. The paint and the colours this time weren't floating so much as simply *plopped* on the page, giving just that little bit more of a tactile quality, a bit more texture – something tangible.

I think the first finished picture I did for the book, as with *Old Pig*, was the image for the opening line of the story: 'Rosie couldn't wait for her baby brother to be born.' It was probably the lightest, happiest picture in the whole book. Rosie is shown from close-ish behind, taking up the whole centre of the image, jumping, and clicking her heels, but there is also a breezy openness and distance in the image. We see the hills beyond, the sky, a cloud, all very lightly touched in.

Then there's the following spread –

> *'I'll teach him how to hop, leap and run – just like me!' she told her mum.*
>
> *'When is he going to be born, Mum? When?'*
>
> *'Be patient,' said Mum. 'It'll be a while yet.'*

– with four images of Rosie hopping, leaping and running all over the place, watched by her mum. It's all about the sheer energy and joy of her body language. The first version of this spread showed no 'props' at all – no spade, wheelbarrow, watering can, no grass even. Later, for reasons I'll come back to, I redid the picture with those additions.

But she was wrong.

"I'll teach him how to hop, leap and run –

just like me!" she told her Mum.

"When is he going to be born, Mum? ⊢——————— When?"

"Be patient," said Mum.
"It'll be a long while yet."

Bobby was born the very next day.
He was the smallest, weakest little hare ever.

The image on this double-page spread is much closer in, enfolded by foliage. The whole tone has changed, the focus is of course on the red-raw baby now, between Mum's front legs, Mum licking, proud Dad looking on. Rosie is off to the side, looking back, with her body turned away. She's a little lost, bewildered – the area immediately beyond her being the only part of the whole image which is left unfinished, uncertain, thinner, cooler…

There follows a sequence in which the parents concentrate on looking after the baby, while trying also to include Rosie. But Rosie is confused, frightened, in denial. She says 'No', she won't push the pram or rock the cradle. Instead she runs after a butterfly, plays on the swing. She stays away.

Then she goes 'out', picking blackberries with her dad, and he asks her the question:

'Rosie,' said Dad, 'why don't you like Bobby?'
'I do!' she said. 'It's just…'
She stopped, then she whispered,
'He's so tiny, it makes me scared.'

Above, and on following pages: sketches from the dummy for *Rosie and Tortoise*

Bobby was born the very next day. He was the smallest, weakest little hare ever.

ROSIE *and* TORTOISE   [259]

'Come and sit next to me, Rosie,' said Dad, 'I want to tell you a story.'

Rosie is forced to acknowledge her fear. And Dad, understanding at last, tells her a story, a version of *The Hare and the Tortoise*, which runs through four double-page spreads. '*Once upon a time, there was a hare and a tortoise who were best friends. One day they went gathering nuts in the forest, each going their own way, but at home-time Tortoise couldn't find Hare anywhere, so he set off alone.*' Tortoise plods through the dark forest, saying to himself, '*Slow and steady does it, slow and steady will get me safely home*', until he sees Hare coming to meet him with a lantern.

It is a story in which Rosie can recognise both herself and her baby brother. Listening to the story, imagining herself as Tortoise (Bobby) going on that lost, lonely walk herself, Rosie enters the heart of her little brother. She finds compassion.

On the next spread she comes out of the story, back from that solitary walk through the dark forest, back into the light of day. Visually, the left-hand page takes us back to the opening of the book. Rosie is even looking back there.

Rosie sat quietly, thinking.

When Bobby was born, he'd weighed the same as an onion. Then a potato, then a turnip.

Having opened her heart at last to her baby brother, she is remembering also how her parents tried to include and help her.

One of these days he would weigh as much as a cauliflower, perhaps a cabbage, even a pumpkin!

On the facing page, Rosie turns to her dad, reaching out her hand to his. It's the first time in the book we see her *touching*... the first time we see her *being* touched.

Rosie smiled.

'Bobby is slow and steady,' she said. 'Isn't he?'

'He is,' said Dad.

In the penultimate spread, it's night-time.

That night Rosie held her brother for the first time.

She could feel his heart beating against hers.

Rosie smiled.
"Bobby is slow and steady," she said. "Isn't he?"
"He is," said Dad.

In its profound simplicity, and because I remember *exactly* that – feeling my own kids' hearts when they were young – this just about turned my heart right over.

————

Because I saw the *Rosie and Tortoise* text as an *answer* to the *Old Pig* text, I was interested in finding not only the right contrast, the right counterpoint between the two in the styles of drawing, the use of colour, the distance or the closeness of the images, I also wanted to reflect that in the overall architecture of the book.

Of course, the writing itself gave me that architecture.

The opening line of *Old Pig* – 'Old Pig and Granddaughter had lived together for a long, long time' – gave me the two of them, Old Pig and Granddaughter, in their garden, on the opening single page. The first line of Rosie – 'Rosie couldn't wait for her baby brother to be born' – gave me just Rosie.

The next sequence of lines in *Old Pig* gives us the two together: 'They shared everything, including the chores …'.

The next lines of *Rosie* give us just Rosie – hopping, leaping and running.

When night fell, he was still plodding on, saying to himself,
'Slow and steady does it, slow and steady will get me safely home.'

Then we go through, in both books, a mix of images – some smaller, some larger – looking at the life; until, in *Old Pig*, we come to the moment where Old Pig has to say goodbye, not only to everything she loves, but to Granddaughter, with whom she shares it all. Old Pig takes Granddaughter on a last long walk, the two of them together, as described earlier. And we have them, throughout a beautiful day, over four consecutive, full double-page spreads, walking through all their favourite places, feasting their eyes; 'Looking and listening, smelling and tasting'.

At a similarly critical point in *Rosie and Tortoise*, listening to her dad's story, we enter the first of four consecutive double-page spreads.

On the first, Hare and Tortoise are gathering nuts in the forest, 'but at home-time Tortoise couldn't find Hare anywhere, so he set off alone'. This picture, set in daytime still, gently refers to those sorts of images where you have to search among the leaves and tree trunks to find hidden things.

When night fell, he was still plodding on, saying to himself,
'Slow and steady does it, slow and steady will get me safely home.'

In the next three spreads it is night-time, unlike the corresponding spreads in *Old Pig*, where it is day. But here, Tortoise is alone. The forest becomes darker, and Rosie is imagining, feeling for the first time how it is for her little brother. Her heart reaches out to his…

> *Little by little, Tortoise made his way toward the edge of the*
> *forest…*

The forest is coming closer in this picture and Tortoise is surrounded by huge organic forms that appear to be moving – the very ground he is walking upon seems to be moving, uncertain. But up ahead is a calmer, more 'readable' area –

> *where he saw what looked like a yellow moon moving through the*
> *trees.*
> *And there, coming to meet him, was Hare, with a lantern.*

Here we have – contained and held in the moment, illuminated and enfolded in light and leaves, grounded in recognition – a *knowing* of place. Certainty.

Hare reaches across the gutter of the double page towards Tortoise.

Then, moving out of the story within the story, out from those four double pages, we come back into the day, into that light and airy single page where 'Rosie sat quietly, thinking'. And where, on the facing page, Rosie reaches across to her dad.

Coming to the final pages, in *Old Pig*, Old Pig and Granddaughter get home late from their last day-long walk. Out of those four autumn-coloured double pages we move into quieter, cooler colours, to two single-page pictures, one with Granddaughter helping the exhausted Old Pig into bed, and opposite, in slightly warmer colours, an image where she remembers how Old Pig used to cuddle her in bed to help dispel bad dreams.

> *'Tonight,' said Granddaughter, 'I'd like to come into your bed and*
> *hold you tight. Would that be all right?'*
> *'That would be very all right,' said Old Pig.*

Towards the end of *Rosie and Tortoise*, we move into another full double-page spread:

"And there, coming to meet him,

"And there, coming to meet him was Hare,
with a lantern."

That night Rosie held her brother for the first time.
She could feel his heart beating against hers.

Embracing, finally welcoming her brother, Rosie has taken him to her own special dark and private place, a variation on a hole in a hedge I remember from Mallacoota Primary School, and reminiscent of the place where Tortoise and Hare meet in that special, held moment at the edge of the forest. The night and stars shine through and, for the first time, Rosie holds her brother, a bit bigger now, sitting in the wheelbarrow we saw her in on the title page.

In *Old Pig* also there's a corresponding spread, with colours just a touch cooler, showing how Granddaughter says goodbye in her own way, playing her cello for Old Pig.

The corresponding architecture of the two books is reflected in their very last pages.

In *Old Pig*, 'for the very last time Old Pig and Granddaughter held each other tight until morning.' The last double page, very fully coloured, using the whole palette, from night to day, from cool to warm – it's almost a dreamscape of their whole world.

That night Rosie held her brother for the first time. She could feel his heart beating against hers.

"Hey, Bobby," she said.
"Hey there, Little Tortoise!"

And then a last single page. No text, no dialogue. By contrast, that last
double-page spread of Rosie holding Tortoise for the very first time.

And then the last single page in *Rosie and Tortoise* where Rosie
finally says, '*Hey, Bobby… hey there, little Tortoise!*' She has made
a soft, grassy manger in the wheelbarrow; the young tree from the
half-title page is there, now grown, and the lantern from Dad's 'Hare
and Tortoise' story is hanging from a branch above Rosie and her
baby brother. There is something of the feel of Christmas here. And
yes, the wheelbarrow is the one shown on the last, wordless page
of *Old Pig*.

In the endpapers for *Rosie and Tortoise* – front and back – I decided
to use that earthy and leafy place where Hare and Tortoise meet, to
contain, open and close – to *hold* the whole meaning of the book in
that special moment. In the endpapers for *Old Pig*, by contrast, the
suggestion given by the reflections, by the colours on the water, is of
transience, change, of passing from one place, one time, to another.

———————

There's a postscript to the story. When I was a week or two from
finishing *Rosie and Tortoise*, I stumbled across a copy of *Guess How*

First version,
later replaced,
of the final
illustration in
the book

Much I Love You, by Sam McBratney and Anita Jeram, a lovely picture book which went on to become a massive bestseller around the world – a story about the love and affection between Big Nutbrown Hare and Little Nutbrown Hare.

I realised that there were two double pages in *Rosie and Tortoise* – the 'hopping, leaping and running' spread, and the holding, 'his heart beating against hers' spread; and the very last – the *'Hey, there, Little Tortoise'* page, that were all far too similar in their drawing and colour to some of the images from *Guess How Much*, too similar to the whole tone and feel of Jeram's illustrations. So I redid the 'hopping, leaping and running' page, adding more background and props, but probably didn't change it enough. I also redid the 'went off to play on the swing' page, mostly because the linework in the original was simply a bit crudely done. Even though I really liked the original illustration for the 'she could feel his heart beating against hers' page, I did a replacement, and damn it, liked that one even more. But it was still too similar to Jeram. So I did it again, and again. I think I did four more finished drawings for the 'heart beating' page, before I finally realised I should 'marry' that secret, leafy meeting place with the hole in the hedge from my own childhood. Then I began to redraw the original *'Hey, there...'* page, which I *really* really liked, but realised Rosie's arm was too big, it looked like a log, so I started again and did a third version, which I felt really nailed it. But, with a day or two to think about it, I realised it was still too close, it still had echoes of *Guess How Much...* And at last came up with the image as it now is in the finished book.

Even so, when the book was published, when I talked at schools, students would ask me if I did *Guess How Much I Love You.* I suspect they hoped they were getting to meet somebody seriously rich.

I also did the two *Henry* books, both of which have a bear in them, but did they think I was responsible for *Winnie-the-Pooh*? There are *thousands* of books with bears in them out there. Hundreds of them published over just the last two weeks alone, for god's sake. Did they think Ernest Shepard was still going strong?

Would that he was.

PART THREE

I think it's a mistake to ever look for hope outside one's self.
One day the house smells of fresh bread, the next of smoke and blood.
One day you faint because the gardener cut his finger off,
within a week you're climbing over the corpses of children bombed in a subway.
What hope can there be if that is so?
I tried to die near the end of the war. The same dream returned each night
until I dared not go to sleep and I grew quite ill.
I dreamed I had a child, and even in the dream I saw it was my life,
and it was an idiot, and I ran away.
But it always crept onto my lap again, clutched at my clothes.
Until I thought, if I could kiss it, whatever in it was my own, perhaps I could sleep.
And I bent to its broken face, and it was horrible…but I kissed it.
I think one must finally take one's life in one's arms.

Arthur Miller, *After the Fall*

Fox

Through the charred forest, over hot ash, runs Dog,
with a bird clamped in his big, gentle mouth.
He takes her to his cave above the river and there he tries
to tend her burnt wing;
but Magpie does not want his help.
'I will never again be able to fly,' she whispers.
'I know,' says Dog. He is silent for a moment, then he says,
'I am blind in one eye, but life is still good.'
'An eye is nothing!' says Magpie. 'How would you feel
if you couldn't run?'
Dog does not answer.
Magpie drags her body into the shadow of the rocks,
until she feels herself melting into blackness.

I WAS NOT very healthy, and certainly deeply unhappy at the time the *Fox* text came along. The problems in my marriage – the pain – had begun in the aftermath of *Motor Bill and the Lovely Caroline*, after I had left my teaching position at the University of Tasmania, and continued all through the work on *Old Pig*, the two Henrys, *Honey and Bear*, *Rosie and Tortoise* and beyond.

When did Rosalind Price send me this stunning text by Margaret Wild? Was it way back when I was still working on *Rosie and Tortoise*? I was already quite sick by then, sicker than I knew – struggling by then to even remember *how* to draw, to even *imagine* what it would be like to be *able* to, doing the whole thing almost on some sort of automatic pilot. Or had I even started on that one yet, was I still trying to work, then, on the two Henrys, trying to celebrate the rightness of everything, belonging and family, when my own was falling apart?

When I first read *Fox*, I felt as though I had been punched in the chest, very hard, or that I'd been run over by a truck, a dirty great concrete mixer. It hurt. It was horrible.

Though there was no reason to suppose Margaret Wild knew it, the story was a searingly close parallel to what had happened to my marriage – every single thing about the text so painfully close to what I had done or allowed to happen, to what we'd all gone through. Horrible. It brought the whole thing back.

Not that it ever went away.

———

A little later, when I was able to breathe again, I realised what extraordinarily powerful writing this was. Risky, confronting, courageous, strong... And generous. Biblical almost, in its grandeur, archetypal in its universality, and all too painfully – intimately, beautifully, scorchingly – human. All the blood, sweat, tears and meat of a juicy great novel, honed back to three pages of transcendent typescript. It was amazing. In just a few hundred words, the story told of the friendship between Dog, who had a missing eye, and Magpie, who had a burnt wing. *Then Fox came into the bush and Magpie trembled* – as if she already knew what would happen. Fox tempted Magpie – three times – and the third time she yielded. She went with him. He ran with her on his back, out into the desert; and abandoned her.

I had never read anything like it. For sheer power, certainly no picture-book text I could recall even remotely approached it. I felt, and still do, that Margaret Wild had really broken the form with this text, changed its possibilities – for me certainly, forever. A totally, shockingly *original* piece of work, as true and painful about friendships in kindergarten and school playgrounds as about adult sexual relationships. Or as the Allen & Unwin blurb had it, 'A breathtaking story of friendship, love, risk and betrayal.' I was stunned, floored, by it.

I showed it to my wife; I gave it to her to read.

'It's *horrible*,' she said, 'horrible, I hate it!' She didn't want me to do the book. I understood, and said so; we talked about it many times, but I also said that I had no choice; I *had* to do it – the writing was too magnificent to refuse.

That was when the pain really started.

I had become much more than unhappy. Every day I felt as though there was some massive great weight constantly pressing down on my chest, was barely able to breathe, almost unable to get out of bed.

And that had been going on for some years already.

I'd wake at three or four every morning, the inside of my head like one of those hideous dodgem bumper-car tents at a sideshow – thoughts careering and crashing around into one another, a sheer bedlam of idiocy and noise, an appallingly predictable but utterly unavoidable senselessness. An unstoppable shredding, near obliteration of the self, every morning.

Exhausted from the lack of sleep, more tired than when I went to bed, I would get up early, stoke the Rayburn, squeeze the juices, put out the breakfast things, prepare everybody's school lunches and see them off. Then just collapse back into bed – or, if I couldn't get up the stairs, onto the couch. Unable to get up again, sometimes, until just before they were due to come home again in the afternoon.

None of them knew. And I told no one.

I had the days to myself.

Some mornings, hoping the weight would lift, I would go outside into the garden. I'd planted a lot of things over the years, natives mostly. Acacias, callistemons, eucalypts, grevilleas, hakeas and kangaroo-paws, all good for the native birds. But roses also, I had some wonderful roses, and I'd built a few rock walls.

It was beautiful out there, when I *could* see it, overlooking the whole valley to the east and north – to the apple and cherry orchards on the other side of the river; the hop fields edged with poplars that would become a pool of gold in the late autumn sun, and the hills and mountains beyond. Over it all was the vast sweep of sky, clouds, the light and colours of everything constantly changing. And just down the hill from our place, running through the middle of all this, overhung with a mix of gums, blackwoods and wattles, and reflecting it all – sometimes with a clarity stronger than the original – flowed the tannin-dark Huon River.

To the south and west, immediately behind the house, was a steep hill, with great cataracts of rock and beautiful trees, mostly stringybark and white gum, and underneath them a native cherry here and there, the odd scrappy wattle, native grasses, fallen branches. It is the multi-coloured and white trunks of eucalypts that I really love – standing strong, straight and vertical through it all, giving it structure…the upper branches, twigs and leaves calligraphic against the intense cobalt sky. It was impossible to look at this patch of landscape and not see early Fred Williams, late Arthur Boyd, bits of Nolan and Streeton and, especially, again and again – the background in Tom Roberts' *Bailed Up*, the forerunner to all the others…

And birds, there were always so many birds. The ubiquitous sparrows, starlings and blackbirds, of course, and crows, lots of crows, but always also an assortment of honeyeaters: the elegant eastern spinebill, the crescent, the striped, the strong-billed, the white-bearded and, those larger members of the family, the wattlebirds. Eastern silver-eyes, diamond firetail finches and goldfinches, pardalotes, thrushes, wagtails, warblers, whistlers and a mix of robins and wrens. Sulphur-crested and black cockatoos, kookaburras and kites, hawks, even the occasional grey goshawk. A pair of sea eagles lived just down from us, and I would sometimes see wedge-tails cruising across the valley, or riding the thermals just above our house. And one day, most amazingly of all – a wandering albatross. Sam and I were driving into town, and this magnificent bird came gliding steeply down over the cliff, only a few metres above the car – so close, *huge*, barely clearing us – pursued by a couple of gulls. It rode the breeze across the river, over the valley to the far side, and then we then joined the chase on our side as it turned south, heading back towards the ocean from which it had apparently been driven inland by bad weather. Needless to say, this extraordinary creature took no time at all to leave us behind. And not once did we see it flap its wings.

My favourites were the swift parrots. Found only in Tasmania and some Bass Strait islands, these are perhaps not as spectacular as the crimson, eastern or western rosellas, but I loved them. A mob of them, anything between twelve and twenty, would turn up around October every year – about six months after I'd seen them last – and appearing so suddenly, it would almost always take me by surprise. Flying straight as arrows, they would come low and fast through the trees towards the house, sweeping gracefully, steeply, up into the walnut and birch immediately in front of the verandah; loudly announcing their arrival with a lot of jubilant chattering, bobbing up and down, and much strutting back and forth on the branches. Some of the apparently even more excitable ones – as though wishing to find some extra way of expressing their pleasure, their joy in the sheer triumph of the moment – would swagger right out to the ends of the branches, turning from side to side, this way and that, weighing them down the further they went, all the way out to the twigs – and then flop and swing upside down, hanging there, flapping and chuckling all the while.

This whole ritual of their arrival – for so it seemed, a total performance, happening every year, year after year – would go on for five or six minutes. Then, quite suddenly there'd be a lessening of chatter, one or two of them would have stopped altogether, and there'd be a pause in all the posturing, followed by a complete stilling. The

DRAWN *from the* HEART

attention of those one or two, and then of all, seemed suddenly to be taken elsewhere, by something else – perhaps somewhere in the garden, but more likely by something up among the gum trees behind the house. They'd make a couple of short, sharp statements, immediately echoed by a staccato chorus throughout the whole group, and off they'd all go – checking out their territory, happy as kids returning to a favourite summer playground, to see if special things were still in the special places they had left them in last year, and to see whatever else might have turned up, or changed, while they'd been away.

But it had been a couple of years – longer, a *long* time – since I'd had a day like that. At my worst, I could see none of this. I could see almost nothing. Not the landscape, not the trees, not the garden. Not even the birds. Or if I did see them, if I *could* see them – it was as though I was numb – I didn't *feel* them at all.

I didn't hear anything either. Not the birds, anyway. I even stopped listening to music.

And, not for the first time, I had stopped reading.

I was just about dead.

(THEN THE PICTURES)

Apart from all the personal pain associated with this story – how to step outside all that, transcend it, turn it around, and put it all into the book – I faced the challenge of finding the best way of meeting, engaging and answering this extraordinary text.

It's like that every time, of course – back to square one with every book – but with this text it was particularly hard. It was completely unlike any picture-book text I'd ever read; so much more challenging, so confronting, not just for me, but for any reader. It broke all the rules of the genre. How to go about finding the visual form that would most fully respond to all of that? How would I even *find* the right images, let alone *make* them? What sort of illustrations could match it, what sort of media, what sort of technique, what sort of design, and how would I treat the text itself – what sort of lettering or type?

I had absolutely no idea, for any of it.

Boring, old-fashioned, traditional-mainstream, pale-and-wan me had to see whether I could *answer* that, whether I could come up with something that did justice to, truly *engaged with*, maybe even expanded upon, the writing. I had to find a *total* visual approach and response to the story, not just in the illustrations but with the text also; I needed to find a design for the book that invited – nay, insisted – the reader pay even closer attention to the text, a design that matched the story's power and tone of voice.

I have always loved classical book design and illustration, the heritage and rules of good craftsmanship and legibility, and I've always been reasonably content with the knowledge that I am simply part of a tradition. I have never consciously set out to break any new ground – never thought I had it in me anyway – never tried to do anything flash, or to impress with some new technique. I have simply tried to engage with and answer each text. But with this text, which I believed broke the picture-book mould, I *had* to see what I could do about breaking the form also. Or, at least try to give it a hefty shove sideways, a bloody good kick in the driving side, a damn good dent. Scary.

It had to be utterly unlike anything I had ever done before, or seen, because the text was utterly unlike any I had ever illustrated or read. Margaret Wild had gone where she had never quite gone before, writing so bravely, so originally. I had to also.

It took twelve months of agonising about it, weeping and bleeding all the way.

One day Henry came home from school, and found me sitting at my desk in the studio, doing pretty much just that: weeping.

'What's the matter, Dad?'

'I can't do this book, Henry. I have absolutely no idea of how to go about it. I don't think I am any good at this at all, I don't really think I know how to make books.'

He was silent for a while, and then said, 'That's not true, Dad. Look at all the books you've done already.'

'Yes, well...maybe I've simply forgotten how. I certainly don't feel

DRAWN *from the* HEART

I can make this one, that's for sure.'

After a longer silence, he asked whether I still happened to have any of those blank dummies left anywhere.

'Help yourself. Second drawer from the top, over there,' I said, pointing to a set of plan drawers. 'There are different sizes; what do you want to do?'

He started going through them, and chose one. 'I'm going to make a dummy of *Fox*. My version. And show you how easy it is.'

And he sat down at his desk just across from mine, took out some pencils and, without reading the story again – already knew it well enough, he reckoned – he set to work. Simple as that. And honest to god, he sat there and worked away at it for around two days, with breaks for meals and sleeping; and did it! It was beautiful; nothing like what I might have done – much more free-wheeling, much more joyous. I loved it. Henry was pretty happy about it too.

'See how easy it is?' he said. 'And if *I* can do it, you *certainly* should be able to.'

Wonderful.

It worked. I was so moved by his generosity, by the sheer heart in what he'd done, and so impressed with the finished result, that it helped. Within a day or two, I was able to sit down and begin work at last on my dummy.

It took about three months – going through the text, chopping it up, line by line, or by paragraph, by block or by page; getting the basic images right; deciding what would happen on each page with each line of text, each moment or passage of time, and where the text should go – top, or bottom? Left, right, or middle? – for each and every word; coming up with the layout, design and feel of the whole thing.

And then, when I had finished and sent it off, I collapsed.

––––––––––

The people at Allen & Unwin raved about the dummy, *loved* it, they said, as did Margaret Wild. They were all very excited about me getting to work now on the finished images. But I was exhausted already, unable to do another thing. And although I figured I did have the basic

Sketch from
the *Fox*
dummy, for
*'I see a strange
new creature!'*
she says.

imagery right in the dummy, I really had no idea how I would do the
finished artwork. I was completely lost. What could I do that would
measure up to the text? The more I thought about it, stared at it,
searched for approaches, the more convinced I became that I wasn't up
to the task. Didn't have the necessary originality of vision, the talent,
the skills.

And so I died, again.

I don't think I made another mark for about three months after
that. I walked around and around in circles, staring at the photocopied
dummy, at the desk, my paints, brushes… reading and re-reading the
text, staring for hours at particular passages, trying desperately to find
the trigger, but unable to see a thing.

And all the while Allen & Unwin and Margaret Wild were thinking,
hoping, I was well into it.

But really, I had been going downhill for so long by then already…

Magpie huddles, a scruff of feathers adrift in heat.
She can feel herself burning into nothingness.
It would be so easy just to die here in the desert.

I had ground to a complete halt. For a very long time all I managed to do was housework. Cutting the firewood, carting and stacking it, doing the washing, the cooking. I neglected – found I simply couldn't deal with – all sorts of other things. The mail and paperwork piled up, and the studio became a mess. I would force myself to walk the twenty or so metres from the house down to the studio, and then just keep on walking – unable to go in. Even just looking in there, seeing the mess, made me feel physically ill. But I kept thinking I could work my way through it, that it was just a matter of working my way through it.

It would be so easy just to die here in the desert.

If I could find the energy, I would work in the garden. Sometimes I thought it was only gardening that helped get me through.

But I did know I was unwell, that I was in trouble, and I finally went to our family doctor. I had not been able to talk with anybody else, but with her I could. She listened; it was somehow helpful that *somebody* at least knew. A couple of times she came to see me at home, because I was unable to get myself into the car and drive the one and a half kilometres into the town, to her clinic.

At one stage she referred me to a counsellor, who no doubt tried his best – but I was just so damned sad I couldn't even really talk with him. Sometime later I tried a psychiatrist she recommended, a fellow who had supposedly had some measure of success using cognitive therapy techniques. I went to maybe half a dozen appointments with him, but finally lost interest in sitting there listening to him talk about his family – their trips to the snow with friends, his daughter, their sewerage problems – for what seemed like hours on end. And I couldn't afford his fees.

For a long time – regarding it as an admission of a failure to resolve my own problems – I resisted going onto any sort of medication. I finally did, and it seemed to help. But I would then go off it again...

So I just went round and round in circles.

––––––––––

Eventually I managed to force my way back into the studio, and cleaned it up; I went through all the drawers, shelves, boxes, cupboards, through the kitchen and around the sheds, and collected anything and everything that looked as though it might be vaguely useful for the final images for *Fox*. I laid it all out on my workbenches and desk back in the studio...

Music played a vital role. Bob Dylan, *Time Out of Mind*, over and over; Van Morrison, *Astral Weeks* and everything else; Tom Waits, *Mule Variations*; Arvo Pärt; Mischa Maisky's *Songs without Words* from Schubert; Paul Tortelier playing Bach's cello suites.

God knows how, but finally, something like a year and a half after I had first received the text, I at last managed to get started on an image – on what I call 'the third whispering page'.

And when at dawn Fox whispers to her for the third time, she whispers back, 'I am ready.'

That was the key page for me at that stage; the one I *had* to get done, before I could even begin to think about any of the others.

That first picture was a real mixed-media job: a multi-layered collage of bits and pieces of different papers, heavy impasto, oil paint, acrylic, ink, watercolour, shellac, oil sticks...and instead of drawing with pens, pencils or whatever, I gouged, scratched and scraped my way through all this stuff using kitchen forks, bits of wire, old dental tools, bits of rusty tin, sandpaper – whatever seemed to work – to find my lines. I then worked the oil sticks into and over the whole picture, working and rubbing them in across the entire surface, obliterating the whole image under deep black, red, blue, brown or green oil. After allowing this to dry a little, I rubbed and polished off the higher, flatter, smoother surfaces with soft cloth; laid glazes of acrylic and wash over the top, gouged back in again, varnished again with shellac, added more colour here and there – until I felt the image had everything I was able to find. Until I felt it matched the voice in the writing – the texture of the language.

I disappeared right into it... And when next I looked, about a day and a half later – there it was, on the desk in front of me. Done! It had just come right out of me, from god knows where... And I had danced and sung almost all the way through it, hardly even knowing what I was doing with the paints, the brushes, the bits of tin and wire, or what I was doing on the paper. It just happened. So *easily!*

It felt amazing.

I was ecstatic. I called Allen & Unwin to tell them I had got it – would show them on the way through Melbourne to Perth, where I was booked to do a week at the Fremantle Children's Literature Centre. They were of course all hoping I'd be showing a whole *lot* of the pictures by that stage – were a bit disappointed that it was only the one.

'But it *is* the *right* one,' I said. 'At least (and at last) I now *know* what I am doing.'

But then I went on to Perth, to Fremantle, and spent a week there talking with hundreds of people; busloads of kids, and their teachers. And by the time I got back to my desk, and took that illustration out of the folio, I had no idea at all – literally, *no idea at all* – of how I had done it. I looked at the various tools and media I had used, but I could not remember. I stared at the picture, at its layers, colours, textures – and could not work out how I *could* possibly have done it.

Then I *really* crashed. I think for another three months. Or was it six? I don't know. I was not able to do another picture. It was hideous. Total agony.

———

How long did it take, how long did I struggle with it? This book, the making of which, after all, was my attempt to make my own 'long journey home', to my marriage. Was it three years, three and a half?

Fox whispers to her for the third time...

I'm not sure. It felt like a lifetime.

But I began reading again: May Sarton, *Journal of a Solitude;* Thomas Lynch, *The Undertaking;* Cyril (aka Palinurus) Connolly, *The Unquiet Grave;* Annie Dillard, *The Writing Life;* William Styron, *Darkness Visible;* everything by Michael Ondaatje; Nuala O'Faolain, *Are You Somebody?;* C.S. Lewis, *Surprised by Joy;* Sara Maitland, *Home Truths*, etc., etc. – so many writers whose work and books helped unlock the shackles. But most especially, I returned to James Hillman's *A Blue Fire* collection. The essay 'The Divine Face of Things' had been enormously helpful for my work in *Old Pig*. This time it was his essay 'On Betrayal' that was to serve as a kind of bible for me, all through the making of *Fox*.

But I struggled nevertheless. It is a struggle more often than not, but with this book it was far harder than usual because of the closeness of the story to my own life. There was too much pain.

I kept on with the mixed media. Every image, page and spread became a Queenstown, a mine-site, an exploration, a major arch-aeological dig, through layers and levels of different materials and work, very often in contradiction and conflict with one another. And though this method of working with such a range of tools and layers of materials might sound a little complex, or messy – still, through it all I was trying to keep the images simple, a lot simpler than those I'd done in some earlier books, but somehow, I hoped, a lot more *loaded.*

While I wanted the reader to *feel* a whole lot about the landscape, the setting of the story, I wanted to achieve this by means other than drawing that landscape in detail. I wanted the primary focus to stay on the characters themselves, avoiding literal representation of the setting. My aim with the images, rather, was to suggest an inner landscape – to find the images in the places and spaces *between and behind the words*, in the places *where the meaning and feeling in those words come from.*

Similarly, because Margaret Wild's story so vigorously pushes the limits, I had to come up with something different in the treatment of the text. Initially, I thought there was no way I could or should hand-letter it. My usual style of 'nice' hand-lettering was, well, just far too nice for this text. So I thought I would typeset it, with a classic typeface that had some sort of hard, cut edge to it. I fiddled about with a few different fonts, but somewhere along the way, I abandoned all this and showed the publishers a first rough indication of what I had in mind – a hand-lettered, badly done, very messy kind of thing, which had a lot of capital letters in it. They weren't impressed, and warned me that Margaret Wild most certainly wouldn't like it. I said I'd try to persuade them. They said I would need to.

I had taken the idea from my six-year-old, Henry. I used to bake a lot of cakes, including birthday cakes, in our old combustion stove. Very often Henry would help me – looking up possible recipes, shopping, mixing, and licking the spoon clean. In anticipation of his next birthday, he had written me a little reminder note: 'Dear Dad, could I please have two cakes for my seventh birthday? First I'd like a Chocolate Truffle Deluxe cake, but also a Passionfruit Bonanza,' followed by a PS (in case there should be any misunderstanding), 'I'd still like some presents too!'

What a great little letter. I loved it, not only for its up-front directness, but for his handwriting – a half back-to-front mix of capital and lower-case letters, all over the place!

I stared at it. And I realised – that was it! *That's* how I should do the *Fox* text. Then I thought, 'Hey, I could get *Henry* to do it!' No, that would be too much; it would put too much pressure on him. I'll simply copy his style. So I tried, but could I get my hand to do it? Exactly as Henry had, with all his wonderful awkwardness? I couldn't. I once thought I could be a very successful forger, thought my oh-so-clever illustrator's hand could do just about anything... The harder, the more consciously, I tried, the sillier my version of his lettering looked. The more *fake*.

Finally, because it seemed there was no way I could *make* my hand do it, no way I could make it do the lettering badly enough, insanely enough, riskily enough, I tried it – and then finally did the whole thing – with my far *less* controllable *left* hand. I read the text word by word, line by line – but as if for the very first time, all over again – and wrote the letters, the words and the lines with my *hand and heart fully connected*, and my brain completely turned off.

I wanted the final text in the book to be as confronting to read as I had found the typescript to be. I wanted the reader to feel, as viscerally as I did, all of Magpie's discomfort, confusion and pain. The treatment and arrangement of the printed text would be as confronting as the writing itself, take the same sort of risks, illuminate and extend as much of its inside workings as possible.

And most especially – because I believed this piece of writing, every single word of it, to be so good – *I wanted to slow the reading of it right down*.

Sitting in on many readings of picture book texts – sometimes by teachers, librarians or parents, sometimes by the authors themselves – I have very often felt people throw the language away, waste it, simply by reading too fast.

I thought, 'This writing, this language, is amazing. I want people to *really* read this, carefully. I want to slow them right down, confront them with each and every word. Make it awkward to read – give them no choice – I want them to *have* to slow down, to have to *work* for it. *Feel* it. Have those words go right into them. I want people to realise how bloody gutsy – brave, beautiful and strong – this writing really is.'

––––––––––

There were a couple of parts of the text that caused intense debate and were also critical for the illustrations. The first was the description of Fox's eyes in Margaret Wild's original manuscript:

After the rains, when saplings are springing up everywhere, a fox comes into the bush; Fox with his dead eyes and rich red coat.
He flickers through the trees like a tongue of fire, and Magpie trembles.

There was a *lot* of to-ing and fro-ing on that one, about the 'dead' eyes.

Margaret *really* didn't want to change that; she very much wanted 'dead' to stay, wanted to say something about the very *soul* of Fox; and the *only* word she felt was right for that was 'dead'.

And I was saying, yes, but, have you ever *seen* a fox's eyes, Margaret? Honest to god, they are *so* intense, so sharply focused and alert...so searchlight-lit and driven from within, so much *an innate expression of the animal*, and so beautiful really, that I reckon no matter what damage Fox might be suffering, no matter what he (or she) might be feeling, there is absolutely no way the eyes of a fox would ever, or *could* ever, look dead.

I think Rosalind, the editor Sarah Brenan and I were unanimous that 'dead eyes' should be re-thought; we all felt that 'dead' was too final, suggesting that Fox was irredeemably malevolent. But it was important to show that he also was damaged, not whole. We went backwards and forwards on just that *one word* – Rosalind, Sarah, Margaret Wild and I – on and off for about a year, I think. I still have an old, faded copy of a fax I sent early on in the whole discussion, which has about a hundred different adjectives on it. But *all* of us offered up god knows how many alternatives – other adjectives, words, phrases and expressions – until eventually, we decided to go with 'haunted'.

In picturing Fox, I tried to give his eyes an unmistakable intensity, an expression of the essence of the *animal* – affirming that he simply is, *inevitably*, what he is, and lives in the only way he knows, in the only way he can. Especially on the cover, the 'third whispering page' and the 'creamy with blossom' page, where I gouged deep black lines around Fox's eyes so they focused out, directly and intensely *at* the reader. The colour inside them – the same as the landscape around him – takes us *through and beyond* Fox, to the world in which he lives, suggesting that that threat, that possibility of temptation and betrayal, is *always* there; as much as we might wish to avoid or deny it, it is simply part of the world.

But I did know what Margaret meant, so I tried to show something about the damage to the personality, to the soul, that the text implied. I tried to *take something away*, leaving the colour inside Fox's eyes flat, curiously lifeless; strangely, oddly, dead. It was a simple enough thing to do: put the strong lines around the eyes, let that colour be in there, but have no light in them; no highlight, no reflection of light, no reflection of anything. Desolate, empty, sad, haunted (some of the words we'd tried out in the text, each one part of the truth); but not 'dead'.

To me, the most effective of these images is the one on the 'third whispering' page: *'And when at dawn Fox whispers to her for the third time, she whispers back, 'I am ready.'* Fox dominates not only Magpie, but the whole image, partly accomplished through the intense focus of his eyes, not directed at Magpie, but at the reader.

Most readers seem to be more impressed with the image of the eyes on what I call the 'creamy with blossom' page. At the top we have this text, running the full width of the page:

In the evenings, when the air is creamy with blossom,

In the
evenings,
when the air
is creamy with
blossom …

In the evenings, when the air is creamy with blossom,
Dog and Magpie relax at the mouth of the cave, enjoying each
other's company. Now and again Fox joins in the conversation,
but Magpie can feel him always watching her.

*Dog and Magpie relax at the mouth of the cave, enjoying each
    other's company.*
Now and again Fox joins in the conversation,
but Magpie can feel him watching, always watching her.

In the dummy I had drawn the three of them simply sitting near the
mouth of the cave – Magpie and Dog together, Fox just a little separate,
atop a rock – with trees and rock all around. And the drawing of the
characters, the setting *within* that image was sufficiently okay that I
found it a little hard to let go. But increasingly, as time went on, I knew
the image was wrong. It looked too much like a 'happy family snap' of
the three of them, for god's sake. I finally realised that all I should have
there were Fox's eyes, watching, in a horizontal strip, like a mask.

In essence this is a simple, obvious repeat, if you like, of the
words. What I think gives the image strength is its *counterpoint* to that
exquisite opening phrase, 'In the evenings, when the air is creamy with

In the evenings, when the air is creamy with blossom, Dog and Magpie relax at the mouth of the cave, enjoying each other's company.

Now and again Fox joins in the conversation, but Magpie can feel him watching, *always* watching her.

And at night his smell seems to fill the cave— a smell of **rage** and envy and loneliness.

blossom'. The phrase itself is *beautifully* creamy; the image of the eyes accompanying it comes as a jolt. *That* jolt, I think, is what readers respond to. Below that strip, that 'mask' with the eyes, are these words, again running the full width of the page:

And at night his smell seems to fill the cave –
a smell of rage and envy and loneliness.

I needed an equally strong image for the page opposite, the picture of the cave. I had painted it initially in the gentle, grey-blue colours of night, and enjoyed creating the textures and marks in the surface of the rocks; but then in trying to find the right colours to go with the words – fill, smell, rage, envy, loneliness – everything just got darker and darker, until almost all those marks I had liked so much, and until absolutely *all* that gentleness of colour, which I had *really* liked, had completely gone.

––––––––––

Another picture that changed was the one after the third whispering page. Magpie has given in to temptation and agreed to go with Fox. Fox takes her running, flying, away from Dog and out into the hot red desert. In this 'flying' picture, I initially showed Magpie riding on Fox's back in the predictable way; in the revised version, Magpie is tumbling upside down, in a sign of things to come. But the picture I had *most* trouble with, the page I knew I had nowhere near right in the dummy – the one I always *knew* would be the most difficult – was the 'silence' page, when they have reached the desert. I called it the 'shaking, stillness, and screaming' page. This was another passage that provoked months of debate. The original text for this page read:

He stops, scarcely panting.
Then he shakes Magpie off his back as he would a flea. Fox pads
    away.
He turns and looks at Magpie. And he says, 'Now both you and
    Dog will know what it is like to be truly alone.'

This passage was the one that gave me most difficulty. The implication is that Fox had always intended to dump Magpie in the desert. This seemed crude, allowing only one interpretation – that his motives were

He stops, scarcely panting.
Then he shakes Magpie off his back
as he would a flea.
Fox pads away. He turns and looks at Magpie.
And he says:
'Now both you and Dog will know what it is like to be truly alone.'

Then he is gone.
In the stillness, Magpie hears a faraway scream.
She cannot tell if it is a scream of triumph,
or of despair.

simply destructive, he was past redemption, and Magpie was entirely the victim of his malevolence. Whereas in life there are always *at least* two sides to the story, aren't there? And I wanted kids reading the book to see that, understand that, and most especially – to *feel* it. I wanted to slow that moment in the story down, so readers would have that bit more time to think about, to *feel*, what was happening.

He stops, scarcely panting. Then he shakes Magpie off his back as he would a flea.

'Is there something about the writing here, Ron,' Margaret Wild asked me at some point, 'that you don't like?'

'Margaret, I love it,' I said. 'But I do think that at this particular point of the story, it is a bit too one-sided, *all* the wrong is with Fox, when really I think it should be a little more complex, more open than that.' I didn't know how she should do that, and wasn't able to suggest anything. 'I'd just like a bit more time, a bit more time and space in there, somehow…'

Just as Margaret hadn't wanted to change the 'dead' eyes, she *really* didn't want to change this bit of the text at all, and fired off a damned effective double-barrelled blast at all of us about it. But after I had said I didn't think I'd be able to do the book the way it was, she gave quite a few goes, and eventually ended up with two new lines between Fox stopping, then shaking Magpie off his back…

He stops, scarcely panting.
There is silence between them.
Neither moves, neither speaks.

While Dog sleeps, Magpie and Fox streak past coolibah trees, rip through long grass, pelt over rocks.

Fox runs so fast that his feet scarcely touch the ground, and Magpie exults, "At last I am flying. Really Flying!"

Then Fox shakes Magpie off his back as he would a flea, and pads away.

Just two short sentences; nine new words – but it gave me all the time and space I wanted. In that moment of 'silence between them' – between the exultation of flying and the cruel shaking off, before the stillness and the screaming – there is reflection, and the interpretive possibilities are wide open.

That picture, that double-page spread – for the 'shaking, stillness and screaming' text – was the very last one I did. I probably did forty or fifty different sketches, just rough little thumbnails mostly, for that spread, before I came up with the final image – in the very last week.

As I've mentioned to kids in schools, it took Michelangelo something like three or four years to paint the whole of the Sistine Chapel ceiling; it took me damned near the same amount of time to come up with just one little picture. Why was that one so hard? Because of what's happening there between the two characters, Fox and Magpie. It's just *so* bloody terrible! *So* hard. There is so *much* pain, for *both of them.* And all this pain – all the blood, all the heart's pumping – is there in Margaret's extraordinary writing. The passage ends:

He turns and looks at Magpie, and he says,
'Now you and Dog will know what it is like to be truly alone.'
Then he is gone.
In the stillness, Magpie hears a faraway scream.
She cannot tell if it is a scream of triumph or despair.

It is a shocking passage of text. A killer. But magnificent too. Incredibly beautiful, powerful writing.

The trouble was that these words were so damned powerful that I just couldn't find anything more to add. With every book my first rule of thumb has been to *not* draw what is there already in the words. I try to find something from behind or between the words, something unsaid, something from the *moment behind and beneath the moment,* something about where those words come from, something *from and about the heart,* to then *add* to the words.

With this 'dumping in the desert' passage, it was all there in the words. There was nothing I could add, the heart of the moment was already right there in the text. So, after three years doing god knows how many different sketches for this spread, I reversed my 'rule': I decided to make *the words themselves* the primary focus. I put them slap-bang across the middle of the spread, and used the painted image area as a frame around *them*.

The language there is so astonishingly *loaded* that all I had to do – all I really *wanted* to do – was draw as much attention as possible to it; sit the image around it, and hold it up front and centre. Strong. Make the words themselves the image. A simple enough idea, but it took me the best part of three and a half years to see it.

Most people, I would say, have a fairly innocent view of those who write and illustrate books for children. They probably think, 'Well, well, that's nice, that must be a nice thing to do.' (I've certainly heard that plenty of times.) 'What a thoroughly nice lucky little order his life must have,' they think, and maybe even, 'What a nice person he must be.'

You know: Big Trike and Little Trike, for the littlies. Cute.

The truth, at least as far as I'm concerned, has got nothing whatsoever to do with nice. The best kids' books aren't what I'd call nice. Even kids – pieces of sun, pieces of moon, maybe – are not always 'nice.' And sure as hell – ask anyone who knows me well enough – I'm very definitely not nice.

So, if nice isn't what makes a good kids' book, what is?

I very often haven't a clue. It is sometimes obscure to me. Enveloped in cloud, buried in sand. On other occasions – thank you, darkness, thank you, light – bits and pieces of the reasons shine gloriously through, and all is right with the world once more.

Why do some people become accountants? Why do others become doctors, mechanics, teachers, librarians, publishers? Why, indeed, artists?

Paul Theroux wrote, 'It is the wounded who become artists.' In a similar vein, somebody once described the various studio departments

He stops, scarcely panting.
there is silence between them.
Neither moves, neither speaks.

Then Fox shakes Magpie off his back
as he would a flea,
    and pads away.

He turns and looks at Magpie, and he says,
"Now you and Dog will know what it is like
to be truly alone."
Then he is gone.
In the stillness, Magpie hears a faraway scream.
She cannot tell if it is a scream of triumph
or despair.

in the Tasmania School of Art as 'a series of sheltered workshops for the walking wounded. Poor bastards.'

Speaking for myself, I have every reason to believe it may be so.

But does it have to be, is it always going to be, so hard?

A Russian poet, Yevtushenko, wrote that the poet, the artist, feels all the sorrow, bears the collective guilt of the sins, large and small, of all humankind. So, the wounded make art out of their need to get well again-to cleanse the sores, to heal the wounds, to ease the pain. To find some measure of innocence. They make art, write poetry, music and books because they need to do it, because it is necessary, to redress the balance. To remake the world anew, and to remake themselves, again and again and again.

———————

I was never confident, ever, that I would actually make it all the way to the end of this book, until I had finished that last picture. Even as I was finishing the last few pieces of the lettering over a weekend with my parents, seated at their kitchen table, my hands shaking with nerves – until the very last words were done, the very last letters, I never really believed it.

And then I drove from my parents' place to Melbourne to meet with Rosalind Price, Sarah Brenan and Margaret Wild, at Allen & Unwin.

I was vividly aware that I had kept them all waiting for a damned long time. I think the 'whispering page' was the only finished illustration any of them had seen in over three years. So I was nervous and, because I'd barely slept for the last month, dead tired. And I had been working on the book for so long now, was so entangled in it, that I really had no idea at all whether the thing was any good or not. I was fully expecting them to reject my wonky, left-handed lettering, and honestly wouldn't have been at all surprised if they'd all been 'a bit sad' about the illustrations also.

We were in Rosalind's office, the artwork in a pile on the table between us. Rosalind, Sarah and Margaret were all sitting; I was standing – slowly turning each sheet, one after another, to give them all time to have a good long look. I had photocopied the lettering onto acetate, and tacked each sheet in place over the respective images so they could see how it would look, how I wanted it to work. It was very like the earlier lettering that Rosalind was pretty sure Margaret would not like.

Nobody spoke. For page after page, image after image, nobody said anything, not a word. There were occasional *sounds* – groans, really, every now and then – as I turned from one sheet to the next.

Okay, I thought – they don't like it. I'm just going to have to take this. I knew I could easily enough get rid of, or change, the hand-lettering; but if they didn't like the illustrations, I really didn't know what I'd be able to *say* even, let alone what I'd then go away and *do*. I was so totally exhausted.

When we eventually got to the end, I just sat down, *collapsed* really, in a chair, utterly spent, pretty sure, now, of what was about to come…

I think it was Margaret who spoke first. 'Oh, *god!* Ron, I'm absolutely flabbergasted! I hardly know what to say. What *astonishing* paintings. They are absolutely beautiful! And the lettering – I really do think you have added so much to the text by the way you have handled it. It's marvellous.' And so on, and so on. It was wonderful. *She* was wonderful.

And then Sarah and Rosalind – having given Margaret the first spot – probably began speaking together, and they were both as complimentary. I could hardly believe what I was hearing.

––––––––––

I cannot recall another thing from that day. But I do remember Rosalind's call a few days later, after I had returned to Huonville.

'It is a triumph, Ron. An absolute triumph.'

But she did go on to say that while they all really loved what I had done, and believed in the book, they were nevertheless thinking they might have to reduce the print run.

'We feel it might just be a very difficult book to sell out there. It is a very confronting story, after all, and, if it's hard to sell in Australia, where it would at least be recognisable, it will be harder still to sell into other countries. So, I'm just trying to prepare you, I suppose…'

'That's okay, Rosalind,' I said. 'Thank you, but I am prepared for that already – in fact, fully *expecting* it.'

I have not known any adult who, upon reading this text, did not express some sort of almost involuntary physical response – gasps for breath, grunts of resistance, moans of despair – and very often quite without realising they had done so. When I showed a neighbour the manuscript, she almost vomited at the line, *'[Fox] shakes Magpie off his back as he would a flea [and] pads away.'*

'It's horrible!' she said. '*Horrible.* You're not going to do this are you? I mean, it's not really a *children's* story, is it?' Her own marriage was in trouble, although I only realised this a couple of months later, when they split up.

I knew what she meant, of course. I did always *suspect* it would be difficult for A&U to sell. It was certainly not the kind of book anybody was going to buy for little Jason's or sweet Kylie's birthday. In fact, I wasn't sure they'd be able to sell it *at all.*

But kids have not yet been down all the potholed tracks we have; they will and do receive this text in their own way. They do not feel personally hurt or threatened by it as some adults do.

When I read *Fox* at schools, from the very opening line, 'Through the charred forest, over hot ash, runs Dog, with a bird clamped in his big, gentle mouth', the kids are all sitting there, absolutely *riveted* to the spot. Waiting, watching, open. Absolutely *engaged.* They know these characters, Fox, Magpie and Dog, they recognise the archetypal truth of them. They know about the daily hurts and changes of allegiance in their schoolyard, in their street. They read the jealousy, the betrayal, the cruelty and the losses, but – and this has something to do with the strength of the writing – they also read it very much as a story about friendship, loyalty and trust. It makes them think about honesty, loneliness, kindness, fairness, about risk, and about courage. All pretty big stuff, worth thinking about.

I am always humbled by the generosity and fullness of what they offer back to me, stunned at what this text draws out of them, at the intensity, depth and range of their responses to it. But I am not surprised. This is great writing – an allegory about the things that make us human, a story that goes straight to the heart.

Fox was published in 2000. I think nobody was more surprised than me when the first print run sold out so fast, and Allen & Unwin had to reprint so quickly, and then again. We ended up with three or four reprints in the hardback. Wonderful.

And the book went on to collect absolutely all the awards it was entered for in Australia, plus a whole lot of very favourable critical attention in the press at the time of its publication. I don't think I've ever published a book that had critics quite so deeply engaged with the work, in review after review, article after article. Many of these I didn't read until years later, because I was too wrecked and depleted at the time, and could barely read anything. I was so completely burnt out by the whole experience of making *Fox* that I hardly left the house for god knows how long.

And meanwhile Rosalind Price and the wonderful Angela Namoi, rights manager at Allen & Unwin, were taking it to the various international book fairs and managing to sell it into many languages, many countries – into many more than even *John Brown* had managed.

Not that I was pleased with everything that happened out there. In the UK edition, for example, they decided against using my hand-lettering, and typeset the text in the most appallingly ugly font, and in such a silly way that it made me wonder why they had bought the rights in the first place, if they had misunderstood the text to that extent. An irony: The book was shortlisted for the Kate Greenaway Medal in England, but didn't win it, somebody informed me, because the judges felt my typesetting let it down. The English publisher had left my name as the designer on the imprint page – thus making me apparently responsible for their typesetting. And – un-*bloody-believable* – they even got rid of some of Margaret's words. Claiming that English children wouldn't be able to understand things and words like stringybark, yellow box, coolibahs and saltpans.

Much later, the English publisher told me, 'Well, I'm afraid English children simply wouldn't recognise any of those names, wouldn't understand what you are talking about. We took advice on all this, we *do* know what we are doing, after all. We sent it out to our readers in England, took advice on all this, and made our decision.'

When *Fox* received the *Deutscher Jugendliteraturpreis*, Margaret Wild and I attended an amazing dinner in Frankfurt with not only Carlsen, the German publishers of *Fox*, but all the other publishers from around the planet who had taken it on and done their very best to reproduce, in their own languages, my wackadoo, broken-left-foot lettering; even the Japanese, who perhaps did it better than anyone (it won their Best Foreign Language Picture Book prize).

Apart from the English, only the French and Chinese typeset it. I didn't mind the way the French did it – they didn't muck and dither about in the same silly sort of way the English had; they just did it, pretty straight. And the Chinese edition in fact became my absolute favourite. All those beautiful Chinese characters, *incredibly* quietly set in the lightest of fonts, barely there even. It's like music. The text is not spoken out loud in the Chinese edition, *it is whispered*, making it all the more powerful. I love it.

The book was still selling ten years later, and Allen & Unwin produced a special tenth anniversary hardback edition. And the Monkey Baa Theatre Company mounted a wonderful theatrical production based on the book. Not too bad for a book none of us held out very much hope for. Especially not too bad when, speaking for myself, I had very much doubted that I'd ever be able to *start* on it even, let alone finish it.

That was the book.

The *life*, after I had finished the book, after Magpie's return to the cave, was something else.

PART FOUR

Behind every beautiful thing, there's been some kind of pain.
Bob Dylan, from *Not Dark Yet (Time out of Mind)*

What remains when all perishes is the face of things as they are.
When there is nowhere to turn, turn back to the face before you,
face the world. Here is the goddess who gives a sense to the world
that is neither myth nor meaning; instead that immediate thing as
image, it's smile, a joy, a joy that makes 'forever'.
James Hillman, *The Divine Face of Things*

The Heart of the Matter

I BELIEVE OUR appetite for life – our interest, and *engagement* with life – is directly proportionate to, reflective of, our relationship to hope. I've been struggling for so long now – for years, attacking and sabotaging my work and my self – that at times I have been able to see no hope at all. Worse than that, I have at times wished it ended.

That is an appalling thing to say, I know. Especially when I have, as I do, three beautiful kids. But it's an even *more* appalling thing to feel. *Much* more appalling – to be in that darkness, in that state of mind, with no visible way out.

What happened? How did I get there? How to get out?

I think my trouble, my problem, goes back a very long way. It's probably congenital. I could bore you to death with speculation and stories…I'll try not to.

Let me just say that I've been in particular difficulty (in my life, with my work) for quite a few years now. The more recent books I have managed to make – from *Old Pig*, through *Rosie and Tortoise*, the two Henrys, the Honey and Bears, to *Fox*…were all done under a deep unhappiness, a *dis*-ease – the crippling horror of what some people might refer to as depression – the slow shredding, and then the pulping, in that 'darkness visible' of the dying self.

For a long time I had tried to tell myself it was just a healthy self-doubt about my abilities, about the quality of my work – or that it was all circumstantial (difficulties with money, for example), and I could work my way through it. But it became much worse.

I tried, but I also made increasingly idiotic mistakes.

Then *Fox* arrived, the story that was absolutely all about what had happened (though Margaret Wild could not have known it), all about what I had done – and allowed to happen – to my marriage.

It hurt like hell reading that text for the first time. It hurt like hell every time I read it over the three and a half years it took me to make the book. It has hurt at every single one of the two or three hundred readings I have given in schools over the years since. It still hurts, over ten years later.

As I have said, my wife didn't want me to make the book. The pain was too raw. But the writing was too beautiful for me to say no to.

I made the book in yet another attempt to make my *own* 'long journey home'. It took me three and a half years – the making, the journey – and almost killed me. Honest to god, I could have died any number of times during the making of that book.

God knows how, but I managed to do it – to finish it. Maybe the book itself worked well enough, and perhaps the 'long journey home' that Magpie begins on the last page of the book is successful for her – but my own journey failed.

––––––––––

Two years after the publication of *Fox*, in the same year that *Special Days with Honey and Bear* was published, and just three days after I finished the first version of 'Mallacoota to Melbourne', my mother died. She was buried on my birthday.

We hadn't always got on very well, my mother and I; we argued – about many things, probably, but mostly about Dad. Her marriage with my father had not been a particularly happy one, for either of them. Neither had had the sort of life, or lived the sort of story, they might have hoped for.

My mother, after being brought up almost as a kind of princess, found herself with five children, not enough money, and a husband who drank, dreamed and talked more than he actually worked at creating a better future. To her great credit she had picked herself up and got on with things. But the losses rankled.

I knew my dad's faults, but I liked him. I think I simply understood (from very early on) that he was unhappy. So I always hated it when my mother shouted at him, when she ranted at me about how useless he was, and always would be.

When I was around twelve years old I finally shouted back. 'I *know* he drinks, but he's *not* useless! I love him. I *love* Dad, and you might as well just *stop trying* to make me hate him, because I never will!' I meant it, and she knew it. We kept our distance a little after that, and she never harangued me about Dad in quite the same way again.

Just as my mother and father worked out some sort of modus operandi over the years, Mum and I also mellowed in our relationship to one another and became quite close. In her last years, she and I would talk on the phone every week, at least.

When she was dying, I visited her in hospital. She had been so huge and strong for us, for so many years – it was a shock to suddenly see how small and fragile she had become. She was, as she said herself, 'pretty tired now, darling'. But she looked lovely, *really* lovely. So clean and clear, and her hair like the softest clouds.

'You look beautiful,' I said.

She smiled, happy at that. Then – so abruptly, it gave me a bit of a start – she began to pull herself up, using her arm and elbow in an effort to twist herself sideways on her bed.

'What are you doing?'

'Oh, just let me *do* it!' she almost snapped, and then, softening, 'Help me sit up a bit, darling, and turn me round. I want to see Dad.'

He had done everything for Mum over the last few years. His whole reason for being (over the last several years of his life) had revolved, finally, around her.

He was at that moment standing across the room by the window, looking a bit lost, confused – like a little boy. The room became quiet, still. It was almost as though the rest of us – Tess, Sam and I – were no

DRAWN *from the* HEART

longer there. And then, across that distance, between the window and the bed, there came, there *grew*, a connection so strong between them… it was like some sort of physical thing you could almost see, touch. My mother was *giving* my father strength; I could *feel* him receiving it.

Mum died later that evening. And there she was – no longer the princess, no longer the war-horse, but still quite magnificent, looking more like some tiny ancient queen now. What a privilege it was to be there with Dad then – to see the way he was able to walk away from us, straight over to her, take hold of her head – and see the way he ran his fingers through that beautiful hair.

I was struck, moved, by how *physically*, how *almost roughly* he did this, again and again, talking to her not quite under his breath but seemingly unaware of anybody else in the room. 'Oh, darling, darling.'

A little later the nurse came in, stood with us for a few moments, and said, 'She *is* beautiful, isn't she?'

And Dad said, 'She always was.'

Just over two years later, my daughter was married. I made a speech, which of course went on too long. I certainly didn't mean to cause any hurt, but in my effort to give voice to things that I felt mattered – speaking from my heart – I evidently said too much, *touched* on too much. Perhaps there had been just too much pain, for everybody.
I lost my daughter, and with all that, I knew I was going to lose – that I *had* to lose – much, much more…

Three months later, my father died.

I was fortunate enough to be with him for his last couple of days – just the two of us, mostly – talking and remembering things together. I showed him photographs of Adelaide and Alexander at their wedding, and put them into his hands. He lay there, barely able to hold them, but unable to let them go either, occasionally brushing his fingers across their faces, their arms, their hands… seeming to want to actually touch them, and simply smiling at them, for the longest time.

Oil and
enamel on
corrugated
iron

We slept, then, he in his bed, me on the floor next to him. He died
the next day, Sunday.

I organised his funeral, wrote and delivered the eulogy for him, and
woke up. Completely. My father had not managed to live a life that could
in any way be described as happy or fulfilled; nor had my mother, even
if they had eventually found some kind of peace. I woke up about what
the absence of love had done to my parents, about how much it had cost
them both for most of their time together. About the lack of forgiveness,
the loss of generosity – about the loss of courage, and of hope.

It was the last thing I would have wished – but I realised what I
had to do. However much pain it might cause, if I wanted to continue
to live and work (even just to *live* – and I had decided I did) I had to
leave my marriage. And risk losing everybody. Everything.

———

DRAWN *from the* HEART

I think I've only ever been able to sort myself out, if at all, through my work. And I've been having trouble with that for years. I've always struggled with the making – each book more difficult to do than the last, never felt the work was good enough – always felt like some kind of a fake, always felt I should be doing something else. (Go and get a real job, Ron.)

But I wasn't very good at the actual life, either. I never was able to separate them – my work, my family, my life. The work I did in books, the later ones especially, were seedlings propagated from my life, my marriage, my family. Then I lost the lot.

Though reading had long been almost a life-source for me, I lost interest even in that. I came to the point of barely being *able* to read. And I lost the impulse to draw – I lost the ability, the impetus, got to the point of not being able, *at all*, to draw. Unable to even *imagine being able* to. Let alone being able to imagine (going through all the pain of) trying to make a book out of somebody else's words. Lost the will to even try… Ever again.

Rosalind Price (perhaps she saw it coming) once asked me – long before *Fox* – 'What would you do, what *could* you do, if you couldn't draw?'

I had been struggling with that for years already, but particularly so in the years after *Fox*. If not drawing and painting, then what?

––––––––

Something happens when our parents die. It is sad, of course, but perhaps there is something in their going that also sets us free, that somehow almost *obliges* us (to at least try) to become who we truly are, or might wish to be. And we take that on, perhaps, partly *on their behalf* – in reflecting on all those things we know they themselves missed out on, or failed to find – we are somehow able to at last take on that responsibility in our own lives. We know that is what they would have wished for themselves, and even more certainly what they would wish for us.

Thinking now of my parents – of their floating, their fragility – I am also reminded of their strength, of how they both had an ear for music, an eye for beauty. I am grateful.

'About time,' Mum would have said.

This might sound a little odd after making books for around forty years, but I never had any ambition to be an illustrator. I have never thought of myself as such. Unlike a lot of illustrators, I've never had one particular style or technique, and I have never felt myself to be in sure possession of any particularly clever skills. Quite the contrary.

The words are the thing, really, to me, what they trigger off within the reader – the ideas, the thoughts, the feelings. My job is to weave in and out and among all that, exploring the threads, looking for the spaces between the lines, looking for the places behind the words – for the places where the meaning comes from. Looking for what is *not* written. Looking for the *unsaid*.

It's hard going a lot of the time – searching for the missing pieces – trying to find the richest, the juiciest possible interplay between pictures and words...but then again, engaging in that struggle, going for that spark which just might ignite it all, is where the magic is, and the exhilaration. In working for kids, I am working for *their* sparks – for their imagination, their compassion, their creativity.

The Bunyip; John Brown; Motor Bill; Old Pig; Rosie and Tortoise; the Henry books; *Honey and Bear* and *Fox* are all texts which offer 'universal truths, universal values'. They all have something of the classic allegory and fable about them, but I cannot imagine how I could possibly impose a common illustrative style on such a rich range of writing. Each text is different; I endeavour to respond to each according to its own unique and particular needs. My so-called 'technique' or style therefore moves around quite a lot, from book to book.

The words are the central thread – the human voice, running from the writer to the reader – around which all else weaves. It is the way the words are written – the particular quality of the voice, rather than merely the story those words tell – that will most strongly influence the way I make the book.

People only get to see the published book, of course. That's *it*, they think. That's the only one there is. And perhaps they are unable, then, to imagine the book looking, or being, any other way.

But when you think of how many different ways there are of dividing up a text and laying out the pages, of handling the text type or (hand-) lettering, of all the different tools the illustrator *might* have used – how many different media, styles, techniques – there could be a hundred different ways, at least, of making a particular book. It is endless. And that's part of the problem. I get excited about *all* these possibilities. But the publishers, after all, are only going to print one. Which one do I do?

My fundamental problem in bookmaking – and this goes way back to the very beginnings of my interest in drawing and painting – has something to do with having too many 'heroes', too many people whose work I admire, covering all sorts of approaches and styles, crossing all sorts of boundaries. Wonderful teachers like Don Wordsworth and Harry Friedman emphasised learning to see and draw in different ways; but as much as I enjoyed all that, and learnt a great deal from it, there can be a downside to it. I never quite managed to find *my own way*. I had no one way of seeing, no one way of drawing. No original vision, no real voice of my own.

And *that*, I think, is what finally ground me to a halt with my work – the fear that I lacked any sort of original vision, that I had no voice that was genuinely my own. And I allowed that to infect the other area of my life that mattered most to me – my family. With deeply unhappy results.

Sometimes I think that if I have any talent at all, it is only that I love other people's work as much as I do. There is almost nothing that gives me so much pleasure, almost nothing that I love so much, as discovering a wonderful piece of work by somebody else. Seeing a drawing or a beautiful painting that stuns me, reading a book, a piece of writing, or hearing a piece of music that gives me a new way of looking at and thinking about the world. All that gives me the greatest and most deeply sustaining of pleasures. It's the same when I come across a beautiful landscape, or watch the light on the river, the trees, or the birds in the garden... These experiences flip some kind of mysterious switch – pull a subliminal trigger, open some hidden valve – and make it possible for me to then try to make and do things...

As an illustrator, I am attracted only to texts that reach to and open the heart, that touch the soul.

With some debt to James Hillman (again), words are not of the tongue, or pen, but of the heart. Nor is beauty held in the eyes, but in the heart. I am interested in how the heart thinks, in the relationship between that and the soul of the world – I might say, indeed – in the *health* of the world.

'Beauty' – an awareness (in the very moment of perception) of the 'divine face of things' – is vital to me, together with an awareness of the fragility of it all... a *knowing* of pain. The beauty and the blessings, sometimes rubbing up pretty damned hard against the losses and pain – *that*, for me, is where most good art comes from.

I love it when an author has found some kernel of truth, the right form in which to express it, and then, using language in some kind of new, fresh or surprising way, has written something *so beautifully...* that it moves and turns my heart around. Or (perhaps, more accurately) *stills* it somehow. Trying to construct a book, trying to make pictures that in some way then *add* to that stillness, is difficult. *Tantalisingly* difficult. But it does feel good to at least get close.

When somebody sends me a story that in some mysterious way catches me like that – which simply opens and enters my heart – first of all, of course, I am stunned, stopped in my tracks by it; then, if I say yes to it, I have to find a way of drawing that answers the voice in the writing. I go into the text to find what it is that moves me. I try to go through and behind the words to where that voice comes from.

My heart is opened to the voice, to the heart within the words.

That, for me, is the heart of the matter.

That's where I draw from.

If I'm very lucky, I might also discover a place that feels perfect for the story, that feels right for the voice, that feels right for the music – as, for instance, with Captain Taylor's Paddock for *Old Pig*.

But I try very hard *not* to simply illustrate whatever the text already says or describes – rather, I try to find images for what is not there in the text, for those things which are left unsaid, for those feelings, for those 'moments beneath the moment' that almost *cannot* be written. I try to find images from *within* those

Oil and enamel on corrugated iron

moments – images for what the words cannot do. I often feel that the best illustration – much more than merely being descriptive – is quite like music: underlying and serving the words (perhaps), but quite independent of the lyrics (the text), bringing something altogether new to the listener, taking the reader somewhere else entirely.

I don't believe I knew what I was doing with my earlier books. I was simply lucky with a couple of them, and downright ignorant with others. Only in some of the later books did I begin to under-stand what it was I was trying to do. Only in the very last few did I realise I wanted to find images for what is *not there* in the written text – that I wanted to find (and try to make) images that would actually take the reader *somewhere else*, take them almost *away* from the words…to another place, probably to their heart, so that it might be opened, so they might (from within their own heart) find a new way of 'looking and, listening, smelling and tasting'…a new way of seeing, thinking and *feeling* about the world, and their own place in it.

———

I don't think of myself as an illustrator, but I'm not really what I would call an artist either. I haven't the original vision, don't have the 'vertical rise' (of any kind of remarkable rocket). I serve the words of others, a bookmaker, a collaborator, trying to make visible something that is not explicitly there in the text, trying to add something that was not there before. Nothing flash, and no great big grasshopper leaps even – when it all comes down to it, a bit more *ant*-like. The thing is to just get on with it. Keep going. Working with (and mutually dependent on) the author's words, the editor, the publisher, the printer, the distributor, the bookseller, the parent, the teacher, the librarian – and most especially, dependent on the readers. A bookmaker, a collaborator who (in the hollow of his log, in the depths of his nights) tries to throw a bit of light onto some beautiful words, and bring something extra to them.

———

But, yes – in the meantime, after *Fox,* I really had come to the point of being unable to even *imagine* doing another book. The book was so hard to make – took so long, cost so much and was so exhausting, that it left me in a blind, dark place, utterly unable to draw. I was sure it was the last picture book I would ever make.

In that darkness, very nearly extinguished myself – almost appalled that I could still be here – I began (only for myself initially) to write… trying to remember how or why I began drawing in the first place. In some of the (re)discoveries I made along the way – surprising myself a little – the writing then became an attempt to write a series of essays about the picture books I had made over the last thirty years or so – trying to remember or see what I'd been trying to do with them – exploring the genesis of ideas, the processes involved, and to see what I had managed (or not) to do with them. Hoping all that might be of some interest and value. I could no longer draw, no longer make books and then I lost my family, and the writing became more desperate.

Slowly it became an attempt then to understand why *all of that* had happened… again, almost just for myself, really… but also (at least in part), for them. For my children, my family. Maybe I could work out why I had crashed – name the losses, understand them – and then find a way through it, and get back to work. Back to work, and back to life. At the same time salvaging, helping in any way I could, whatever remained of my family.

So, we have arrived, finally, at a place different to the one I thought I was going to. A story about books, about book*making,* about my life – a series of illustrations of how *not* to approach any damned thing at all, perhaps. Who knows how interesting or useful it will be to anybody? But it has been a very interesting process for me. I was surprised (from a multitude of directions), rekindled by some of the discoveries, finding I wanted to remain here, and wanted to continue.

I was 'surprised by joy'.

––––––––

In among all this, along came a new text, *The Coat,* by Julie Hunt. An astonishing piece of writing, totally out of left field. A slightly

A double-page spread from *The Coat*: *The coat watched a man approach. He was a disappointed-looking man, and when he came closer he looked even more disappointed.*

bizarre story, it is about a chronically disappointed man being taken by surprise, and then – amazed by the possibilities in life and his own potential – about *allowing* himself to be so. It is absolutely beautiful. *Exactly* the text I needed after *Fox*. I have to admit, the story has been sitting on my desk for a little too long now – a *lot* too long, in fact, while I have been working my way through the life, and trying to finish *this* book first. But I have made a decent start on it, and will be leaping straight back into it the minute this one is away. I can hardly wait.

Not only that, but an exquisite little text, so warm and gentle, *On the Day You Were Born*, arrived from Margaret Wild. It is all about introducing a brand-new baby to the world; all about introducing a brand-new world to a baby.

And more recently still (after initially saying no), I said yes to yet another truly extraordinary text from Margaret, *The Dream of the Thylacine*. An incredibly powerful, almost *sculptural* piece of writing – just 22 lines, a mere 130 words – which I am champing at the bit about. I can see the whole architecture for the book – the text painted on wood, corrugated iron, concrete and wire, juxtaposed with juicy big paintings.

And I met Yvonne. In 2003, when she was living in Baden-Baden, she had been shown a copy of the German edition of *Fox*. *Fuchs*. 'Something stirred in the black mud at the bottom of the billabong' (or perhaps at the bottom of the Oos River that runs through the middle of that famous old town). We met when Margaret Wild and I went to the Frankfurt Book Fair, to receive the *Deutscher Jugendliteraturpreis* for the book. She later moved out here, from Berlin to the Huon Valley, in southern Tasmania, to be with me. Extraordinary.

It is with Yvonne that I have somehow found my way back, begun working again, confident that I can continue to be here for my children, for my family.

With a bit of luck – just maybe – we didn't all lose everything.

———

In December 2004, I wrote a letter to Margaret Wild:

My dearest Margaret,
I do think life can at times seem utterly bewildering, frustrating, unreadable...
It can sometimes be heartbreaking.
Equally, I think it can also be extraordinarily beautiful, absolutely delightful in the surprises it sometimes holds, and then throws up for us.
And I have to say, I personally do still believe – completely – in beauty, and in love...
'Beauty is an epistemological necessity...it is the way the Gods touch our senses, reach the heart and attract us into life.'
I completely believe in what love can and does do for people, for all living creatures, and for the places we all live in. I believe it can bring about, cause and create what might appear to be absolute miracles.
I really do believe that love can, and does, save lives.
Equally, I believe that without love – in the absence of love, things....creatures, places, and people can and do die.
Am I, my dear Margaret – my favourite picture book writer – am I an altogether hopeless case?
A lost cause? An irredeemably old-fashioned, completely anachronistic, totally unrealistic Romantic?
Why else – for what other reason – does anybody make any kind of art?
For what other reason do you and I write stories and make books?
If not for beauty?
If not for love?

––––––––

Life, family, work – they are all, *it is all* a process. This book – more words than pictures, this time – for me, has been part of that process, some sort of an attempt to better understand some of its mysteries and difficulties. God knows whether I've seen, recognised or really

Seeking the mouth of the river
A double-page spread from *The Dream of the Thylacine*

confronted all the questions I should have done. Much less whether I've managed to pin down any of the answers. The big difference for me, now, is that I find I'm not quite so worried about whether I have done so. I'm more concerned about whether I've genuinely attempted to engage in the struggle. I think, I hope, that I have at least given it a good go.

———

Recently, after years of financial struggle, juggling and pressure, over the last five years particularly – and simply because I wanted to get out of the house, out of my studio – at the tender age of sixty – I decided I needed to go and find a job, work with other people, out there in the world. I didn't bother with a five-page resume or c.v. (none of the people I would be giving it to would be interested anyway); I typed up the simplest of notes, six or eight lines, and printed out a dozen copies headed *Looking for a job. Ron Brooks* That was it.

I remembered our time in New York, where every second waiter and waitress, shop-assistant and bagel-maker was a writer, musician, singer or artist (of some kind or another); I thought about one of my own favourite writers, Thomas Lynch (poet, essayist), who obviously does an equally fine job as a funeral director in the family business; I was thinking of all the German writers, artists and film-makers in East Germany, who (considered, as they were by the regime, as non-citizens) could get jobs *only* as waiters, street sweepers or as cemetery caretakers, and of an artist I know in Prenzlauer Berg, in the old East Berlin. Among his many fine capabilities, he is very good with stone; he spends some of his time restoring the stonework of old churches, and chooses, still, to continue renovating and caring for the headstones in Jewish cemeteries.

The first place I handed my note into was one of the local service stations. I saw they had advertised a night position – not exactly for the job of 'petrol pump attendant', but for a nightshift 'console operator' – which would leave my days free. A bit further up the street, I dropped another copy of my note into the small supermarket and local delicatessen, then to the hardware store, and the bigger supermarket. I left one at the local 'fish factory', where again I was hoping a night or evening shift might be possible, and a little further along the road, at one of those huge apple cool-stores, and a couple of orchards. I left one at the Huon Mushroom Farm, overlooking the rapids on a bend of the lovely Huon River (down which I've paddled with my kids). And yes, I also tried the Huon Cemetery, and called the person in charge. I had heard they might want some sort of nocturnal caretaker...

At the end of the day, I had given out ten sheets.

Next day I had a call from the smaller supermarket and deli, and I've been there two, three, four days a week ever since – working behind the console, serving customers, stocking the shelves – and loving it. It's not exactly any kind of world-saving or earth-moving kind of work; but it's straightforward, simple and honest. I'm out in the world – I'm at least (and at last) out of my otherwise isolated and sometimes gloomy old hollow log up on the hill; I'm down the hill there, in the town, meeting and greeting and getting to chat and deal with a whole lot of people. It's fun, and it's good for me too. The bread-and-butter income and the flexibility in the shifts gives me the opportunity to continue with my own work – making books, painting, writing.

I should have done it years ago.

Ten years after I thought I was finished, this book is at last about to go to the printer. Ten years after *Fox* was first published, it has been reissued with a magnificent new cover, and made into an opera. Unbelievable. Next week I'll be down in the studio, back into *The Coat, The Dream of the Thylacine* and *On the Day You Were Born* – enjoying the discoveries, and seeing what I can do.

It does feel *so good* to be back from the almost dead – to be living and especially working again – a little bit (nay, a very *big* bit) like some kind of miracle.

Acknowledgements

I AM NOT a writer. Nevertheless, the Australia Council (way back when) liked my ideas for another couple of picture books, and they liked the original idea of this book. They funded my next two years of wrestling with it all, which I greatly appreciated, and still do.

Throughout the writing of this book, Allen & Unwin has shown nothing but good faith; they have been extraordinarily patient. I greatly appreciate that, too. Over the last months of what had become almost unmanageable, Sarah Brenan (for whom this book was just one of many) has hung in there, and her steadfastness has been invaluable.

My thanks also to Allen and Unwin, Penguin, Walker Books and Hachette, etc., etc., etc., for allowing me to access images from their books, and to Ursula Dubosarsky, Julia McClelland, Margaret Perversi, Jenny Wagner and Margaret Wild, for allowing me to use extracts from their texts.

Most of all, and most extraordinarily – throughout tears, tempest and tumult, through almost unnavigable wastes, facing with me all the monsters that dwell therein – Yvonne Burger has been my raft, the warm breeze in my sail, and my island.

I'm not sure the book would be here; I'm not sure that I would ever have got here, or there, without her.

List of Books

The Bunyip of Berkeley's Creek, written by Jenny Wagner, Longman Young Books in association with Childerset Pty Ltd, Harmondsworth, UK 1973; Penguin/Childerset, Melbourne, 1975; paperback Penguin, Melbourne, 1978

Aranea, written by Jenny Wagner, Kestrel Books, Harmondsworth, UK, in association with Childerset, 1975; paperback Penguin, Melbourne, 1979

Annie's Rainbow, written by Ron Brooks, Collins, Sydney, 1975; paperback Collins, Sydney, 1982

John Brown, Rose and the Midnight Cat, written by Jenny Wagner, Kestrel, Harmondsworth, UK, 1977; paperback Penguin, Melbourne, 1980

Timothy and Gramps, Collins, Sydney, 1978

Go Ducks Go!, written by Maurice Burns, Andre Deutsch, London, 1987; paperback Scholastic, 1987

The Macquarie Bedtime Story Book, edited by Rosalind Price and Walter McVitty, The Macquarie Library, Sydney, 1987; paperback Penguin, Melbourne, 1990

Motor Bill and the Lovely Caroline, written by Jenny Wagner, Viking Penguin, Melbourne, 1994 paperback Penguin, Melbourne, 1994

Honey and Bear, written by Ursula Dubosarsky, Viking Penguin, Melbourne, 1998; paperback 2000

Special Days with Honey and Bear, written by Ursula Dubosarsky, paperback Penguin, Melbourne, 2002.

The two books reissued by Penguin as *The Honey and Bear Stories*, paperback, 2010

This Baby, written by Julia McClelland, Oxford University Press, Melbourne, 1992; Hodder, Rydalmere, New South Wales, 1995

Old Pig, written by Margaret Wild, Allen & Unwin, Sydney, 1994, new cover edition 2009; paperback Allen & Unwin, Sydney, 1997

Henry's Bed and *Henry's Bath*, written by Margaret Perversi, Viking, Melbourne, 1997; paperback Penguin, Melbourne, 1998; paperback Walker Books, Newtown, New South Wales, 2007

Rosie and Tortoise, written by Margaret Wild, Allen & Unwin, Sydney, 1998

Fox, written by Margaret Wild. Allen & Unwin, Sydney, 2000; paperback 2004; new cover hardback 2010

For use of images and text extracts from the following books, Allen & Unwin would like to thank:

Penguin Books: *The Bunyip of Berkeley's Creek*; *John Brown, Rose and the Midnight Cat*; *Honey and Bear,* and *Special Days with Honey and Bear*

Walker Books: *Henry's Bed* and *Henry's Bath*